ANTISEMITISM

ANTISEMITISM

HISTORICALLY AND CRITICALLY
EXAMINED

by
HUGO VALENTIN

Translated from the Swedish
by A. G. CHATER

BOOKS FOR LIBRARIES PRESS
FREEPORT, NEW YORK

First Published 1936
Reprinted 1971

INTERNATIONAL STANDARD BOOK NUMBER:
0-8369-5914-0

LIBRARY OF CONGRESS CATALOG CARD NUMBER:
79-164630

PRINTED IN THE UNITED STATES OF AMERICA

PREFACE

In this book I have been chiefly occupied with the Antisemitism of to-day. But as the present cannot be understood except as a product of the past, I have also given a brief account of Antisemitism through the ages. I have sought to define the causes of Antisemitism as I conceive them, and to show the true value of the charges now most usually brought against the Jews. As Germany is at present the antisemitic country *par excellence*, and the antisemitic ideology has been mainly developed by Germans, I have dwelt especially on German Antisemitism.

It has not been my purpose to write a book on the Jewish question, still less to trace the history of the Jews. My investigation only concerns Antisemitism. I have therefore not been able to devote much space to the position of the Jews in non-antisemitic countries—Scandinavia for example—nor to those epochs in which the Jewish and the non-Jewish world have met in the advancement of civilisation and in fruitful co-operation, nor to the many proofs of sympathy and noble philanthropy which non-Jewish men and women have shown the victims of Antisemitism, especially during the last two years. It is obvious therefore from the nature of the subject that the pictures of the past and the present here displayed to the reader will be predominantly sombre in their colours.

Antisemitism is no longer a problem which concerns only the Jews and their enemies. It concerns everyone. It has therefore a stronger claim on the attention of the public than has been the case hitherto. In the consciousness of this I have written the present book, the result of many years' study of Jewish history and of contemporary Jewish problems.

If this work—its objective facts and its subjective points of view—should contribute to lift the discussion above the plane of vulgar Antisemitism, it will certainly have achieved an object.

I have not denied the complicated character of Antisemitism, still less the existence—in certain countries—of a Jewish question, which is a consequence of unfortunate circumstances and tragic mistakes. But at the same time I have tried to indicate the danger with which hatred of the Jews, like all national hatred, threatens our civilisation. In proportion as the eyes of the nations are opened to the true nature of Antisemitism, as democracy is educated into immunity against national psychoses, and as the individual realises his duty to test before passing judgement, in such proportion will the power of Antisemitism decline.

Hugo Valentin

Upsala, *January 1935.*

CONTENTS

ANTISEMITISM: ITS MEANING, AND THEORIES REGARDING ITS CAUSES

The expression Antisemitism is misleading to this extent, that the hostility of the Antisemites is directed only against the Jews, the majority of whom moreover are undoubtedly not " Semites," and for the last two millenniums have not used a Semitic language as their mother-tongue. The expression Antisemitism however is preferable to any such word as *Judenhass*, since it denotes that the Jews are not attacked in their quality of a religious community but as a race. In this sense the term seems to have originated with Wilhelm Marr in his pamphlet *Der Sieg des Judentums über das Germanentum* (1873). For the sake of simplicity I here use the word as synonymous with *Judenhass*—hatred or persecution of the Jews—although in speaking of former times it is of course an anachronistic term and is at the same time misleading as regards the " Antisemitism " of our own day.

Concerning the ultimate cause, or rather causes, of Antisemitism—for obviously we are here dealing with a complex of causes—opinions are much divided. The orthodox Jews regard the overthrow of the Jewish State and the exile of their nation as a punishment for their sins and Antisemitism as an inevitable result of the Dispersion, so long as the non-Jewish peoples are not penetrated by the knowledge, justice and love of God; that is, until the coming of the Messiah. A number of neo-orthodox Jews on the other hand believe in a gradual reconciliation between the non-Jewish world and the believing Jews—a view which is accepted to a certain extent by the Christian, anti-Jewish theologian Gerhard Kittel, in his remarkable work *Die Judenfrage*, published in 1933. Many liberal Jews regard Antisemitism as an outcome of atavistic habits of thought, doomed to disappear with increasing enlightenment and humanity; while others attribute it mainly to the fact that Jewish assimilation has not everywhere made such progress as to enable the non-Jewish world entirely to overcome its feeling that the Jews are aliens.

The Zionists as a rule regard Antisemitism as a result of existing national or cultural disparities between the Jews and the traditional anti-Jewish bias of the non-Jewish world, which thus, according to the theory of racial Antisemitism, consciously or unconsciously defends itself against alien influence; and above all as a result of the abnormal position of the Jews as a nation without a State. Only a Jewish land, where the Jews can lead a normal national life and which is capable of absorbing the " superfluous " Jews of Eastern and Central Europe, will be able, in the opinion of Zionists, to mitigate or destroy Antisemitism. Theodor Herzl, the founder of Zionism, considered Antisemitism inevitable in all countries where the Jews form a considerable proportion of the population, and this, he thought, was largely independent of their behaviour. In the introduction to *Der Judenstaat* (1896) he characterises the Jewish question as a pre-eminently national one, in the solution of which both Jews and non-Jews were interested, and which therefore ought to be treated as a political question in " the council of civilised States." Antisemitism, which he views " as a Jew, but without hatred or fear," was in his opinion a complicated movement, the elements of which were not merely brutality, business jealousy, religious intolerance, but also " presumed self-defence." In words to which the events of 1933 in Germany have lent special significance he pronounces against the Liberal view of assimilation and Antisemitism. " We have everywhere made an honest attempt to merge ourselves in the population surrounding us and to preserve only the faith of our fathers. This is not permitted. In vain are we loyal and in many cases exaggerated patriots; in vain do we make the same sacrifices of blood and treasure as other citizens; in vain do we strive to promote the honour of our native country in the arts and sciences, or to increase its wealth in trade and industry. In our native land, in which we, too, have lived for centuries, we are denounced as aliens, often by those whose families were not living in the country when our forefathers were groaning there. The majority is able to decide who is an alien and who is not; this is a question of power like everything else among the nations. . . . Thus we are everywhere good patriots in vain, as was the case with the Huguenots, who were also forced into exile. If only they would leave us in peace ! . . . But I do not believe they will ever leave us in peace." In the concluding words of *Der Judenstaat*, Herzl expresses his conviction that Antisemitism is bound to increase, and that its eruption will be the more violent, the longer it is delayed.

In contradistinction to Liberalism and Zionism, Socialism regards the Jewish question as of social nature. According to the Marxists' view Antisemitism arises as a product of competitive jealousy and as a means adopted by those in power to exploit ancient prejudices and popular ignorance, diverting the fury of the impoverished classes from their real enemies. It is sought to entice the workers away from the class war by giving them the illusion of a real national solidarity and at the same time stamping oppressive capitalism as " Jewish." Artisans, small capitalists, petty tradesmen and other members of the lower middle class, ruined or hard pressed by financial and industrial capitalism—the " lower middle class " in Germany is estimated at twenty-three and a half millions: a third of the population—are incited against the department stores, the Jewish " Bourse-jobbers " and Jewish " robber capitalism," although the designation

Jewish is entirely misleading, seeing that Jewish and Christian capital form an indissoluble whole, of which the Jewish share is the less powerful. Those engaged in the liberal professions—doctors, lawyers, and so on—are taught to see in their Jewish competitors the cause of their embarrassment; in reality brought about by the depression, that is to say, by the capitalist system. Those employed in offices and shops are taught to turn their hatred against the Jewish exploiters, overlooking the equally dangerous and mischievous non-Jewish, whereby a race-war front is substituted for the class-war front. In dealing with the small and medium farmers, or the agrarian victims of tariff and finance policy, the anti-semitic agitator has a relatively easy task, since he can avail himself among the peasantry of anti-Jewish ideas surviving from a long-vanished economic epoch. The farmer, groaning under the yoke of mortgage slavery, is made to imagine himself the victim of Jewish bloodsuckers—a view which has been actually propounded by the present German National-Socialist Minister of Agriculture, Darré. Thus, according to the Socialists, the hatred of Jews is a creation of the individual-capitalist order of society and a phenomenon destined to disappear with the substitution for this of a socialist-collectivist system. Those Socialist Jewish workers who are at the same time Zionists consider the position of the Jewish proletariat as exceptional, and conceive the causes of Antisemitism, or, as the case may be, the means of destroying it, in accordance with their Socialist-Zionist ideology.

According to another view the inmost cause of Antisemitism is a sense of inferiority with regard to the Jewish competitor, who is hated for his cleverness, and therefore slandered and abused. This in the opinion of many people was the case in Germany, where, according to what the Nazis would have us believe, 600,000 Jews were on the way to wresting power from 60,000,000 Germans, and therefore had to be forcibly repressed, after the public had first been convinced of the Jews' power and inferior value by means of

" instructive " propaganda. The earliest sanguinary persecutions of the Jews during the Middle Ages took place significantly enough just where civic life and commerce were
developing—on the Rhine and at Venice, for instance; and
it was only when the Christian burghers had begun to
compete with the great Jewish merchants, who previous
to the Crusades had been the intermediaries of trade between
East and West, that an intensive antisemitic agitation was
inaugurated, accompanied by legislation for the suppression
of the Jewish competitor. The American, Walter Hurt, has
drawn an interesting parallel between Antisemitism and
the anti-Japanese movement in California. He quotes one
of the leaders of the latter movement as openly admitting—
a rare thing in similar cases—that the Japanese must be
resisted not so much for racial-political reasons as for
economic, since their thrift, industry and progressive spirit
give them the upper hand in free competition.

According to another view, whose best known representative is probably the convert from Antisemitism, Count
Heinrich Coudenhove-Kalergi—a view with which his son,
Richard Coudenhove-Kalergi, the leading exponent of
the Pan-European idea, is in agreement—the ultimate
cause of Antisemitism is religious fanaticism, a thesis
which this author developed in a work published in 1901,
Das Wesen des Antisemitismus, since reissued in several
editions, revised by his son. In classical antiquity the Jews
irritated the non-Jewish world by denying all gods but God
and by voluntarily severing themselves from the pagans.
During the Middle Ages the cause of Antisemitism was
Christian intolerance of the Jews, who were regarded as
the murderers of the Saviour. But modern, ostensibly a-
religious Antisemitism has also a similar cause, though this
appears under the protective disguise of racial antipathy.
At the same time, as children learn to love Christ, the
Saviour and the friend of children, they are naturally
seized with indignation against those whom they deem to

have hated, tortured and killed him. When the child hears the word Jew, he associates this conception with the passion of Christ. This very often has a decisive influence on the individual's subsequent attitude towards the Jews. In Christ he does not see a Jew who loved his people and whose whole being bore the stamp of religious and ethical inheritance from his forefathers. He sees in him the anti-Jew, a conception which is supported especially by the tendency of the later Gospels. (As has been emphasised by the Danish religious historian Ditlef Nielsen, among others, the authors of these Gospels—to say nothing of the post-canonical— seek to throw the blame for Jesus' death on the Jews instead of on Pontius Pilate, since obviously " it must have been a stumbling-block to the Romans that the founder of the religion was executed as a rebel against Roman sove-reignty.") The child's pliant and impressionable soul is, according to Freud, quoted by the younger Coudenhove-Kalergi, a retort in which a great part of our instincts and feelings comes into existence, and the antisemitic instinct arises " almost always " from infantile prejudices. Children who receive a non-religious education are inspired with the same antisemitic prejudices through scornful or spiteful utterances about the Jews from the lips of their relatives, nurses, teachers and friends. Thus the instinctive and emotional life of the child is infected with an anti-Jewish spirit. In particular the words, " His blood be on us and on our children," though they must appear psychologically improbable—no angry mob thinks or speaks in this way— have contributed in a great degree to give children the idea of the Jewish people as the murderers of Christ, as an incarnation of the principle of evil, and not merely the generation contemporary with Christ, but all succeeding generations down to the present day. It is by no means fortuitous that the Antisemitism of the Mohammedan countries has never been so embittered as that of the Christian.

As a rule, no doubt, the youth or the grown man drops the faith of his childhood, but not his antisemitic antipathies, which, in ignorance of the history of their genesis, he supposes to be " innate." He then looks for an explanation of them and finds it in pseudo-scientific articles and books, in which the Jews are depicted as an inferior race. The racial Anti-semites gain a new supporter. " Religious prejudice is primary, antipathy secondary, racial prejudice tertiary."

It must, however, be pointed out in this connection that the influence of elementary Christian religious education is by no means necessarily antisemitic. In the mind of many a clergyman and teacher the circumstance that Jesus is asserted rightly or wrongly to have been put to death by the Jews, or rather by certain Jews, is of small importance compared with the fact that he and all his disciples were Jews, and that their conception of the world, their thoughts and feelings, were shaped by Jewish tradition. For this reason, particularly, though by no means exclusively, in Free Church circles it has often been felt that a debt of gratitude is owing to the Jews; they are treated in word and deed as brothers. And the hatred of Jews has been vigorously denounced as unworthy of Christian people.

A typically modern view is that initiated and developed by F. Bernstein and Arnold Zweig, that the ultimate source of Antisemitism is an instinctive feeling of hostility, which exists in embryo in every group of persons in relation to a group differently constituted. Or, as Pascal long ago ex-pressed it: " Différence engendre haine." The title of Bern-stein's book, published in 1926, sums up the whole theory: *Der Antisemitismus als Gruppenerscheinung*. Zweig's book (1927) bears a no less expressive title: *Caliban*.

The inhabitants of one parish like to appear superior to those of the neighbouring parish, and this engenders a cer-tain antagonism, such as may be felt by the children of one farm towards those of another, by one company towards another, by the cavalry towards the infantry, and so on. The

members of one group have a feeling of mutual solidarity.
They are swayed by what Zweig calls " the centrality-
emotion," and feel in relation to the other group a " difference emotion." The individual who is infected by hatred of
another group, and considers himself badly treated by a
member of that group, regards the latter's actions as typical
of the group in question. It often needs no more than that a
person should have unpleasant experiences with a single
Jew to blow his latent Antisemitism into full flame.

A well-known Swedish writer, Carl G. Laurin, opens his
book *Folklynnen* (" National Characters," 1915) with an
anecdote which gives an excellent illustration of the theses
just mentioned. " Here," say the little peasant lads, " the
boys are good, but there "—pointing indignantly to the
next village, a few stone's-throws away—" there they are
wicked." And the author adds: " I heard this when I was
a child, and since then I have always thought how unsympathetic is the untutored mind towards what is strange.
A great deal of culture and of the objectivity it begets is
required before we can grasp that a foreign national
character may be sympathetic." He supplements this by
another no less typical story told him by a Swedish-speaking
Englishman who, on passing through a railway station, had
witnessed the reactions of a number of Swedish peasants
on seeing the meridional gesticulations of a party of Frenchmen. " They're not men, they're monkeys," said an old
countryman. " And," remarked the Englishman, " he was
right there." The author adds that, in all probability, the
Frenchmen were telling each other how like orang-outangs
these peasants, and possibly also the Englishman, appeared
to them. Such apparently humorous but in reality very
serious stories obviously have their place in an account of
Antisemitism.

Among primitive Jews also we naturally find cases of
trying to repay contempt with contempt, of a fondness for
drawing an exaggerated picture of the oppressors as less

noble, gifted, cultured and humane than the oppressed. But it is clear that the cultured Jews of Western and Central Europe would have reason to plume themselves on the dispassionate way in which they react to their slanderers were it not that they themselves were troubled with an equally repulsive spiritual disease: the Jewish hatred of self, of which more in another connection.

Upon the difference - emotion depends the tension among nations. So long as nations have geographical frontiers, this tension can follow a normal course. When crises occur the opposition discharges itself in war, after which a relatively tolerable *modus vivendi* is established between the antagonists. But the peculiar position of the Jews, disseminated among various peoples, renders them the object of a practically permanent antipathy, the intensity of which varies with the influence of various factors on the difference-emotion of the surrounding nation.

The more dissatisfaction there is in the country the greater the risk of enhanced Antisemitism, since every feeling of dissatisfaction has a certain tendency to transform itself into hostile feelings towards some given person or group. We seek, as it were, to divert our own feeling of dissatisfaction upon someone else. It is not the case that one group after objective inquiry arrives at the result that a certain other group is harmful or inferior. The primary thing is hatred. The argument furnished by reasoning is secondary.

By characterising all subversive powers as Jewish, " Jewish " materialism, for instance, and " Jewish " egoism, it is sought by suggestion to get rid of one's own consciousness of guilt. It has been said not without reason that what the Nazis are persecuting among the Jews is really what they ought to persecute among themselves, and that what they are trying to silence is really the voice of conscience.

What is true in the field of morality is also true in that of politics. During the World War the chief object of German

Ba

hatred was England. The " Gott strafe England " agitation
was the forerunner of National-Socialist Jew-baiting. The
Germans loved to think that Sir Edward Grey with Satanic
guile had caught their country in his toils and then brought
the boundless misery of war upon peaceful Germany. But
German fury collapsed in impotence before the superior
power of the Entente. When during the peace negotiations
at Versailles the French proved to be Germany's most
irreconcilable opponents, and especially after they had
occupied the Ruhr, German fury chose them for its object.
But here again, their hatred found no release. Then it was
turned upon the defenceless Jews—according to the law of
least resistance. They could be vanquished, coerced, dishonoured. A release was found for malicious feelings and—
at last—a sense of victory, triumph. The triumph was felt
to be so much the greater in that the Germans succeeded
in making themselves believe that the weak, unorganised
and disunited Jews constituted a powerful people and were
the real rulers of Germany. They succeeded in compensating
their own inferiority complex through the delight it gave
them to humiliate the Jews to the utmost. The victorious
Powers had chastised the Germans with whips; now the
Germans chastised the Jews with scorpions. They were not
content with crushing German Jewry. They denounced
the whole Jewish " race " as inferior, defiled its honour,
deprived the German Jews not only of their civil rights but
their human dignity, while at the same time lauding their
own race to the skies—a shining example of the modern
Caliban's difference and centrality-emotions.

At different times and in different classes of society one
or another of the causes of Antisemitism has dominated the
discussion. The motives alleged for it vary. Now the Jew
is attacked as a dissenter, now as a business rival, now as an
alien. Antisemitism clearly follows the same laws as hatred
directed against other minorities. When the minority is
relatively small, and attracts relatively little attention,

Antisemitism is feeble. When primitive passions are quelled by humanity, reason, religion, philanthropy, they are kept under, but at great crises they burst into flame. The Jews' quality of a permanent minority renders Antisemitism permanent. In reality Antisemitism is merely a special case of the hatred of foreigners. A brief survey of the history of Antisemitism through the ages will prove this.

CHAPTER II

ANTISEMITISM IN ANTIQUITY

UNTIL THE JEWISH NATION was scattered abroad it was no more exposed to hatred than other peoples. Antisemitism was born of the Dispersion. It is true that our knowledge of the state of things during the Assyrian and Babylonian-Persian captivities is only insignificant, but regarding the Græco-Roman period we are comparatively well informed.

The first " Antisemite " in the world's literature is Haman, who, according to the book of Esther, tried to exterminate the Jewish people, and, addressing the Persian king Ahasuerus, characterised it in the following terms : " There is a certain people scattered abroad, and dispersed among the people in all the provinces of thy kingdom; and their laws are diverse from all people, neither keep they the king's laws: therefore it is not for the king's profit to suffer them." Although the book of Esther was certainly not written before the time of the Maccabees, and cannot be used as an authority for the Babylonian-Persian period to which its action is assigned, this utterance nevertheless deserves to be quoted on account of its typical character. The scattered people, holding fast to the religion handed down from their ancestors, is accused of want of respect for the laws of the kingdom—though no evidence is brought forward—and the intervention of the State is demanded.

By the middle of the second century B.C. the Jews were already scattered over practically the whole of the Roman Empire. A hundred and fifty years later, Philo describes the situation in the following words : " On account of their number the Jews could not be contained in a single country. Therefore they have established themselves in most of the countries of Europe and Asia, and in the most favourable ones. No doubt they regard Jerusaiem, where the temple of their chief god is situated, as their mother-city, but as their native land they regard the country where their fathers, grandfathers, great-grandfathers and even earlier generations have lived and where they themselves were born and brought up." As early as the second century B.C. a fateful conflict arose between Judaism and Hellenism owing to Antiochus Epiphanes' attempt to hellenise Judæa and the victorious revolt of the Maccabees. This involved tension between the Jewish and the Greek (hellenised) world, especially in Egypt. After the Roman conquest of Egypt in 30 B.C. this tension became specially acute owing to the Jews being favoured by the Romans. In Caligula's time it came to an actual pogrom in Alexandria, when the Jews refused to set up the emperor's statue in their synagogues. The war against Rome, which broke out in 66 B.C. and ended in the destruction of the Jewish State, brought about a further aggravation of the relations between Jews and pagans. The Jewish congregations in Egypt, Syria and elsewhere were now wholly or partly broken up. The disappearance of the Jewish State made the position of the Jews in the Dispersion still worse than before. They were no longer members of a relatively free nation, but were *dediticii*, that is, persons who had surrendered at discretion. In the minds of the ancients the political defeat of a people was proof of the weakness of their god and of their own inferiority. The disarmed and defeated were objects of contempt. The final exasperated revolts—under Trajan and Hadrian—bear witness, it is true, to the brilliant courage of the Jewish people, but contributed to the further deterioration of their position in the Græco-Roman world.

Here as in the World War the propaganda of hate went hand in hand with the military conflict. From the third

century B.C. Egypt became the anti-Jewish country *par
excellence*, much as Germany in our time. It was in particular
the Egyptian antisemitic authors who later furnished
weapons to the Greek and Roman Judæophobes and influenced opinion in the Roman Empire in an anti-Jewish
spirit. Some of the accusations, especially those derived from
the Alexandrine Antisemite Apion, the Theodor Fritsch of
that time, were purely fantastic, alleging, for instance, that
the Jews were descended from Egyptians who had been
expelled on account of leprosy, that they worshipped an ass,
and so on. That the Jews, in contradistinction to all other
nations, refused to worship other people's gods, and that their
cult was imageless, led to their being accused of godlessness,
blasphemy and impiety. Apion's question, how the Jews
could regard themselves as citizens of Alexandria when they
did not worship the city's gods, is significant of the mental
attitude of antiquity. Circumcision and the prohibition of
swine's flesh were used to show them in a ludicrous light.
The Sabbath, which is surely one of the Jewish people's best
gifts to mankind, was unintelligible to the pagans; they
squander a seventh part of life in idleness and inactivity,
Seneca declared. The preponderance of the ceremonial law
in the life of the Jews appeared to the pagans, especially the
sober Romans, as superstition, as an absurd extravagance.
The barriers to intimate intercourse with non-Jews due in
particular to the ritual laws about clean and unclean food
were interpreted as an attempt at seclusion on the part of a
people which despised non-Jews—a sign of national arrogance
and misanthropy. Their course of life was different from that
of other people. It was advanced against them that they did
not sit at table with others, did not marry non-Jewish
women, did not take part in public worship and sacrifices.
The accusations of hating all others, refusing to do them any
service, and so on, were of course as prevalent as in modern
antisemitic writings. Tacitus, well known as a bitter Antisemite, asserted among other things that the Jews were

unrestrained in sensuality, although they abstained from non-Jewish women, and that they taught their proselytes to despise the country of their birth and to count their parents, their brothers and their children as nothing. Apion tells us that the Jews had a secret law commanding them annually to fatten and slaughter a Greek, to eat his entrails, and in so doing to pledge themselves by oath to hate the Greeks. It was thus the lie of ritual murder, so often exploited since, which was originated by this author. After this it goes without saying that he represents the people of Isaiah and Jesus as unintelligent. They have no men like Socrates, Zeno and Clearchus, he assures us. Another antisemitic author contemporary with Apion—Apollonius Molon—speaks in the same breath of the Jews' cowardice and of their foolhardy courage.

In the ancient world the Jews were predominantly an agricultural people. As traders they were surpassed by many other nations. They were not particularly wealthy, nor were they reproached for any injurious influence on economic life. This in itself shows that ancient Antisemitism was of a different nature from mediæval and modern. But there is evidently a certain modern touch in the Antisemitism of the great city of Alexandria, which for several centuries was the metropolis where Jews were most numerous and the centre alike of the Jewish Dispersion and of Antisemitism. Here the Jews held high official posts, had absorbed Hellenic as well as Jewish culture and at the same time were evidently troublesome rivals of the Greek merchants. Ancient Antisemitism acquired a " national " complexion, in so far as the Jews' refusal to allow themselves to be hellenised like other contemporary peoples was felt by the Greeks to be an insult and an impertinence. Such stubbornness on the part of a barbarian people was bound to rouse the antipathy of those who held that the barbarians, at least those who were not hellenised, ought to be treated " as beasts and plants," in accordance with the advice Aristotle is said to have given Alexander.

In Egypt an additional factor for a long time was the Jews' partisanship for the Romans against the Greeks. And a religious complexion appears in ancient Antisemitism in so far as the Jews' refusal to acknowledge any god but their own and to take part in foreign cults was interpreted by the pagans as defiant self-sufficiency. A similar view, as mentioned above, was taken of their relative seclusion, imposed by the ceremonial law. This, moreover, has often been deeply regretted by writers of the assimilation period, both Christian and Jewish, and of course not without reason. But without protective isolation, that is, without the ceremonial law introduced by Ezra, the Jewish people would undoubtedly have gone under in the ocean of the peoples of antiquity. Furthermore, to cultured pagans the imageless cult was an incomprehensible thing, the sublimity of which they did not grasp, and they regarded the Jewish religion as superstition. The statement of Tacitus is valuable: " Portents and prodigies announced the ruin of the city; but a people (the Jews), blinded by their own national superstition, and with rancour detesting the religion of other States, held it unlawful by vows and victims to deprecate the impending danger."[1]

It is curious, by the way, that no Greek author, whether antisemitic or not, seems to have had any knowledge worth mentioning of Jewish religion and ethics, in spite of the facts that the Jews were living in the midst of his own countrymen, that a copious Jewish literature—apologetic and polemical—existed in the Greek language, and that for over three centuries—approximately from 200 B.C. to A.D. 150 (Bar Kochba's revolt)—the Jews carried on a successful mission. The Jews studied the literature of the Greeks and learned from them, but not *vice versa*. According to Benno Jacob, whose account in the *Encyclopædia Judaica* I have followed in the main, the highly cultured Hellenes and their like considered it in general unnecessary to take account of

---

[1] Arthur Murphy's translation.—(Tr.)

the writings of barbarians, an assertion which, however, is open to discussion. Not until the second century A.D. is a pagan (Celsus) thought to have read the Bible.

But it must be noted that no general feeling of hostility to the Jews prevailed in the ancient world, except possibly in Egypt. Individual antisemitic writers existed, but no anti-semitic movement. Assertions to the contrary, which still occur both on the antisemitic and the Judæophile side, are baseless. The fact is not merely that several of the greatest statesmen of antiquity, such as Cyrus, Alexander the Great and Cæsar, pursued a clear Judæophile policy, which was undoubtedly due to their seeing in the Jews a talented, useful and conservative element in the State—a point of view to which I shall return in another connection—but the peoples themselves proved friendly disposed. For centuries the Jews lived peacefully among them in the Babylonian-Persian Dispersion and in the Roman Empire. The pagans embraced Judaism in great numbers, either completely or as " proselytes of the gate," as is attested both by the Jewish apologist Josephus and the hostile Seneca in words which have often been quoted. This shows not merely that the hatred of Jews had by no means become general among all pagan nations, but also that intercourse between Jews and non-Jews must have been far more intimate than we are led to conclude from antisemitic complaints of the Jews' exclu-siveness. It is also to be noted that by no means all the ancient writers who mentioned the Jews were biased against them, and that other peoples of antiquity, the Egyp-tians, Syrians, Greeks, were also objects of detestation—not to mention the Romans themselves, whom the oppressed peoples regarded with savage hatred. In the year 88 B.C., 80,000 Italians were massacred in Asia Minor in a single day. And the hatred which was directed against the Christians seems to have been even more violent than the hatred of the Jews. The accusations hurled against them were to some extent similar to those against the Jews. They were charged with godliness, libertinism, incest, ritual murder, and so on. When Rome was burning, the cry was not " It's the Jews' doing " but " It's the Christians' doing." If Christianity had not triumphed and extirpated paganism, it is probable that the Christian minority would have been exposed to this day to an oppression as harsh as that suffered by the Jews.

CHAPTER III

ANTISEMITISM IN THE MIDDLE AGES

I N THE ANCIENT WORLD Antisemitism was more a literary than a popular phenomenon, whereas in the Middle Ages the masses of the people were imbued with hatred of the Jews in proportion as the Church through rites and education inspired them with her view of the Jews as a race accursed of God. Until this came about the European peoples had left the Jews in peace. If in later antiquity the Jews had been *dediticii*, they now appeared as *deicidæ*—God's murderers. The tendency, already apparent in the New Testament, to represent the whole Jewish people as the murderers of Jesus —fully developed in the latest Gospel, that of St. John— now colours the whole ecclesiastical way of thinking. The hostile agitation of the Church culminated especially at Easter, when the story of the passion of Jesus was often represented with the force of suggestion and in the spirit. To the simple-minded people the living Jewish generation appeared as the torturers and murderers of Jesus, and to them was attributed the same savage hatred of Jesus, the Saviour and Redeemer, the friend of the poor and oppressed, as was ascribed to the Jewish contemporaries of Jesus. It was believed that the Jews loved to pierce the host until it bled. The little bacterium *Micrococcus prodigius*, which on contact with the air produces a blood-like stain on certain foods, the wafer among them, has been the cause of many mediæval pogroms. The accusations of ritual murder, which the pagans of the old world had launched at the Christians, were now directed against the Jews. In the twelfth century and later it happened repeatedly, that a dead child was placed in a Jewish house in order to turn the resentment of the populace against the Jews. It is true that the existence of the latter was permitted, in order that its misery should be a living witness to the truth of Christianity and at the same time a punishment for their *deicide*. In agreement herewith the Jews, who since A.D. 212 had been fully qualified Roman citizens, became after the triumph of Christianity the object of a canonical and temporal exceptional legislation, which gradually transformed them into a pariah people, " against whom anything was permissible, and who in many cases were not regarded or treated as human beings in a Christian sense, but simply as an object, like a slave, a beast or a prostitute." The isolation of the Jews from the non-Jewish world, which in antiquity and during the first seven centuries of the Middle Ages had only been relative and by no means precluded intercourse between Jews and non-Jews, was now drastically put in force by the Christian State and Church.

With the Crusades, the cancelling of debts, the expulsion of Jewish congregations, compulsory baptism and massacres of Jews, which previously had only occurred sporadically, began to be usual. Why should we spare the enemies of Christ in the West, when we are setting out to fight them in the East? was the thought in men's minds. The armies of the first Crusade were filled with a wild hatred of heretics, and this feeling spread to the populace. In France, it is true, the authorities protected the Jews from attack; only in Rouen do we hear of their community being put to death or coercively baptised as the case might be. It was otherwise in Germany. The German crusaders marched southward through the Rhine valley, and then eastward by Ratisbon into Bohemia, everywhere putting an end to the Jewish congregations and murdering their members with frightful tortures. Only those who accepted baptism were spared, but almost all preferred a martyr's death. In many places the

Jews defended themselves to the last, sword in hand; in other places they killed each other to escape the crusader's torture. A contemporary Jewish chronicler thus describes the destruction of the congregation at Worms: " One man slew his brother, another his kinsmen, his wife and his children; the betrothed slew their affianced brides, tender women their little darlings. All accepted with a whole heart the judgement of heaven upon them. Recommending their souls to their Creator, they cried: ' Hear, O Israel, the Eternal is our God, the Eternal is One.' " It was above all the steadfastness of the mediæval Jews when faced by the horrors of the stake and the torture-chamber which drew from Coudenhove-Kalergi the exclamation of admiration and amazement, that there is no people in the history of the world that surpasses the Jews for courage.

The Crusades mark the turning-point in the history of Western Jewry. Their consequences, it has been said, extend even to our own day. Before them the persecutions of the Jews had not only been relatively rare, but were also, generally speaking, more marked by the desire of the spiritual and temporal authorities for religious conformity than by hatred of the Jews. Popular feeling had not been inordinately antisemitic, and neither in France nor in Germany had the Jews on the whole occupied an exceptional position politically or economically. But now, under the stress of the general heresy-hunt, the masses were filled with a hatred of the Jews which in greater or less degree has survived to our day. The Jews' prosperity was broken up, partly by pogroms, partly by enforced cancelling of the crusaders' debts, partly by antisemitic legislation the practical effect of which was to expel the Jews from the community, and partly by the fact that Christendom, which now owing to the Crusades came directly in contact with the Levant, no longer required them as intermediaries. Congregations with proud traditions and important Jewish centres of learning were annihilated, whereby the level of Jewish culture was reduced.

From the close of the Crusades the separation of the Jews from the Christian world, demanded by the popes of the thirteenth century, may be regarded as complete. Since the governments of the different States were alone able to protect them by force, they became entirely dependent on them. They became the property of the Emperor, *Kammerknechte*, and were afterwards made over by him for a consideration or as a mark of favour to cities and princes who undertook to protect them, for which service the Jews had to pay annual fees. Thus they became a source of income, a commodity in fact, which the emperors and princes, cities and estates, which had promised them a problematic protection in return for payment, could at their pleasure give away, mortgage, sell, or, if they judged it economically advantageous in connection with their financial obligations, entirely destroy. The governments made use of them as sponges with which to draw money out of the people and which were afterwards squeezed; and thus the hatred of the populace was turned against the Jews instead of against the taxing government. On their journeys the Jews had to carry a special safe-conduct, and from this custom was derived the notorious poll-tax, which put them on a level with cattle. The Jews were compelled to wear a special badge, usually yellow, on their clothes, special hats, and so on, whereby they were branded as pariahs and were the constant object of contempt and ill-treatment on the part of the mob.[1] Even in antiquity, the Jews of the cities had often leased or bought houses near to one another, as is the case to-day with Chinese and Italians in foreign places—New York for instance. It was now ordained in a series of synods that the Jews were not to live among the Christian population. In many places the Jewish quarter was isolated by a wall, making it a " ghetto " in the strict sense, which was closed at night like

---

[1] The decision as to a distinctive dress for Jews (and Mohammedans) was made in 1215 by the fourth Lateran Synod on the initiative of Pope Innocent III. Before that date certain fanatical Caliphs had distinguished their Christian and Jewish subjects in a similar way.

a prison. Even more demoralising than the repeated outrages was the consciousness of being continually dependent
on the whim of rapacious authorities. At any moment the
governments could conjure up a pogrom spirit through
rumours of ritual murder, defilement of the Host or the like,
and could afterwards extort the uttermost farthing from the
panic-stricken Jews in return for offers of protection.

In the earlier Middle Ages the Jews had been not merely
traders but also agriculturists and craftsmen. In the sphere
of credit and finance, they do not seem to have played any
very important part. They were now excluded from practically all occupations, except those which were thought
degrading and a very small number of handicrafts whose
members were not formed into guilds (such as seal-engravers
and makers of lenses). Their exclusion from commerce was
disastrous from an economic point of view, as it appears that
previously they had here played an important part, especially
during the ninth century—the period of the great Jewish
merchants, when a large proportion of the trade between
the mutually hostile Christian and Mohammedan worlds
passed through their hands. It was the sad fate of the Jews
to render themselves superfluous. A Christian mercantile
class arose, which, partly by Jewish example, had learned
the art of trading. Their teachers became competitors and
were driven out. The Jew, who had no country to fly to,
was compelled to choose the only callings that offered. He
became a petty tradesman, a middleman or—a usurer, as in
those days everyone was called who lent out money at
interest. The canonical law as we know did not forbid
Christians to exact interest from non-Christians, but only
from one another. Thus was the Bible's prohibition of usury
among Israelites transferred to canonical legislation. But
how was Christendom to get on without borrowing at
interest? The accomplishment of great undertakings, such
as Crusades or the building of churches, called for large
capital sums, but nobody would risk them without a return.

The problem was therefore solved by giving the Jews an actually recognised position as moneylenders. For the Bible permitted them to exact interest from non-Israelites. It is evident that, thanks to this truly macabre privilege, the Jews made a real contribution to civilised life and effectively assisted the transition of European society from an economy of barter to one of finance, and that they fulfilled a necessary function in the economic life of the time. It may be added that in all probability the Jews would have starved to death without the profits accruing from their trade in money. From the close of the eleventh century it became the very foundation of their existence in most countries where they were permitted to reside, but at the same time an additional cause of their degradation and of the intensification of hatred against them. By employing in loans the capital acquired mainly in trade during previous centuries they saved their own lives and thereby those of future generations. But when in the thirteenth century the Christians, who previously had practised " usury " in secret, began to compete with the Jews—this refers particularly to the Italian bankers, the " Lombards," who enjoyed the powerful support of Rome, and to their German successors in Augsburg and Nuremberg—they again felt the pinch. The Jewish bankers, who accommodated princes and cities with loans and farmed taxes and customs, had always been few in number compared with the numerous petty usurers operating among the lower classes and especially among the peasants. These latter were now altogether preponderant. Even to-day this sad survival from the Middle Ages is not entirely extinct—in Galicia, for instance. The Jewish pawnbroker, also not entirely extinct, can trace his descent from this period, as well as the Jewish pedlar and old-clothes man, since their callings doubtless originated in the trade in unredeemed pledges.

The Jewish usurer, a stranger among strangers, who followed a trade regarded as unchristian, often turning the distress of others to his own profit, became the object of a savage hatred which was directed against the Jews as a whole. Drained to the dregs by emperors and princes, whose tools and taxable subjects they were, and who therefore were rightly designated " arch-usurers," fleeced, expelled, recalled when convenient, beaten, humiliated and baited, they returned hate with hate. They would not have been human if they had not done so. With all their energy, intelligence and will-power they defended themselves against a hostile world. For them it was literally your money or your life. For a Jew without money was a helpless being without rights. Thus arose the idea of the Jews' unquenchable thirst for gold, which still flourishes as a widely spread misrepresentation. Their teachers and rabbis preached a lofty morality in accordance with great and binding traditions. But in war the laws, even the moral laws, are usually silent.

It is not for us to judge. But as we still hear the assertion that the Jews are by nature worshippers of mammon and usurers, it must here be insisted once more that the calling of usury was forced upon the Jews and that relatively late— rabbinical literature bears witness to their internal conflicts —and that in classical and mediæval literature up to the twelfth century, otherwise abounding in antisemitic accusations, the Jews are not once charged with usury or extortion and only occasionally with love of gain. This also applies to the writings of the Church Fathers, rich as they are in antisemitic assertions. Coudenhove-Kalergi points out that in the two-volume subject-index to Thalhover's well-known edition of the Fathers in German translation, a work of eighty large volumes, the word Jew does not occur a single time under the following headings: usury, covetousness, avarice, exaction of interest. (On the other hand the Fathers speak of usury on the part of clerics; very naturally, since it was by no means rare for the Church and the convent, the greatest capitalists of that time, actually to practise usury under various legal fictions.) The Sephardic Jews, who were

CA

not forced to adopt usury, never did so. Nor is there anything
to show that the Jewish usurers exacted higher rates of
interest than others. On the contrary: Bernhard de Clair-
vaux, who in his appeal to Christendom before the second
Crusade is the first to mention the Jews as moneylenders,
exhorted the populace to forbear from persecuting, killing
or expelling the Jews, since the Christian usurers were even
worse than they. Examples might be multiplied. The Christian moneylenders, being less exposed, could evidently
permit themselves greater liberty, and a credit system was
indispensable after society had outgrown its primitive
agrarian form. Nor can it be asserted with justice that the
Jews, themselves bled to the bone, exploited the population
more than the landowners sweated their dependants, the
ragged, toiling, starving villeins. If the Jews were more
hated than the lords of the soil, which by the way is open to
discussion, it was due to their being regarded as aliens, and
to the generally antisemitic attitude of the Church, which
taught the people obedience to the temporal authority;
though it must not be overlooked that the Popes not infrequently issued bulls against the persecution of Jews,
sometimes in return for a monetary consideration, but often,
no doubt, from Christian humanitarian motives.

The massacres of Jews, or their expulsion from various
countries or cities—from England in 1290, from France in
1306, from a number of cities in Germany and Austria in
the fourteenth and fifteenth centuries—were due as a rule
to economic causes: when the Jews were thought to be no
longer necessary they were proscribed in order to lay hands
on their property and their bonds. As a rule they were only
tolerated until their places could be taken by Christians.
The Jews expelled from Germany were well received in
Poland where, together with the contemporary German
immigrants, they fulfilled most of the functions of a non-
existent middle class. They farmed the royal taxes and
customs as well as a great number of the estates of the

nobility, the products of which they were well able to dispose of, and thus they incurred the hatred which otherwise would have been directed against the royal tax-gatherers and the landowners themselves. But when a middle class began to arise their position rapidly deteriorated.

Particularly at periods when the economic state of affairs rendered them less necessary the Jews all over Europe had to serve as scapegoats. The terrible pogroms in the middle of the fourteenth century were brought about by the rumour that the Black Death was due to the Jews having poisoned the wells. The Antisemites of the time believed this just as firmly as their modern German compeers believe that the Jews brought about the World War and the defeat of Germany.

This dark picture, however, has its bright spots. Here and there the relations between the Jews and the population were of a relatively patriarchal character. The wealthy and far-famed Jewish congregation of Ratisbon, which possessed valuable imperial privileges and enjoyed the protection of the city council and burghers throughout the pogrom period of the fourteenth century, flourished until the close of the late Middle Ages (in 1519 the Jews were banished from the city). In Italy the Jews on the whole were treated comparatively well, until those in authority became possessed with the spirit of the Counter-Reformation. Jewish physicians, many of whom were attached to the papal household, were held in great repute, as were Jewish silk-weavers. It was the Jews brought in by the Judæophile Norman princes who founded the Italian silk industry. Raphael's tapestries were worked by Jewesses. The period from 1230 to 1550 marks a culmination in the history of Jewish culture in Italy. In Spain, especially the Moorish part, and in Portugal the Jews of the Dispersion enjoyed a prosperity previously unknown. Here as later in nineteenth- and twentieth-century Europe we find not only great rabbis and merchants but also Jewish scientists, physicians, philosophers and statesmen of pre-eminence. But there again the situation grew worse towards the close of the Middle Ages. In 1492 all Jews were expelled from Spain except those who accepted baptism, and among these, the Marranos as they were called, the Inquisition wrought gruesome havoc. In 1498 all Jews in Portugal were compulsorily baptised, unless they preferred martyrdom, and after a few decades (in 1531) they too were handed over to the Inquisition.

Behind the walls of the ghetto, in the midst of boundless misery, learning was nevertheless held sacred. It was above all the study of the holy scriptures and their family life hallowed by religious rites that saved the Jews from intellectual apathy and moral ruin. Profound learning was valued above wealth, not only in theory but in practice—in contracting marriage, for instance. But of this the outside world had little inkling. It saw merely the degradation of the Jews and judged accordingly. The Jew was excluded from mediæval Christian culture.

CHAPTER IV

ANTISEMITISM IN MORE RECENT
TIMES, UP TO THE RISE OF MODERN
ANTISEMITISM

At first the Reformation made no change in the position of the Jews. It is true that at the commencement of his career Luther adopted a Judæophile attitude. He declared that the Christians treated the Jews so badly— " like dogs "—that a good Christian ought to wish himself a Jew. And yet they were the blood-relations, cousins and brothers of the Saviour, favoured as no other people by God, who had entrusted the Holy Scriptures to their hands. They had been exposed to outrage and it had been asserted that they consumed Christian blood to cure their bad smell. They had been forbidden to work side by side with Christians and excluded from human intercourse, thus forcing them to practise usury. How then could they amend their ways ? They ought to be received with kindness, not with popish but with Christian charity, they should be allowed to support themselves by work, in order that they might see for themselves and get to know the Christians' life and doctrine. But when the Jews declined to accept Christianity in its Lutheran form, thus disappointing Luther's hopes, he was seized with indignation. All his inherited hatred of the Jews burst out in full flame. They poisoned the wells, committed ritual murder, practised black arts, reviled Christianity, conspired with the Turks against Christendom. He urged the princes to resort to the most cruel measures against them. His hostile attitude naturally influenced opinion in the Lutheran countries. The fanatical Counter-Reformation tended in the same direction. On the other hand the Reformers' greater estimation of the Bible and the deeper insight into Jewish mentality which resulted therefrom were calculated to counteract Antisemitism, and in fact gave rise in the puritanical England of the seventeenth century to a pro-Jewish feeling, which was destined to be a factor of some importance not only in England itself but in religious movements abroad, especially the Free Churches, which were under English influence. Humanism again caused the study of the Hebrew language to flourish, which tended in the long run to remove false anti-Jewish ideas. In his conflict with the baptised Jew Pfefferkorn and his adherents, the " Dunkelmänner " as they were called, who sought to make a clean sweep of all copies of the Talmud, Reuchlin (1517) expressed himself in a way which anticipates the age of liberalism : the Christian ought to love the Jew as his neighbour, he declared. Moreover it resulted from the Protestants' rejection of the Catholic doctrine of transubstantiation that in the Lutheran and Reformed countries the Jews were no longer accused of misusing the Host and making it bleed, an idea which even as late as 1492 had led the authorities of Mecklenburg to burn twenty-five Jews and two Jewesses alive on the hill now known as the Judenberg and to banish the rest, and the authorities of Brandenburg to burn publicly in Berlin thirty-six Jews who had had the misfortune to survive the horrors of the torture-chamber and to banish the others.[1] It is true that accusations of ritual

[1] In spite of his hatred of the Jews the Catholic chronicler is unable to conceal his admiration of the Mecklenburg Jews' courage and spiritual nobility. " With complete self-control they went to their death," he writes. " Duke Magnus turned to the Jew Aron, whom he had previously known, and said : ' Why do you reject our holy faith, why will you not share the salvation reserved for us who are baptised ? ' Aron replied : ' Noble prince, I believe in God almighty, who created all things. He it is who created me as man and Jew. Had it been in accordance with His designs to make me a Christian, He would not have made me come into the world in our holy faith. Had it been His will I might have been born a prince even as you ! ' . . . The others also went to

murder continued to occur, although as early as 1541 they were refuted by the Protestant preacher Osiander. Persecutions began to be less numerous in Central and Western Europe, apart from those of the Marranos in Spain and Portugal. Instead the sixteenth and seventeenth centuries became the classical period of regulations and safe-conducts. By means of these the Jew was just as much branded as before, but his position was made less insecure.

The still violent Antisemitism of this epoch found its classical expression in the great work of the orientalist Heidelberg professor Eisenmenger: *Entdecktes Judentum* ("Jewry Unmasked"), first published in 1700. The book was written not in Latin, like other learned works of the time, but in German, in order that it might be generally read.

Eisenmenger accepted without question the most preposterous lies about the Jews, even those which had already been disproved, and thus thanks to his authority renewed the belief in them and gave them wider circulation; the stories, for instance, of the Jews' reviling of Christianity and its founder, of ritual murder and the poisoning of wells. He " proved " that according to the Talmud it was forbidden to save a Christian's life, nay, that it was the duty of a Jew to try to kill the Christians. When the Talmud speaks of " religious martyrs, who died for God's sake " he vocalises[1] the words in a way no Jew would ever have dreamed of doing, and translates: " ritual murderers, who slew from religious motives." And so on. Although Eisenmenger was certainly guilty of many mistranslations and misinterpretations, he was nevertheless according to his lights a learned Protestant Hebraist. But he was blinded by hatred. Thus his book became a counterpart to many learned Catholic

their death with courage unbroken, without resistance, without a tear, and breathed their last with the singing of psalms." The Brandenburg Jews died with similar dignity. When the fire was lighted their rabbi, bound to the stake, recited the prayer of the dying. All died with prayer and psalm-singing. Only a people of lofty moral rectitude dies thus.

[1] As Hebrew is written without the insertion of vowels, a word may be read in different ways.

fanatics' libels on Protestantism. With good reason has Marcus Ehrenpreis said of *Entdecktes Judentum* that it ought rather to be called *Verfälschtes Judentum* and declared its author to be the father of Talmud falsification. As such however he has acquired an immense importance, in spite of the fact that Christian theologians and Hebraists of the eighteenth and nineteenth centuries (Michaelis, Delitzsch, Dalman, Siegfried) have exposed his arbitrariness. *Entdecktes Judentum*, a new edition of which was published in 1893, became to a certain extent the canonical book of Antisemitism, an arsenal for all those who wished to attack the Jewish religion and particularly the Talmud.

Entdecktes Judentum may be paralleled from Poland, where for reasons already stated Antisemitism became violently intensified after the close of the fifteenth century, but it is significant that Polish antisemitic literature was based in the main on German models both earlier and later than Eisenmenger. The march of Antisemitism was accompanied by charges of ritual murder and defilement of the Host with their attendant wholesale executions, by expulsion from various towns and districts, by slanders, cancelling of debts, despoliation, maltreatment and pogroms. The pupils of the Jesuit schools specially distinguished themselves in attacking and ill-treating the Jews. The Jews were blamed for all the misfortunes of Poland. They were described as sympathising with the Turks, the Swedes, the Protestants, and when the Diets broke up and were unable to agree, that of course was also the fault of the Jews. As already mentioned they had been rendered to some extent superfluous by economic developments; they were therefore looked upon as parasites but were forbidden other means of livelihood. Tradesmen and artisans hated them as competitors—in Poland they had been allowed to become artisans and had availed themselves very largely of the opportunity—the common people hated them as the tools of the landed aristocracy. For they were middlemen, buffers in reality, between

the peasants and the gentry. Thus the Jews found themselves
between the hammer and the anvil. The Swedes' relatively
humane treatment of the Polish Jews was interpreted as due
to collusion between them and the Swedes, and after the
withdrawal of the Swedish troops Polish Antisemitism burst
forth unhindered like a torrent. " The bloody decade "
1648–1658, initiated by Chmielnicki's Cossack revolt, is one
of the most gruesome pages in Jewish history. The material
welfare of Polish-Lithuanian Jewry was then destroyed
amidst terrible massacres, and for a long time its intellectual
vitality also. This once flourishing Jewish centre now suffered a fate similar to that which three centuries earlier had
overtaken German Jewry. From now on, despite all legislation, a steady stream of impoverished, begging, peddling
Eastern Jews poured out over Western Europe, especially
Germany, where they combined with the persecuted and
almost starving Jewish proletariat. Europe had acquired its
" Eastern Jew question," which to this day plays so important a part in the history of Antisemitism. But as yet the
Eastern Jew did not represent a type distinguishable from
the German Jew.

Nevertheless for the Jews of Central Europe the sixteenth
and seventeenth centuries mark an improvement in the
situation. From the mercantile point of view the Jew no
longer appeared so harmful to the State. Clear-sighted
statesmen recognised that the Jews might enrich the treasury
not only as payers of taxes but also by benefiting industrial
life. The economic point of view was beginning to compete
with the fiscal, though the latter was still dominant. While
the orthodox zeal of the clergy and the hatred of the multitude combined to keep the Jews out of the country and to
limit their freedom of movement when they had entered it,
the statesmen's hostility towards them was becoming mitigated by considerations of political economy. Thus one
prince or city after another began to permit a certain number
of Jews, strictly limited as a rule, to establish themselves,

which did not prevent their being expelled time after time from various places. But although it is evident that religious hatred decreased in intensity as the end of the seventeenth century was approached, there was nowhere any idea of incorporating the Jews with the Christian community. The Jews were regarded as aliens and the Jewish congregations (*kahals*) as a kind of foreign colonies with their own laws and invested with a certain degree of self-government. It was the stimulating influence of these aliens on economic life, commerce in particular—notably the mercantile contribution of the Jews expelled from Spain and Portugal in the cities which offered them a refuge, such as Amsterdam, Antwerp, Hamburg, Leghorn, Bordeaux—that prompted statesmen in the name of expediency to protect them from the burghers who feared their competition and from the zealous clergy.

It was obvious that economic life could only benefit by the Jews' international or interurban connections, which on occasion provided the Jewish business man with a staff of collaborators, since, to quote a writer of the end of the eighteenth century: the Jew never did business " as an isolated individual, but as a member of the world's most extensive trading company." The German and Polish Jews, the Ashkenazim as they were called, through their business and matrimonial connections and through their similar culture and language, formed a net spread over Central and Western Europe, which on the south was in touch with the Spanish-speaking, Sephardic Jews, who in their turn had connections with the Jews of America and North Africa, a fact full of importance to the then budding colonial trade of Europe. It was thanks above all to this solidarity that they had been able to endure the murderous struggle against a hostile outer world during the later Middle Ages and were better fitted than others during the mercantile period to perform certain economic and mercantile functions to the advantage of the States which tolerated them. It was the Jewish army contractors, bankers, court factors, bill brokers, in short Jewish high finance, which now brought about a change in the assessment of the Jews' value. But it must be noted that the great mass of the Jewish people consisted of petty tradesmen and hawkers, who were as much despised as before, and that legislation governing Jews seems to have been based on the assumption that the Jew was a noxious animal, who must be prevented by a number of insulting laws from following his criminal inclinations. Only those Jews who had been able to scrape together enough money to buy a so-called safe-conduct, which gave them the right to stay in the country and to engage in certain trades and professions, enjoyed a position of relative security. And lest the Jews should become too numerous in the country, only the elder sons as a rule were allowed to stay there.

In the later mercantile phase it became usual to try to engage Jewish capital in State-protected trade and industry. The establishment of factories was frequently enjoined as a condition for a permit of residence. The Jew, who in his capacity of a granter of credit for consumption had been regarded as a usurer, appeared in quite another light as a granter of credit for production. The old mediæval system, which compelled the Jews to live apart from the Christians and confined them to certain callings, was thus undermined and a beginning was made towards a community of economic interests between Christian and Jewish industrialists. At the same time, under the stress of freer national-economic and political tendencies, the view gained ground that by their enterprise and by their methods of competition the Jews counteracted in a valuable way the tendency of Christian commerce to stagnate, which led to an improvement in the situation even of those Jews who were not actually wealthy. The Jews aimed at a rapid turn-over of capital, which was in accordance with the mercantile demand for a rapid circulation of money, and it was considered that through their activity as intermediaries they expedited the exchange of goods, which was regarded as

highly desirable. Their business methods, based on adver-
tisement and competition, their view of the justification of the
profits of credit and speculation, which had been regarded
as reprehensible so long as public opinion was governed
officially by the mediæval principle of the " right " value,
justum pretium, of goods, were in agreement with modern
ideas of political economy, and especially with the economic
Liberalism derived from Adam Smith. But the privileged
representatives of the old system of production and consumption regarded the Jews with displeasure, nor did the general
public share in the relatively high estimation in which they
were held by leading politicians and statesmen.

At the commencement of that epoch of history which
opens with the Jewish emancipation and the French Revolution, the situation of the Jews all over Central and North-
West Europe had appreciably improved. The pedlars had to
a great extent become shopkeepers in the towns, the number
of usurers was much reduced, and so on. In various ways they
were financially more closely incorporated in the State,
before becoming so in other senses. It is significant that a
bookkeeper in the employ of the Jewish silk manufacturer
Bernhard of Berlin worked out proposals for the Prussian
Government regarding the technical improvement and
extension of the silk industry. His name became illustrious,
but not in the commercial sphere. It was Moses Mendelssohn. In many places rich Jews enjoyed a favoured position,
socially approaching that of the Christian burgher. The
ghettos were being given up. In most places the enforcement
of the yellow badge had become a dead letter. In certain
quarters the poll-tax was abolished. The more well-to-do
Jews in Germany and Western Europe gradually became
less distinguishable outwardly from their Christian environment. They too were benefited by the advance of the middle
class and the higher social estimation of trade and industry.

We have arrived at the epoch-making phase in the history
of Antisemitism, which according to the point of view one

takes is termed the age of assimilation or of Jewish emancipation.

Even down to the middle of the eighteenth century the
Jews had unquestionably lived as a people isolated from
others, with their own religion, their own customs, dress,
language, reckoning of time, their own self-government and
laws of marriage and inheritance. Their contracts and wills,
their account-books and private letters were written in
cursive Hebrew characters. They associated and married
only among themselves. They still constituted a unity, more
or less independent of national frontiers. The only deep
cleavage was between Sephardim and Ashkenazim. The
world of the Christians was to them a foreign world. To
read a German book appeared to many of them as the first
step on a path which might lead to apostasy, and therefore
as an ungodly act. Now the more intimate contact with this
Christian world involved the partial destruction of the walls
of the ghetto—I am referring more particularly to the state
of things in Germany. One might call it a fateful chance
that this took place simultaneously with the penetration of
the Western upper classes by the ideas of the age of enlightenment, if it were not that precisely the same material development which rendered possible the improvement in the Jews'
position also prepared the way for the emergence of the ideas
of enlightenment.

In 1754 Lessing and Moses Mendelssohn made each other's
acquaintance. Their intimate friendship, which was of the
greatest significance to both, appeared to many as a promise
of a coming reconciliation and productive co-operation
between Christians and Jews in the name of the religion of
toleration and humanity. Moses Mendelssohn's German
translations of the Pentateuch and later of the Psalms were,
it has been said, of an importance to the Jews almost as
epoch-making as was Luther's translation of the Bible to the
Germans. Not the least of its results was that the German-
Jewish young began to read German. By the end of the

century a very large proportion of German Jewry, previously Yiddish-speaking, became actually German-speaking. And in *Nathan der Weise*, Lessing, taking his friend Mendelssohn as a model, created an ideal figure of the Jew who exercised a great influence on the formation of opinion. Both considered that the Jews ought to adopt the Christian culture, while remaining faithful to the Jewish religion, that is, what Mendelssohn meant by Jewish religion, which was in reality a deistic religion of reason and humanity, though Mendelssohn himself lived according to the Jewish law all his life. In other writings of an apologetic and philosophical nature Mendelssohn laid the theoretical foundations of Jewish assimilation, which actually had already begun.

More and more Jews and Jewesses began to play a part in German culture, which just at that time was peculiarly rich. Rahel Varnhagen's salon became a rendezvous for the most notable Christian personages in German cultured life. Both the Kantian philosophy and the young romantic movement found enthusiastic adherents among the younger highly educated Jewish generation. Nowhere did Goethe and Schiller receive such warm acceptance. In 1797 one of Schiller's correspondents in Berlin characterised the cultured Jewish circles as the only ones where literature was discussed. In contradistinction to Mendelssohn these Jews and Jewesses as a rule adopted either for themselves or for their children not merely Christian culture but also Christianity, rarely from any religious conviction but rather in order to make themselves fully acceptable in society. In those days there were no German racial theorists to oppose mixed marriages. Nor did any prominent German intellectual oppose the entry of the highly educated Jews into German cultural life. Sentences of repudiation belong to a much later date. In 1934 a Nazi writer recalls in indignant terms that Friedrich Schlegel married Mendelssohn's daughter, that Wilhelm von Humboldt wrote love-letters, in Hebrew characters into the bargain, to Henriette Herz, and that, as he expresses it, "Schleiermacher and many more were whining like dogs around this Jewess." It looked as if nothing could check this process, which by degrees was removing the outer sheath of German Jewry. During the first eighteen years of the nineteenth century more German Jews were baptised than during the previous eighteen hundred years put together.

Hand in hand with the Jews' assimilation, that is to say, their incorporation with Western culture, went their political emancipation, that is, their legal incorporation with the State and society. The men of the age of enlightenment proclaimed the " natural " rights of man, and as the Jews were unquestionably men, they ought also to share in these rights. In the name of humanity and religious toleration the abolition of the Jews' exceptional status, regarded as ignominious, was demanded. Among the public at large, however, who were not affected to any extent by the ideas of enlightenment but at the same time had little political or social influence, anti-Jewish conceptions persisted as strongly as before, a fact which was not without importance, especially during the inevitable periods of reaction. But even among educated people no very clear pro-Jewish feeling was prevalent as yet. It is true that the ideas of emancipation were often put forward by men of warm feeling and impassioned pathos, but were carried through at this time—nineteenth-century Liberalism had a different trend—from paramount utilitarian considerations and as a consequence of the abstract ideas of liberty which were prevalent. And it was required in return that the Jews should sacrifice the autonomy of their congregations, which meant the whole of their national culture, and become purely and simply Frenchmen, Prussians, Austrians, an atomising of Jewry which obviously was felt by many Jews to be a heavy price to pay for emancipation, and which was in fact opposed by the Eastern Jews, but not by the Western. We should give the Jews everything as individuals but nothing as a nation, declared a French advocate of emancipation. The lack of an historical sense, often attributed to the age of enlightenment, betrays itself strikingly in the attitude of its best men towards this eminently " historical " people, whom it was proposed suddenly to emancipate and render politically useful by means of laws regarded as most excellent—Joseph II's so-called patent of toleration, for instance. But a people which had lived for centuries cut off from others could obviously not be expected to give up in a day its habits and special character and become like all the rest, which was what was asked of it. This brought about its nemesis, especially in those countries where the Jews in general had not been assimilated. Eastern Europe, Austria included, became a brutal penitentiary for the Jews. But in other countries also it became apparent that the incorporation of the Jews in the Christian order of State and society was a far more difficult problem than the men of enlightenment had imagined.

In 1781 Moses Mendelssohn's friend Christian Wilhelm von Dohm published his celebrated work *Ueber die bürgerliche Verbesserung der Juden*, in which he demanded in the name of humanity, justice and political expediency the gradual emancipation of the Jews, pointing out at the same time that their " corruption " was the result of the unworthy treatment they had suffered at the hands of the Christians. The latter point of view was amplified in the following year by Moses Mendelssohn in the introduction to a translation by Marcus Herz of Manasse ben Israel's *Vindiciæ Judæorum*, written in 1656. " We are still excluded," he wrote, " from all arts and sciences and other useful professions and human activities, all roads to improvement are barred against us, and then our lack of culture is made an excuse for continuing to keep us down. Our hands are tied and then we are reproached for not using them." He confuted at some length the then current assertion, no doubt derived from the physiocrats, that trade was an unproductive occupation and that the Jews were merely " consumers." The discussion

concerning Jewish emancipation was well in train. It was
only to end with the complete accomplishment of emancipation several decades later—to be resumed with renewed
vigour after the Franco-Prussian war and in the Germany of
our own day, where the whole work of emancipation is now
in process of nullification.

The Antisemites replied by representing emancipation as
incompatible with the fundamental Christian character of
the State, and insisting on the impossibility of making
patriots of the Jews, who were haters of the Christians and
revilers of Christianity, incorrigible cheats, usurers and
parasites. But the opponents of Mendelssohn and Dohm
forbore to repeat the accusations of ritual murder and torturing of the Host, charges which still flourished in Eastern
Europe, long keeping the Polish congregations in a state of
unspeakable anxiety and leading to trials accompanied by
torture and wholesale executions of the accused by methods
of refined cruelty.

After the death of the Judæophobe Frederick the Great a
royal commission was appointed to draw up suitable
measures for improving the position of the Jews. It reported
in 1793: " Experience has shown that the Jew is capable of
practising every social virtue. When his heart is not hardened
and rendered unfeeling by misery and persecution he is
capable of showing benevolence, magnanimity, unselfishness, sacrifice of personal advantage for the good of his
fellows without asking about their religion. . . . Rather is
there reason to consider him given to exaggerated kindness."

Free America was the first modern State which, relying
on the idea of religious liberty, made no legal difference
between Christian and Jew. To this extent the Declaration
of Independence marks the beginning of Jewish emancipation. But revolutionary France was the first European State
to enact this emancipation. The law of September 27th,
1791, sanctioned on November 13th of the same year, the
    DA

French Jews' " Magna Charta," gave full civic rights to every Jew who took the oath of citizenship, while at the same time abolishing the autonomy of the Jewish congregations. In 1806 Napoleon summoned Jewish notables and prevailed on them to work on the Sabbath in order to show that the French law was more important than the Jewish, and to pass a number of resolutions which in the following year were confirmed by a great Jewish representative assembly, " the Great Sanhedrin," summoned for the purpose. " As regards nationality we belong to the surrounding nations," this assembly proclaimed. " There is no Jewish nation, but only Germans, Frenchmen, Englishmen, who profess the Jewish religion." Thus Napoleon, the emancipationist Jews and their Christian friends imagined they had cut the Gordian knot of the Jewish question. But the great mass of the people did not welcome their new compatriots. They despised them and were by no means willing to facilitate that choice of new callings demanded by the times, their *Berufsumschichtung*—to use a German catch-word of to-day. The master craftsmen would not accept them as apprentices, and so on. The Jews on their side, who were specially numerous in Alsace, clung from force of custom to their old callings, including that most melancholy survival from former times, rural credit. Napoleon, whose conception of the Jews verged upon that of vulgar Antisemitism and who was vexed at the " usury " of the Alsatian Jews, therefore subjected the rights of the Jews in Northern and Eastern France to certain restrictions (the so-called " infamous decree " of 1808), which however were to be annulled after ten years, if they behaved well. Only a few years later he modified these decisions, since the reports of prefects spoke in favour of the Jews, and the decree was never renewed. In France emancipation was accomplished once for all.

In most German and West European countries the French example was followed in the main during the last years of the

eighteenth century and the first fifteen years of the nineteenth; in Prussia, for instance, in 1812 and in Denmark in
1814, though it must be remarked that in many places
emancipation was largely confined to the repeal of those
laws and regulations which from considerations of economic
policy limited the Jews' freedom of movement.

But with the fall of Napoleon the antisemitic reaction
broke out in full force and destroyed the work of emancipation in Germany. From this time on Germany becomes the
citadel of Antisemitism. A deluge of malicious and libellous
antisemitic pamphlets was let loose and for a time over-
flowed all bounds. At the same time Germany became a vivi-
fying source for the Antisemites of the neighbouring countries.

In many ways this reaction reminds one of what happened
in Germany after the World War. The fall in prices, which
like Antisemitism had already begun before Napoleon's fall,
the crisis of the Peace, which involved the further aggravation of the economic defeat, gave rise as always in similar
cases to a *Der Jud ist schuld* atmosphere. Hatred of the Napo-
leonic national oppression resulted in a violent increase not
only of anti-French feeling but also of anti-Jewish, since
every alien who might be supposed to exercise an un-
German influence was looked upon as an enemy. Modern
nationalism was born. Its motto, " one State, one nation,"
aimed its sting at the Jewish inhabitants of the State, even
if these had lived in the country for centuries and like the
assimilated German Jews were fervent German patriots.
Simultaneously a general reaction set in against the free
thought of the age of enlightenment, and this, too, found
anti-Jewish expression. Precisely in those quarters which
would hear nothing of the new-fangled nationalism, namely
in reactionary legitimist circles, the fundamental Christian
character of the State was vindicated in a way which often
represented Jewish emancipation to be a godless work. Thus
Jewish emancipation was rejected both on national and
religious grounds.

Hatred of the Jews was now the height of fashion. When in 1788 *The Merchant of Venice* had been given at the National Theatre in Berlin, in order to avoid any appearance of hostility to the Jews the performance was introduced by a specially written prologue in their favour. In 1820 a German translator of Byron's *Hebrew Melodies* had to guard himself by a prefatory note against the suspicion of appearing friendly to the Jews. It became a favourite popular amusement to ill-treat and insult Jews. In some places it went as far as pogroms. Then, as in 1933, the transition from anti-semitic theory to actual persecution seems to have taken the German Jews by surprise.

Among the many writers hostile to the Jews three deserve special mention. The Berlin professor of history, Friedrich Rühs, an adherent of the theory of the Christian State, recommended a return to mediæval Jewish restrictions. The Jews constituted an alien nation of extortioners, of a nature different from the Germans, and ought to be subject to alien laws. They ought to wear special badges on their clothes, in order that Germans might recognise at once " the Hebrew enemy." Only the baptised Jew ought to be eligible for German citizenship. The Heidelberg professor, J. F. Fries, went further. " Led astray," as the author expressed it, by the humanism of the eighteenth century, they had committed the grave error of admitting the Jew to civil life. The mass of the people, who still saw in the Jews a hostile nation, had alone been guided by a true instinctive feeling in regarding them as corrupters of the people and stealers of their bread. Fries proposed even more Draconic measures than Rühs. If the Jews were not checked, " the sons of Christian houses would soon be drudges in those of the Jews." This point of view, that the Jewish competitor, if he were allowed economic liberty, would make himself master of the Germans, is to be met with in many anti-Jewish writings of the time. Most notorious was Hundt-Radowsky's pamphlet *Judenspiegel*, 1819, which openly advocated massacres, the castration of

Jewish men, the relegation of the women to brothels, and so on. The Prussian Government, which was certainly anti-Jewish but not " popularly " so, did not appreciate this pamphlet, free of all " misleading humanitarianism " and based on " popular instincts," but ordered its confiscation.

With the 1830's began the triumphal progress of Liberalism throughout the world. The laws directed against the Jews appeared in the light of a challenge to the ideas of equality, liberty and philanthropy which the young Liberal generation of that day embraced whole-heartedly. The struggle against reaction became at the same time a struggle for Jewish emancipation. Everywhere the educated middle class, the flower of the Liberal army, took the lead in championing the Jews' cause. So long as the producing and trading organisations inherited from the Middle Ages remained in existence, every right conceded to a Jewish tradesman or craftsman had seemed an encroachment on the rights of the burghers and the Jew had been looked upon as an odious usurper. Now on the other hand the liberal burgher saw in the Jew an ally against absolutism and feudalism. To the Jews, as to the Liberals in general, the fight for Jewish emancipation wore the aspect of a fight for the sacred cause of religious liberty. In Gabriel Riesser, a fervent German patriot, the German Jews found an eminently gifted leader. Their opponents again took their stand on the principle of the fundamental Christian character of the State, a view which was now formulated and expanded by the baptised Jew, Stahl, the great theorist of Prussian Conservatism, or, less commonly, on the old ideas of the Jews' unnational turn of mind or their moral inferiority. During the seven days' debate which the Prussian Diet in 1847 devoted to the question of emancipation, the young Bismarck declared that he was indeed no enemy of the Jews but that he would feel it a humiliation if he had to acknowledge as his superior a Jewish official appointed to represent the King's sacred majesty. " I share this feeling with the great mass of the

people," he added; " and I am not ashamed of being in
their company." On account of diversity of tradition the
attitude of the Prussian nobility to the Jewish question was
entirely different from that of the Swedish nobility, for instance. But before the end of the 1860's Jewish emancipation
was accomplished, broadly speaking, all over Central and
Western Europe: in Austria in 1867, in the North German
Confederation in 1869. After the unification of the Empire
it was extended to the whole of Germany. It was soon to be
seen, however, that Antisemitism was still alive in the depths
of the people. It was repressed but not extirpated.

.   .   .   .

In Eastern Europe, more definitely Russia and Poland,
the course of events did not follow the same lines as in
Central and Western Europe. The Jews, it is true, consisted,
apart from a rabbinical aristocracy of learning, on the one
hand of tradesmen and industrious artisans, all eminently
useful members of society, but on the other (if we except
a number of innkeepers) of all kinds of middlemen, whom
circumstances had rendered partly, but by no means entirely,
superfluous. To provide this swarming proletariat with
worthier and more useful means of livelihood was obviously
a matter of public interest, a task for statesmen. It was therefore of ominous significance, for Russia as well as for Russian-
Polish Jewry, that the Russian politician who first saw the
necessity of transforming Russia into a really judicial State
and at the same time understood more clearly than others
the difficult complex of problems known as the question of
the Russian and Polish Jews, Michael Speranski, was overthrown in 1812 by his opponents, partly, beyond doubt, as
a result of his Judæophile views. He regarded it as a mistake
to attempt to change the Jews' immemorial customs by
means of Draconic laws and regulations. Instead an attempt
should be made to render them happy and useful to the
State by, as he expressed it, " opening the road for them to

their own advantage," by keeping watch over them at a distance, lest they should go astray, all according to the principle of the minimum of prohibition and the maximum of liberty. But his opponents, beguiled by anti-Jewish doctrines, evidently had visions of the people subjugated and " fleeced " by the Jews, whom they took to be parasites by nature, the masters of economic progress instead of its lamentable victims. We may recall the prophecies of evil that were showered upon Western European statesmen when they proposed to abolish bond-service. Just as little as the opponents of its abolition foresaw that the free peasant would be a different man from his fettered self, did the anti-Jewish Russian statesmen understand that the Jew like any other human being would be radically changed if he were allowed to live as a free man, not as a hounded criminal.

Instead of letting the Jews themselves take charge of their " improvement," as Speranski had intended, the State did so—in a direful way under Nicholas I. The most notorious measure was perhaps the conscription of Jewish children for a military service of twenty-five years, in reality for twenty-five years of torture with baptism as its aim; an experience which, if they survived its physical and psychical ill-treatment, the young soldiers had to undergo in separation from their families, in strange and hostile surroundings among the most brutal of tormentors—one of the most shocking pages in the history of the martyrdom of Jewish children. The atrocious reprisals inflicted on anyone who failed in his duty to the State during the hues and cries which, together with a demoralising system of informing, resulted from this " military inquisition," threw the already harassed Jewish population into despair. But the majority preferred this martyrdom to deserting the sanctified customs of their forefathers. The Government sought to amalgamate them by force and complained of their " insolubility." Actually they were defending their threatened national particularity, just as the Poles were doing against the

Russians and Germans, and as the Danes of South Jutland were soon to do against the last-named. At the same time they were defending the faith of their fathers. Banished since the time of Catherine II to the western governments, ten Polish and fifteen Russian—a measure which, by the way, met with the disapproval of East Russian governors, who had come to know them as an industrious and economically useful people—hunted by Alexander I from the country districts to the crowded Jewish quarters of the towns, and excluded by Nicholas I from the frontier districts, a measure which reduced half Russian Jewry to pauperism, they offered a bitter and finally successful resistance to the Tsarist policy of Russianisation.

Under the liberally-inclined Alexander II pressure was relaxed. Educated and wealthy Jews were granted an extension of their rights, such as the right of settling outside the prescribed area. The military inquisition was abolished, after having existed for thirty years, and universal military service took its place. The Jews did not distrust Alexander, as, not without reason, they had distrusted his father. Russian schools and universities were attended by more and more Jewish students. A certain assimilation with its resultant apostasy from Judaism took place among the upper classes, as in Germany, in the early days of the movement. But the great mass of Russian Jews were still as much outside the law and culturally isolated as before.

In Poland the course of events was similar. The cleft between the small Polonised Jewish upper class and the rest of Polish Jewry was profound and ominous of the future; the former as a rule being extremely assimilationist, while the latter defended itself fanatically against all foreign influence.

Russian and Polish society was markedly hostile to the Jews. The leading authors, with the exception of Adam Mickiewicz, almost always depicted the Jews in dark colours, often caricaturing not only the old-time Jew but also his modern descendant, the stockbroker, the *nouveau riche* and the railway bondholder, types which had not previously existed in Russia-Poland. The greatest of Russian novelists, the conservative Panslavic Dostoievsky, attributed to the Jews, though without the slightest reason, the same aggressive nationalism as he himself professed, and saw in the modern, free-thinking Jew the supporter of "disintegrating" Western ideas: liberalism, free trade, socialism, anarchism, atheism. During Alexander II's reign a certain relaxation of the tension between Russians and Jews may be noted, and, especially after the revolt of 1863, between Poles and Jews. But almost every reform in the Jews' favour gave rise to an antisemitic reaction, as was the case in Central Europe during the first decades of the assimilation period.

Such was the situation in the great Jewish centres of Eastern Europe when Antisemitism broke out anew in its proper fatherland, Germany.

CHAPTER V

MODERN ANTISEMITISM PREVIOUS TO THE WORLD WAR

ANTISEMITISM in the new German Empire was upheld mainly by three distinct classes of society. The aristocracy of landowners, officers and government officials, a group politically and socially powerful up to the fall of the monarchy and one which, as we know, is still by no means without importance, saw in the Jews above all a social group critically disposed towards its own feudally coloured opinions. The aversion it felt for the advancing middle class and for Liberalism was turned with redoubled force against the Jewish bourgeoisie. Of still greater significance was the Antisemitism of the lower middle class. The member of this class saw in the Jew a great capitalist who threatened his welfare. The development of capitalist society towards different forms of combines—great department stores, huge factories, bank syndicates, trusts—threatened the welfare of the small tradesman and artisan, and as usual the Jews were blamed for this. No doubt many Jews were included among the financial and industrial magnates of the time, but their importance was recklessly exaggerated, and, as will be shown later, capitalism itself was wrongly characterised as Jewish. It was not perceived that the Jews were not those who directed the economic course of affairs. Bebel had in his mind more particularly this animosity of the lower middle class when he described Antisemitism as " the Socialism of blockheads." When later the socialist working class became a political power in the State and the lower middle class thus found itself between the anvil of the upper middle class and the hammer of Labour, Socialism too was naturally characterised as " Jewish "—with what justice will be examined later—and the hatred of the middle class for the Jews was greatly increased. Thus by degrees the harvest was ripening for Hitler. The third antisemitic category was the academic world, which was irritated at the growing number of Jewish students in the university lecture-rooms and in academic careers. The young Eastern Jews could no longer satisfy their inherited thirst for know-ledge in the Jewish schools, but only a small proportion of them were admitted to the universities of Eastern Europe. They then began to flock to those of Central Europe, especially Berlin, Vienna and Budapest, with a correspond-ing intensification of Antisemitism. It was above all in academically educated circles that the antisemitic racial theories, which provided new arguments for the old hatred of the Jews, gained adherents.

The two first-named categories, the nobility and the lower middle class, soon to be joined by the third, the academic, were preponderantly conservative. The liberal and socialist Press, in which of course Jews were prominent (see below), was characterised as a " Jews' Press " and regarded as " disintegrating." When the Antisemitism of the conservative parties drove the Jews over to their non-antisemitic opponents, the idea arose that the Jew was " by nature " radical, hostile to all that German tradition valued and held sacred, that he was an enemy of the Ger-manic outlook on life and a friend of religious, social and political revolution.

Liberalism gave way to Imperialism, the ideal of peace and the brotherhood of nations to that of chauvinism and the worship of the State. In Germany, united by Bismarck's blood and iron, this view found enthusiastic champions. As the Jews were scattered over the whole world they were regarded as an " International " and therefore as enemies of the national State—like the Freemasons, the Catholics (the Black International) and the Social-Democrats (the Red International). Every " foreign " element in the German Empire was to be wiped out, including the Jews. The high priest of German nationalism, Heinrich von Treitschke, professor of history, invented the notorious catch-phrase: " The Jews are our misfortune." It made no difference that the German Jews declared their wish to be Germans pure and simple, though of Jewish faith, and that they gave evidence in word and deed of their patriotic sentiments, often indeed in an exaggerated degree.

In 1873 German Antisemitism burst into full flame, when the reaction set in after the boom that succeeded the Franco-Prussian war (*Die Gründerzeit*). The middle class, which was most severely hit by the slump, gave the Jews a great share of the blame for it, and at the same time the Catholic Church, which was just then engaged in its struggle against Protestant and Liberal Germany—the *Kulturkampf*—opened a campaign against the Jews, for which Pius IX had given the cue in the previous year. He declared that the Jews and particularly the Jewish journalists were at the bottom of all the Church's troubles. Already in 1871 the theologian, Professor August Rohling, had published his notorious book *Der Talmudjude*, which represented Talmudic Judaism as a devilish doctrine. This work, of which more in another connection, circulated by the hundred thousand and, although most strikingly refuted, contributed to an enhancement of Antisemitism in much the same way as the Protocols of the Elders of Zion in our day. In 1878 the Court preacher Adolf Stöcker of Berlin, a Protestant in contrast to Rohling, founded what was called the Christian Social Labour Party, an antisemitic party of mainly conservative and lower middle-class complexion, which became intensely active with its leader as chief agitator. Stöcker described the Jews as harmful to the realm, of alien nature and more influential than was warranted by their number. It was he above all who made the Jewish question a common topic of debate in the German-speaking countries. His language was wildly passionate, but his Christian convictions did not allow him to go to such extremes as the leaders of the more radical Antisemitism. The same was true of cultured persons of antisemitic proclivity like Treitschke, who declared that there never could or ought to be a question of reversing Jewish emancipation, and the philosopher von Hartmann, who defended the relegation of Jews in the State and in society and demanded their conversion to Christianity and complete abandonment of all Jewish solidarity, but dissociated himself from the fanatics' blackening of the Jews and Judaism, as well as the academic Socialist Adolf Wagner, long the Antisemites' authority on political economy, who finally arrived at the view that the Jews were not so much the cause as an effect of the prevailing state of things, and urged the Antisemites to look for the root of the evil in themselves rather than in the Jews.

But the relatively moderate Antisemites were shouted down by the fanatics, who for the most part embraced racial Antisemitism and dissociated themselves from the conservative Junkers. They adopted a scurrilous tone hitherto unknown in public life, excelled in retailing private scandals, which moreover were mostly untrue, forged documents to prove the Jews' plans of world conquest and falsified or distorted quotations from the Talmud in order to prove their turpitude, besides making use of the ritual murder lie on various occasions. Although of course Christian theological authorities were unanimous in demonstrating the absurdity of the last-mentioned accusations, Germany was to witness two ritual murder trials (Xanten 1891, Konitz 1900), which helped greatly to inflame popular feeling against the Jews. Best known among these demagogues was a schoolmaster named Ahlwardt, discharged for irregularities, who, although a person of more than doubtful morals, for a long time played the part of a highly esteemed popular leader and member of the Reichstag, until in 1909 he was exposed as a blackmailer and became politically dead. On the theoretical side Professor Eugen Dühring, expelled from Berlin University, deserves mention as the man who perhaps more than any of his contemporaries anticipated National-Socialist Antisemitism. To his mind race was the all-determining, unalterable factor in the human character. He rejected both the Old Testament and Christianity, which he designated as " the stain of millenniums." An Antisemite of greater personal significance was the eminent orientalist Paul de Lagarde. According to him the Jews were a people bound to the soil and intellectually sterile, their monotheism did not profit humanity and their whole nature was alien to that of the Germans, which found its most unadulterated expression in mediæval culture. Their emancipation, a result of un-German Liberalism—according to de Lagarde Liberalism is nothing but secularised Judaism—was a disaster. Now that it was an accomplished fact the Jews must either be completely absorbed in the German nation or expelled. In contradistinction to Dühring he was not opposed on principle to intermixture of blood between Jews and Germans. The saying often quoted, especially by assimilated German Jews, that Germanity is not inherent in the blood but in the disposition, *nicht im Geblüte sondern im Gemüte*, is due to him. A younger man, still active in German cultural life, the historian of literature Adolf Bartels, endeavoured in a number of works to brand all well-known German-Jewish authors and particularly Heine as inferior.

Of active politicians the University librarian Otto Böckel must be specially mentioned as a forerunner of Hitler. He held aloof from Conservatism and devoted himself to winning over the middle class and particularly the distressed peasantry of Hesse to Antisemitism. Theodor Fritsch, who lived long enough to witness the triumph of Naziism, carried on an intensive propaganda against the Jews and

Judaism, including the Old Testament. The Hammer-
Verlag, of which he was the chief, became a centre of
Antisemitism. His *Antisemitenkatechismus*, drawn up in 1887
for antisemitic agitators and afterwards reprinted under the
title of *Handbuch der Judenfrage*, a work of pronounced paranoic character, full of the most absurd Munchausen stories,
went through many editions. According to the last of these,
printed in 1933, the number of copies issued is 104,000.
Probably few books have poisoned men's minds as this one.

Houston Stewart Chamberlain's pseudo-scientific work,
of high literary merit, *Die Grundlagen des 19 Jahrhunderts*
(1898), of which more later, became the canonical book of
intellectual racial Antisemitism. In comparison with that of
the post-War period, however, this Antisemitism was relatively weak. The so-called Antisemite petition presented to
Bismarck in 1881, which demanded amongst other things the
prohibition of the immigration of foreign Jews and the
removal of Jews from all Government services, obtained
rather less than 300,000 signatures, and the number of
Antisemites in the Reichstag never exceeded twenty-two.
Their constituents were for the most part small tradesmen,
but especially in Hesse and Saxony the peasantry also
supported them. The movement was weakened by mutual
dissensions among the Antisemites. Another significant
factor was that the Catholic Church, after the settlement of
the *Kulturkampf* and the frequent assumption by Antisemitism of an anti-Christian attitude not merely in practice
but also in theory, sided against the movement and to a
certain extent took the Jews under its protection.

A majority of cultured Jewish personalities came forward
in defence of the Jews, as did a large number of Christians,
mostly of liberal leanings. Seventy-six prominent Christian
scholars, scientists, parliamentarians and business men,
among them Mommsen, Gneist, Droysen and Virchow,
were moved by the Antisemite petition to urge their fellow-
countrymen to keep watch over the inheritance left them by

Lessing. The first-named, replying to Treitschke in his pamphlet *Auch ein Wort über unser Judentum*, declared that Providence doubtless knew better than Stöcker why the metal of Germanism required a certain percentage of Israel for its shaping. In his *History of Rome* he had called the Jews of the Roman Empire " a ferment of cosmopolitanism and national decomposition," whereby he by no means intended to describe them as having a disintegrating effect on the power of the State or society—the quotation, torn from its context, has often been used in this sense by anti-semitic agitators—but on the contrary as a means of over-coming particularism and the centrifugal forces. He would now assign a similar rôle to the Jews of the German Empire. As a final goal he had before his eyes their total absorption in the German population. Eugen Richter prophetically warned the Antisemites against rousing the passions of the mob: " Do not wake the wild beast in man, for then it will stop at nothing ! " In 1891 the *Verein zur Abwehr des Anti-semitismus* was formed by Christians and Jews. Gneist, Heinrich Rickert and a large number of other Christian leaders of culture were at its head. This society, which lasted until the triumph of National-Socialism made its existence impossible—significantly enough its assets were confiscated by the new masters of the State—carried on an active journalistic work of educative aim. The *Centralverein deutscher Staatsbürger jüdischen Glaubens*, founded in Berlin in 1893, worked in the same spirit.

Nietzsche's attitude to Antisemitism was a singular one. In the eyes of this enemy of Christianity its mother-religion was naturally bound to appear antipathetic. And, of course, the Jews were responsible for the " slave morality " which Nietzsche so passionately combated. Before his breach with Wagner he expressed antisemitic opinions both about Judaism and the Jews. But after that he conceived an aver-sion for Antisemitism, which found one of its most prominent leaders in his brother-in-law Bernhard Foerster, and thought

highly of the Jews as a people, though he was by no means
blind to the inferiority of certain Jewish types. " Unpleasant, nay, dangerous qualities are found in every nation,
every human being; it would be cruel to demand that the
Jew should be an exception to this rule. Even if these
qualities in him are in a special degree dangerous and
repulsive—and perhaps the young Jew stockbroker is on the
whole mankind's most obnoxious invention—I should like
to know how much, in a final summing-up, one ought to
overlook in a people which through no fault of ours has had a
history more painful than any other, and which the world
has to thank for the noblest man (Christ), the purest of
sages (Spinoza), the mightiest of all books, and the most
effective moral law." The Jews yearned for a permanent
abode on earth, for an end to their wandering life, and we
ought to meet their wishes in this. The Jews of modern
Europe have reached the highest form of spirituality. " To
meet a Jew is a blessing, especially if one lives among Germans." The fight against the Jews had always been a
distinguishing mark of bad, jealous and cowardly natures,
and a man who took part in this fight must possess a fund of
vulgar propensities. " It does not make an Antisemite any
more respectable that he lies on principle." " What a
quantity of mendacity and dirt is needed to bring forward
racial questions in the Europe of our day, which is a racial
hotchpotch . . . Maxim: do not associate with any person
who has a share in the lying racial swindle." He expected
great contributions from the Jews of the future and considered Antisemitism so far useful in that it must force the Jews
to aim at higher goals and to regard absorption in the
national States as all too low an object.

William I sympathised to a certain extent with Antisemitism, at least in its more moderate forms, which was
doubtless what restrained Bismarck from attacking it.
Bismarck, who in his young days had supported the doctrine
of the Christian State but had afterwards carried Jewish

Ea

emancipation in Germany, denounced several times during his Chancellorship the Jew-baiting agitation as well as Antisemitism in general. He considered that the produce of " a German stallion " and " a Jewish mare " ought to be good—explaining that he was uncertain what advice he would give his sons in the matter—and that the Jews, when mixed with the German stock, would act as an effervescent, a property which ought not to be underrated. He was personally associated with several Jews and valued them highly as men. But the necessities of domestic politics obliged him as a rule to depend on the support of the more or less antisemitic conservative parties.

Unbaptised Jews, although nominally eligible, were practically excluded from the corps of officers—in Bavaria, however, Jews were allowed to become reserve officers—from regular professorships in many universities, Berlin for example, and from the higher Government appointments. The Emperor Frederick, in contradistinction to his father and his son, was liberal-minded, but as we know his reign was a very short one. His definition of Antisemitism as the blot on the nineteenth century is often quoted. William II was one of Houston Stewart Chamberlain's devoted admirers, which, however, did not prevent him from esteeming individual Jews. In daily intercourse the German Jews, who had been on the way to complete amalgamation with the rest of the people, were now more isolated, especially in the country districts. Some Jews abandoned their despised Judaism—during the period 1880–1900 the annual number of Jewish baptisms in Prussia increased from 76 to 480—while others were stirred to Jewish self-consciousness and self-defence. We cannot speak, however, of any effective social boycott: in 1880 mixed marriages in Prussia amounted to a tenth part of purely Jewish marriages, twenty years later they were a fifth part. The process of assimilation still went on in spite of Antisemitism.

In Austria-Hungary, where at the commencement of this

century the Jews amounted to nearly two millions, that is, four and a half per cent. of the population, about three times as many as in Germany, Antisemitism had in part the same causes—particularly the success of the Jews in various careers which had been opened to them by emancipation—and in part it followed the same course. The centres of Anti-semitism were Vienna and Budapest, to which cities a number of Jews had emigrated from the eastern parts of the monarchy, above all from Galicia. The conflict was inten-sified by national rivalries within the monarchy. Thus the Czechs' reason for attacking the Jews was that as a rule they were German-speaking and the vehicles of German culture, while the Austrian Germans, especially in Bohemia and Moravia, attacked the Jews because they regarded them as allies of the Czechs. The leading Austrian Antisemites were Germans: the above-mentioned Professor Rohling, Georg von Schönerer, who in Austria took up the mantle of Stöcker and founded the Christian Social Party, and the advocate Lueger, who became mayor of Vienna in 1897. Here the supporters of Antisemitism were for the most part the lower middle class, the students and large sections of the aristocracy. Student Antisemitism in Austria took the form of numerous riots at the universities. In 1897 the German students' organisation declared their Jewish colleagues to be devoid of honour (*der Ehre bar*), and thus not qualified for duelling, a resolution which is still in force. Contrary however to what was the case in Germany, the Emperor sided against Antisemitism, which was of no small significance. Here again two ritual murder trials, one in Hungary (Tiszla-Eszlar) in 1882–83 and one in Bohemia (Polna) in 1899, contributed to inflame antisemitic feeling. In the latter case the Anti-semites scored a great success, since the accused was found guilty of murder, though not of ritual murder. Thomas Masaryk's courageous effort for a revision of the trial, a parallel to Zola's conduct in the Dreyfus case, was unsuc-cessful. In all parts of the monarchy Antisemitism helped to limit the political, and later also the economic freedom of the Germanised, Polonised or Magyarised Jewish upper class, and to hinder the productivity—that is, the transference to handicrafts and agriculture—of the Jewish proletariat, especially of the impoverished masses in Galicia. In the 1890's a ruinous anti-Jewish boycott was organised in Galicia. The Catholic Diet of Warsaw proclaimed in 1893: " The Greek-Catholic faith and Judaism are our enemies," and recommended the adoption against the latter of " Christian " measures, in other words a boycott. Any Catholic who sold or leased land to a Jew was branded as a traitor. Masses of Jews, reduced to beggary, were only saved from a catastrophe of unparalleled dimensions by wholesale emigration to America. In Hungary, where the Government required the support of the Jews against the contentious non-Magyar minorities, the Jews were admitted to official posts, though the highest were only open to those who accepted baptism. Here assimilation had penetrated deeply among the masses, of which more in another connection.

In Austria-Hungary as in Germany Christians made a stand against Antisemitism and formed societies to this end, which followed the same lines as the German, apparently without much effect. Nevertheless, Austrian pre-War Antisemitism seems to have declined somewhat after Lueger's death (1910), partly on account of the advance of Social-Democracy.

．　．　．　．　．　．　．　．

Not long after the outbreak of Antisemitism in the victorious, heavily-armed German Empire it began to spread to the vanquished, disrupted French Republic, where up to that time the movement had been feeble and had borne a predominantly academic and literary stamp. Wounded national vanity was looking for a scapegoat, and the Jews answered the purpose, in spite of their constituting a relatively small proportion of the population: 100,000 in France itself (and 50,000 in Algeria). Being for the most part of German-Jewish birth they could be represented as the tools of the hated hereditary foe, the most effective of all ways of getting them hated and of letting loose popular passions not only against them but against the Republic, which was obnoxious to the Antisemites and was naturally made out to be a " Jew Republic." The Rothschilds were represented as the real masters of France. The *Alliance Israélite Universelle*, founded in 1860, which had undertaken the task of combating Jewish persecution and through its philanthropic activities and the establishment of schools helping the distressed Jews in Eastern Europe and the Levant, was described as a conspiracy having for its object the founding of Jewish world dominion. The aim of anti-semitic agitation was the inauguration of a monarchical and clerical régime. Antisemitism was supported in the main by the aristocracy of birth, which was hostile to the plutocracy, by extreme nationalist circles in the army and in journalism, by Catholic priests and congregations hostile to Jews and Protestants, and by a number of clerically-minded members of the lower middle class. The Union Générale, a bank started in 1876 by several wealthy Catholic families with the intention of counteracting the influence of the Rothschilds, failed in 1885, bringing ruin to a great number of aristocrats. It was perhaps more than a coincidence that French Anti-semitism blazed up in earnest immediately after this. In 1886 Edouard Drumont published his notorious *La France Juive*, one of the most preposterous lampoons ever written in French, which however did not prevent its having an enormous circulation. The Jews, according to the author, would have been masters of France as early as the Middle Ages, if the Government and the Church had not suppressed and finally expelled them, but in the latter part of the eighteenth century they had again become a power. They and the Freemasons together had brought about both the banishment of the Jesuit Order and the French Revolution. He declared that Marat, the man of the Terror, was of

Spanish-Jewish descent and had people guillotined in order to take revenge on Catholicism for the Inquisition's persecution of the Marranos. And after the Revolution the French Jews, financed by Rothschild, had tried to murder Catholic France and had brought about the disastrous war with Germany. In short: the Jews worked hand in hand with Protestants and Freemasons to extirpate the Catholic faith and enslave the French nation to the Germans. A number of antisemitic pamphlets by Drumont and others followed in quick succession. In 1891 Drumont and other Antisemites founded the newspaper *La Libre Parole*, which became the chief organ of attacks on Jews and Protestants. The enterprise was financed in part by the Jesuit Order.

Among the Catholic writers who opposed Antisemitism the historian Leroy-Beaulieu is specially notable; one of the best known scholars in France, whose most celebrated polemical work bears the title *Israél chez les nations* (1893). The author pointed out the error of regarding the Jews as champions of " dechristianisation," which was an achievement of eighteenth-century enlightenment and a result of the French Revolution; he showed that historical theories based upon racial conceptions are untenable, and that to charge the Jews with constituting a State within the State was no more correct than making similar accusations against Catholics, Jesuits and others; that the talk about the Jews' enormous wealth was nonsense, and that the Jews engaged in business and professional work were no more parasites than Christians who lived by other than manual labour. With the applause of the majority in the Chamber the War Minister Freycinet in 1892 branded the antisemitic agitation as a crime against the country. It was evident that hatred of the Jews had not yet obtained sufficient hold on the mind of the French people. To stimulate it with a ritual murder trial would have been useless in so enlightened a country as France. Then at last the right opening was found. The curtain rises on the Dreyfus affair—an event of extraordinary importance for a knowledge of the nature and methods of Antisemitism, and one which in many respects anticipates the antisemitic psychosis of post-War Germany. Here we shall only dwell on those facts which are of symptomatic interest from this point of view.

In September 1894 it became known to the secret service department of the French General Staff, that the German military attaché in Paris, Schwartzkoppen, was receiving secret military documents from a French officer. This appeared from a piece of paper, the famous *bordereau*, which a French spy had picked out of Schwartzkoppen's waste-paper basket. In the General Staff, which was a centre of Antisemitism, suspicion was directed against Captain Alfred Dreyfus, who held an appointment there. It was true that the man was very rich, which made it difficult to understand why he should have undertaken espionage for the Germans, especially as after the cession of Alsace he and his family had left that province in order to remain French citizens. Dreyfus was a fervent French patriot, a " revanche " man and a hater of the Germans. The fact that he was a Jew was certainly a matter of complete indifference to him. But *La Libre Parole* had not agitated in vain for a couple of years against French officers of Jewish birth, describing them as traitors. Subconsciously Dreyfus's colleagues were pre-disposed to suspect him, partly because he was a Jew—the only Jew, by the way, on the General Staff—and partly because it seemed to serve the honour of French officers best that he, " the foreigner," and not a Frenchman should be pointed out as the traitor. The wish, as we know, is father to the thought.

Dreyfus was examined and placed under arrest, but nothing detrimental was forthcoming against him. The handwriting experts called in disagreed as to the possibility of the *bordereau* being due to Dreyfus. Probably the whole intended trial would have fallen to the ground, if an anti-semitic officer on the General Staff, Colonel Henry, had not informed the *Libre Parole* that Dreyfus had been arrested on suspicion of treason. The paper gave the alarm and the whole nationalist and antisemitic Press started a violent campaign against Dreyfus, who was treated as an unmasked traitor, and against the Jews, who were described as the corruptors of France and the paid servants of the Emperor William. Anyone expressing a different opinion was stigmatised as bought by the Jews. Mercier, the War Minister, had not the courage to oppose the proceedings against Dreyfus. The court martial, which consisted of officers not specially versed in the law and was deliberately misdirected by Mercier—for example by withholding documents from Dreyfus, one of which was forged by Colonel Henry and falsely asserted to allude to Dreyfus—unanimously condemned the accused on December 22nd, 1894, to degradation, imprisonment for life and deportation. On January 5th, 1895, he was degraded on parade, while the mob roared with rage at the Jew—the traitor. The epaulettes and buttons were torn from his uniform and his sword was broken over his head. The dishonoured man cried: " I swear by the heads of my wife and children that I am innocent. I swear it ! *Vive la France !* " The mob shouted in answer: " *À mort ! À mort !* " After the degradation, as Dreyfus was led past the newspaper men, he said: " Tell France that I am innocent." Their answer was to hurl derision and antisemitic insults at the desperate man. Does not this remind us of the Jews in Nazi Germany ? It is significant that in 1890 and 1892 similar affairs of espionage had occurred without attracting much attention and that the culprits, who of course were neither Jews nor Protestants, received relatively lenient sentences: five years' imprisonment in one case, twenty years' penal servitude in the other.

Public opinion demanded a sentence of refined cruelty. A special law designated the Devil's Island as the place of deportation. This was a little island off the coast of French Guiana. Its climate was deadly. Here Dreyfus was buried alive, so to speak. His guards were not allowed to speak to him, and he was subjected to a torture, psychical and physical, which would certainly have shattered him, if he had not been sustained by the desperate hope that sooner or later the stain would be wiped from his name and that of his children.

In 1895 a new chief of the Intelligence Department was appointed, Major Picquart. Like practically all officers of the French General Staff at that time he was no friend of the Jews. On the contrary. But he was an honest man. By a fortuitous circumstance it came to his knowledge in 1896, that the *bordereau* was written by a notorious scoundrel, Major Esterházy. He reported the matter to his superior officer. General Gonse, *sous-chef* of the General Staff, demurred: " If you keep your mouth shut, nobody will know anything about it." To which Picquart replied: " Monsieur le général, that is an abominable suggestion, but I don't intend to take this secret with me to the grave." The result was that Picquart was sent to Tunis in the hope that he might meet his death there, but his commanding officer, who was ignorant of the causes of his transference to the fighting line, refused to employ him in positions of too great danger. From this time on the chiefs of the General Staff were firmly determined at any cost to protect Esterházy and prevent the rehabilitation of the innocent man. Rather let an innocent Jew be tortured to death on Devil's Island than that the honour of the French army should be soiled. Thus one after another of the officers of the General Staff and successive War Ministers were drawn into this affair and were forced to adopt an attitude in Parliament contrary to their better judgment. One forgery and perjury succeeded another, until finally the whole edifice of lies collapsed.

Even before the public had heard anything of Picquart's discovery, Alfred Dreyfus's brother Mathieu and several other Jewish and Christian men had moved for a revision of Dreyfus's sentence, and when on November 10th, 1896, a few days before Picquart's departure for Africa, *Le Matin* published a facsimile of the *bordereau* enabling it, contrary to the paper's intention, to be examined also by foreign handwriting experts, the Dreyfus affair again became a burning question. It is the less surprising that several Jews, notably Bernard Lazare and Joseph Reinach, took part in the struggle for truth and justice, since Dreyfus's sentence was represented to be a sentence upon all the Jews of France; but, as Dubnow remarks, they acted as they did, not as representatives of outraged Jewry, but as Frenchmen. The antisemitic Press, which now had the ear of the French people as never before or after, made out that the Jews were a secret International, a collection of antipatriotic dastards —much as Hitler has done in *Mein Kampf*—rendered powerful by their boundless wealth and personal connections. Everyone who was in favour of a revision of Dreyfus's sentence was said to be bought by the mighty Jewish " syndicate." The more the struggle passed into a conflict between the monarchist-clerical and the democratic-republican parties, the more savage and brutal did the antisemitic agitation become. The passions of the mob were whipped up. Royalists and clericals launched their attacks not only against the Jews, but against the Republic itself, which was depicted as a corrupt " Jew Republic." Thus the hounding of Jews—and Protestants—was at once an end and a means. As in post-War Germany, Antisemitism assumed a markedly hysterical and paranoic character.

Mathieu Dreyfus, who knew nothing of Picquart's discovery but who had been informed by an acquaintance of Esterházy that the writing of the published *bordereau* conformed to the latter's hand, accused Esterházy of having committed the crime for which Alfred Dreyfus was sentenced. In a trial which was a mockery of all law and justice Esterházy was unanimously acquitted by a court martial on June 11th, 1898. The country echoed with the cries: " Long live the army ! Long live Esterházy ! Down with the Jews ! "

Two days later Zola published his " *J'accuse* " in the paper *L'Aurore*. It was a gauntlet flung in the face of the whole " military league of criminals." " I have only one passion," thus Zola concluded his pathetic appeal; " the desire for light in the name of humanity, which has suffered so much and has a right to happiness. My burning protest is only a shriek from my heart. Let them dare to hale me before the courts and let the investigation take place in the light of day ! I await it." A storm of insults was now let loose upon the man who had been bold enough to take the part of an innocent victim against the idol of the nation, the army. In many towns demonstrations of hostility to the Jews occurred, which often ended in rioting. In Algiers they took the form of a regular pogrom. But at the same time there were men who did not hesitate to take their place courageously by Zola's side, among them Jaurès and Clemenceau. Zola was prosecuted and sentenced in 1898 to one year's imprisonment. " All seem to be against me," he said; " the two Chambers, the civil power and the military, the great newspapers, and public opinion, which they have poisoned. On my side I have only the ideal of truth and justice, and I am perfectly calm. I shall be victorious. I would not have my country left in the power of lies and injustice. I may be punished here. One day France will thank me for having saved her honour." Before the sentence became valid Zola made his way to England in order to continue the struggle from there. Picquart, who in spite of threats refused to give false evidence, was cashiered and afterwards arrested. The parliamentary elections resulted in a defeat for the republicans and democrats. Neither Jaurès nor Reinach was re-elected. Many deputies had to promise their constituents that in no circumstances would they vote for a revision of Dreyfus's sentence. But on August 13th, 1898, Henry's forgeries were exposed, on August 31st he took his own life, and on September 1st Esterházy fled to England. On September 3rd Madame Dreyfus appealed for a revision of the sentence on her husband. Henry was hailed as a national hero, and a subscription was got up for his widow. With the presidential election of February 1899 passions reached their climax. The Republic was shaken to its foundations. The choice fell upon Loubet, who was a supporter of revision. On June 9th, 1899, Dreyfus was brought back from Devil's Island, and on the same day Picquart was released. On August 7th the trial for treason was re-opened, and this time it was held in public. To the astonishment of foreign countries it ended, not in the acquittal of Dreyfus, but in his being sentenced contrary to all justice and common sense for " treason in extenuating circumstances " to degradation and ten years' imprisonment, after which he was pardoned. Only two out of the seven members of the tribunal dared to vote for acquittal.

But truth was on the march. In the year 1900 a general amnesty was proclaimed for all concerned in the Dreyfus affair, a measure dictated by political motives, with the object of burying *l'affaire*. But Dreyfus was not satisfied with being merely pardoned, and everywhere in France a growing number demanded full justice. In 1903 Dreyfus appealed for a new revision. On July 12th, 1906, the Court of Cassation declared him innocent, on the following day he re-entered the army as a major, and on July 26th, 1906, he was solemnly rehabilitated and decorated in the presence of the same regiment which had witnessed his degradation eleven and a half years previously.

No impartial person could any longer doubt Dreyfus's innocence, especially as Esterházy finally admitted that he was the author of the *bordereau*. But hatred of Dreyfus lived on in many circles. During the transference of Zola's body to the Panthéon in 1908—he had died in 1902, and thus did not live to see Dreyfus's complete rehabilitation—an antisemitic journalist fired a shot at Dreyfus, who, however, was only slightly wounded. The jury acquitted his assailant.

The Dreyfus affair led to a purgation of the French army

and its Intelligence Department. The power of Clericalism was broken. French Antisemitism slowly ebbed away.

We have here described the Dreyfus affair mainly as a phase in the history of Antisemitism in France; it might also be called a link in that of anti-Protestantism. For the Antisemites spoke of " Jews and Protestants " as well-nigh one and the same, much as the German Nazis speak of " Freemasons and Jews " or of " Marxists and Jews." Both Jews and Protestants were represented as the corruptors of the soul of the French people; together they composed " the Jewish-Protestant monster." They tried to undermine confidence in the army, then to bring about war with Germany, and afterwards they would rejoice over the defeat and shame of the French ! In a pamphlet hostile to Dreyfus, " The Protestant Danger," we read: " Protestantism is a German importation and therefore anti-French. This explains why the Protestants, in spite of all the privileges granted them, are always endeavouring to do as much harm to France as possible. It is quite certain that the Jews, the Freemasons and the Protestants have formed an alliance against the Catholic nations in order to establish their dominion over the world. The real culprit is Protestantism." This train of thought reminds one strikingly of that which pervades the anti-Jewish pamphlets of Hitler's Germany. Whether the Protestant or the Jew is depicted as the guilty party is of minor interest; the main point is that " the other," the foreigner, is made a scapegoat.

The Dreyfus affair had the effect of awakening many French Jews, who were on the way to forgetting that they were Jews. Many a Jew in and outside France, who had believed in the extirpation of Antisemitism through enlightenment, Theodor Herzl for instance, had occasion to revise his views. To others again the final outcome of the affair and the resulting decline of Antisemitism in France appeared to warrant optimism.

One may ask oneself in conclusion why things turned out

otherwise in the Germany of 1933 than in the France of a generation earlier. In both cases we find a violent *Der Jud ist schuld* agitation; in both cases there was a determination not only to destroy " the Jew " but also to dishonour him. Perhaps it was chiefly due to the Germans being more accustomed to obey than to act on their own responsibility and to their not venturing like the Dreyfusards of France to offer a brave and determined resistance to the antisemitic liars and agitators. Or was it that, in spite of all, the lofty ideals of Truth and Justice had more vitality in the Third French Republic than in that of Weimar ? Thus in Germany Drumont triumphed over Zola. Germany's Jews were branded as traitors and degraded amid the frantic cheers of their enemies.

· · · · · · · ·

In many countries of Western and Central Europe Antisemitism never gained a firm footing. It is true that attempts were made in the 1870's to introduce Marr's and Treitschke's antisemitic ideas into England, and antisemitic arguments played a certain part in the opposition to Disraeli and his Turkophile policy directed against Russia, the persecutor of the Jews. Turkey, in fact, treated its Jews well but persecuted the Christian Armenians, who there served the same purpose of lightning-conductors and scapegoats as did the Jews in Russia. But when Disraeli showed himself to be an extraordinarily gifted foreign politician, who brought honour and power to England this anti-Jewish talk was quickly silenced. Nowhere in Europe did the Russian persecutions of the Jews arouse such indignation as here. When in 1883 Stöker visited London in order to speak in the Guildhall on the four hundredth anniversary of Luther's birth, the Lord Mayor declined to be present out of regard for London's " honourable Jewish citizens." The vast immigration of impoverished Eastern Jews after the Russian pogroms of 1881, which in a couple of decades trebled the

number of Jews in England—at the commencement of this
century they numbered 200,000—no doubt gave rise to
apprehensions in certain quarters, but did not occasion any
antisemitic movement.

In the United States, where millions of Eastern Jews found
a home and a refuge from Tsarist tyranny, there arose an
Antisemitism of a more particularly social character, which
however could not be compared with that of Russia or
Germany either as regards its intensity or its significance. It
usually expressed itself in the exclusion of Jews from certain
hotels, fashionable clubs, schools and colleges. Politically
the United States were not merely non-antisemitic but
definitely anti-antisemitic. The persecutions of the Jews in
Russia here roused a storm of indignation. After the October
pogroms of 1905 Congress unanimously adopted a resolution
expressing its concern at what had taken place and its profound sympathy with the Jewish victims. And when the Tsar
refused to allow Jewish Americans the same rights as
Christian, the Republic in 1911 denounced its commercial
agreement with Russia. During the debate in Congress
which preceded this practically unanimous resolution the
American Jews were praised on all sides as citizens and
promoters of culture. The immigration law adopted at the
beginning of 1914, with the object of reducing the stream of
immigration, was mitigated in an important point in favour
of Russian and Rumanian Jews. But in the course of the
heated Press campaign evoked in many places by the
immigration question, and the resultant attacks on aliens,
antisemitic tendencies were apparent, especially among
German-Americans. The authorities, however, did not allow
these to influence them. America, the country where the
Jews enjoyed their liberty long before they attained it in
Europe, lacks the politically antisemitic tradition which in
so many countries of Europe furnishes the most favourable
antecedent for a revival of Antisemitism.

After the assassination of Alexander II, which of course it was sought to represent as an act of the Jews, reaction burst all bounds in Russia. It fell like a bolt from the blue upon the younger generation of Jewish intellectuals, who, educated in Russian schools, had passionately gone in for Russification and adopted the ideals and slogans of young Russia. It is true that here reaction was not directed against Jewish emancipation, for the simple reason that no such measure had been enacted in Russia, but the increased prosperity of the Jews and their commercial and intellectual progress under the relatively mild rule of Alexander II, in other words their " intrusion " in various spheres, had excited the anger and apprehension of the many, and Alexander III and his advisers, the " Grand Inquisitor " Pobiedonostsev and Ignatiev, the Minister of the Interior, hated the Jews. They proposed to russify all the national minorities of Russia by compulsion, but as they regarded the Jews as insoluble, they intended to destroy them as far as possible. Pobiedonostsev is said to have declared that one-third of the Jews of Russia were to emigrate, one-third to die, and the remainder to disappear without a trace in the surrounding population. In any case his policy bears this out. Russian policy now became what in spite of all its brutality it had not been before: anti-Jewish on principle. Both Alexander III and his son Nicholas II regarded the Jews as incorrigible parasites and extortioners against whom the people must be protected. They did not or would not see that the evil was not due to any innate desire on the part of the Jews to " fleece " the population, but to their fathomless material distress coupled with a perverse code of laws, above all to their being packed together in the districts assigned to them. They were not acquainted with the tragic circumstances which had created this crowd of Russian-Jewish tavern-keepers and superfluous middlemen of every sort, and above all they were ignorant of the ethical forces which were alive in this down-trodden and ill-treated people. So they decided upon a policy of brutal tyranny, which cannot be matched for cruelty. With good reason the petition presented to the Government in 1905 by thirty-two Jewish congregations characterised the aim of the Tsarist policy as synonymous with the transformation of the Russian Jews into " a mass of beggars without means of subsistence, education or human dignity." And it must be noted that this policy was not directed only against the Jewish tavern-keepers and hawkers —that would in any case have been explicable—but also against Jewish artisans and peasants, not to mention the Jewish intellectuals. Thus the rulers drove a large proportion of Jewish youth over into the revolutionary camp—which in its turn gave them a fresh pretext for attempting to destroy the Jews and at the same time making the struggle for liberty appear detestable to the people by representing it to be the work of the Jews.

As we know, the methods of Tsarist Jewish policy included pogroms, those wholesale raids and massacres which were often set going with the goodwill of the Government, and indeed in many cases were demonstrably due to its contrivance. Police and military were employed, certainly—to defeat the Jewish attempt at self-defence and to check the bloodthirsty mob, when after a day or two it had accomplished its work. The trials which succeeded the pogroms only deepened the impression of the Jews' outlawry.

The first pogrom broke out, after careful preparation, in Elizavetgrad in 1881, significantly enough during Easter, the classical pogrom season, and was followed at short intervals by pogroms in Kiev and about a hundred other places in South Russia. Masses of Jews were wounded, maimed, blinded, murdered, tortured to death, women were ravished, many thousands of families were ruined, the sacred rolls of the Torah were torn and soiled. Officially the Government adopted the point of view that the pogroms were the people's spontaneous reaction against the " extortion "

FA

of the Jews and set up committees in sixteen of the Governments inhabited by Jews, whose business it was to inquire to
what extent the activities of the Jews had a harmful effect on
the " original population." These committees were composed not merely of fanatical Antisemites, but even of those
who were directly responsible for the pogroms. " Thus this
monstrous thing came about: the ruined, plundered Jewish
population, which had a right to call the government to
account for its grave sins of omission, was itself placed in the
prisoners' dock " (Dubnov). Eleven of the committees
recommended fresh repressive measures against the Jews,
while five were bold enough to face right-about and recom-
mend the abolition of the restriction of domicile. Even before
the Government had had time to draw up the anti-Jewish,
so-called provisional regulation of May 3rd, 1882, a great
pogrom under Russian leadership had been staged in
Warsaw, which by the way occasioned angry protests from
the Polish national leaders and from the Catholic archbishop, and another in the Podolian town of Balta, where
troops and police made common cause with the drunken
mob, after the authorities had openly incited to violence.

With the " provisional " regulation, which in the end
lasted for thirty-five years, we come to the " legitimate "
pogroms, that is, measures adopted by the Government to
destroy the Jews by administrative edicts. The first blow was
an exceedingly hard one: the Pale of Settlement, already
narrow, was reduced in a disastrous way, since the terms of
the regulation made it impossible for millions of Jews to
reside in the country and in towns, thus ruining them and
depriving them of employment. After the Jews had been
thus crowded together, fresh restrictions regarding the right
of domicile and the choice of occupation followed one after
another. The Jews, it has been strikingly said, were confined
as in a leaden chamber, the walls of which were pitilessly
closing in on them. The historian would need the pen of a
Poe to describe the torments of the victims. This was worse

than murder. It was an outrage on the soul of a whole people.

Vast masses of Jews poured out of Russia to other countries —above all to the United States, which thus became the greatest Jewish centre in the world. This, the greatest Jewish migration in history, took place after the first pogroms in conditions of wild panic, but afterwards in a more orderly way. During the first years of Alexander III's reign about 100,000 Russian Jews emigrated annually; later on the numbers increased. Simultaneously Jews were pouring into America from Galicia, Poland and Rumania. As usual in the history of the Jewish Dispersion this upheaval and emigration of the Jewish multitudes marked a new epoch.

Western opinion reacted violently against this bestial policy, and the Tsar dropped its real leader, Ignatiev. But the course that had been entered upon was still followed. In 1884 the Government closed the Jewish industrial school at Zitomir, candidly giving as its pretext that, as the Jews formed the majority of the artisans in the province and no Christian industrial school existed there, the Jewish school served for "fleecing the original inhabitants." Jewish fleecing had thus come to mean the carrying-on of trades which might have been carried on by non-Jews. It was laid down that in future only a certain small percentage of the students in colleges and schools might be Jews, as a result of which masses of young Jews thirsting for education had to apply for admission to foreign institutions or give up their studies.

A committee of Government officials—usually known from its chairman as the Pahlen Commission—appointed by the Tsar for the co-ordination of Jewish legislation, severely condemned in its report of 1888 the policy of repression pursued up to that time: " How can a State," the Commission wrote, " treat a section of the population amounting to five million souls—a twentieth part of its subjects—differently from the rest of the people, even if this section is of alien race ? In the eyes of the State the Jew ought to enjoy equal rights. So long as this is not the case he cannot properly be held under the same obligations to the State as others. Violations of justice and restrictions of liberty, denial of equality and persecution have never ameliorated a human community or rendered it more friendly to its rulers. No wonder then that the Jews, who for centuries have been ground to pieces by repressive legislation, are among those subjects who try to avoid their duties to the State and are to a certain extent alien to Russian life. Our statute book contains nearly 650 exceptional laws directed against the Jews, and the natural consequence of this has been that the Jews as a rule are badly off. Ninety per cent of the Jewish population consists of an entirely impoverished body, which, not unlike a proletariat, lives from hand to mouth, a miserable existence in the most impossible hygienic and other conditions. These proletarians are not infrequently exposed to outbreaks of mob fury and live in constant dread of pogroms and violence. And the law itself classes the Jews, like the heathen Samoyeds, as men of alien race. In short: the situation of the Jews is obviously unbearable. And yet they are not aliens in Russia, but have been a component part of the Russian Empire for centuries." From all this the Commission drew the conclusion that a break ought to be made with the existing system of repression and a policy of reforms substituted. But neither Alexander III nor Nicholas II, who were both swayed by vulgar antisemitic illusions, would hear of such a thing. Equally fruitless was the action of Russian leaders of culture in favour of the Jews in 1890, as was the approximately contemporary English protest, headed by Cardinal Manning. The only reply was new blows aimed at the tortured and despairing people. Like the leaders of Nazi Germany, the Russian Government confounded the actual Jews with the fantastic image they themselves had conjured up. In a conversation with Arnold White, who had opposed in the House of Commons the immigration of Eastern Jews and had been sent on a mission to Russia by the great Jewish philanthropist, Baron Moritz Hirsch, Pobiedonostsev characterised the Russian Jews as parasites and a cross between rogues and usurers. But after White had carefully studied the condition of the Russian Jews on the spot he came to the conclusion that the type of Jew referred to " is evolved from the inner consciousness of certain orthodox statesmen, and has no existence in fact." Everywhere he met with thrifty, industrious people, enterprising tradesmen and excellent artisans, whose appearance, it was true, often spoke of malnutrition. " If courage—moral courage—hope, patience, temperance are fine qualities, then the best Jews of Russia are a fine people," White wrote. He considered that under good guidance the Jews might make efficient agriculturists. But as the Russian Government no longer desired to make the Jews productive, but on the contrary aimed at their further pauperisation, it opposed their agricultural training and their settlement on the land. In the early years of Nicholas II the numerous Jewish tavern-keepers were deprived of their occupation—a measure which would deserve nothing but approval, if only they had been given the chance of a more worthy means of livelihood.

In the spring of 1902 Plehve became Minister of the Interior, one of the most brutal representatives of Russian despotism, an enemy of all national minorities in the Empire, but above all of the Jews. It was he more than anyone else who tried to make the revolutionary movement of the workers and students detestable in the eyes of the people by representing it to be the work of the Jews. His watchword was that it was to be drowned in Jewish blood. Thus the town mob and the unenlightened masses of the peasants were given the idea that the Government was eager for pogroms. At Easter 1903 a carefully prepared massacre was set on foot at Kishinev (now Chisianu in Rumanian Bessarabia), of huge dimensions and shocking bestiality. The Jewish defence force was disarmed by the police, and then the drunken mob was let loose on the Jewish population, the men were flogged, blinded, tortured, maimed and killed wholesale, as were the women, many of whom were also ravished; the little children were thrown out of windows and shattered amid the derision of the crowds in the street. Plehve's secret order given in advance to the governor of Bessarabia not to use force to suppress possible anti-Jewish " disturbances " came to be publicly known and roused a storm of indignation within and without Russia. Leo Tolstoy charged the Government with being guilty of the misdeeds committed at Kishinev. But Plehve did not allow himself to be influenced. A fresh pogrom in August 1903, this time in the White Russian town of Gomel (Homel), was evidence of this. The Jewish defence force was defeated by the troops, whereupon the pogrom was officially described as a Russian action of self-defence against this Jewish force, and the Jews of Gomel were arraigned. The outbreak of the Russo-Japanese war with its accompanying nationalist agitation resulted in new pogroms, which however were partly initiated by conscripts exasperated at the war, who turned against the Jews according to the law of least resistance. The *Novoye Vremya* and other reactionary organs naturally represented the victories of the Japanese as the work of vindictive Russian Jews.

Against the growing revolutionary movement the reactionaries organised the notorious " black hundreds," which afterwards furnished the cadres for the well-known fighting organisation, The League of the Russian People. Their mentality, methods and objects may be characterised by a quotation from a leaflet published by them in 1905: " The cry of ' Down with the autocracy ! ' comes from the bloodsuckers who are commonly known as Jews, Armenians and Poles. Beware of the Jews ! They are the root of all evil, the sole cause of our misfortunes. The glorious moment is already approaching when there will be an end of all Jews in Russia. Down with the traitors! Down with constitutions!" The country was flooded with antisemitic pamphlets, many of which were produced in the printing-office of the police department and financed from the Tsar's so-called privy purse. The result was a great number of pogroms during 1905, the most terrible of which occurred in Zitomir and Odessa. In the latter town over 300 Jews were killed, thousands were maimed and wounded, 600 children were made orphans and more than 40,000 Jews were ruined. Between the 18th and 29th of October 690 pogroms took place, all except 24 in the Pale of Settlement. Nearly all were carried out according to a similar plan, drawn up in advance.

In the first Duma (1906), in which the Jews had twelve representatives, mostly belonging to the Cadet Party (constitutional democrats), the Antisemites composed a small minority. In connection with a great pogrom at Bialystok, in June 1906, and the part played by the authorities in arranging it, the Duma adopted an order of the day in which the terrorist methods of the prevailing system were branded as " unexampled in the history of civilised countries " and the resignation of the Government was demanded. Two days later the Tsar dissolved the Duma. The Prime Minister, Stolypin, tried in vain to persuade the Tsar to adopt a policy of reform in relation to the Jews. The elections to the second Duma were held under intense pressure from above. Only two Jews were elected. The number of Antisemites rose to 100, among whom Kruszevan, the organiser of the Kishinev pogrom, was prominent. The third (and last) Duma, in which again the Jews had only two representatives, was on account of the new, undemocratic electoral system even more reactionary and anti-Jewish in its composition. Stolypin, who was being forced more and more towards the Right, stormed against the revolutionaries, among them, of course, the Jews, with threats of deportation and the gallows, and struck one administrative blow after another at the Russian-Jewish people, until like a Plehve, a Bobrikov and so many more of the terrorist statesmen of

Tsarism he was laid low by an avenging bullet. The Jewish deputy, Friedmann, had good reason in 1910 for characterising the treatment of the Jews as even harsher than in Plehve's time. In the following year the reactionaries had recourse to an often-used but rusty weapon: the ritual murder lie. The accused was a Kiev Jew, Mendel Beilis. But this trial, which stirred public opinion so violently, concerned in reality not only Beilis but all his co-religionists. More than a hundred Christian theologians of note in Europe and America demonstrated the absurdity of pretending that the Jews made use of Christian blood for ritual repasts, seeing that they are forbidden to partake of any sort of blood. In spite of the Government having chosen extreme Antisemites to judge the case, with a jury consisting of ignorant petty tradesmen and peasants, Beilis was acquitted in 1913. The Government took its revenge by instituting proceedings against twenty-five Russian and Jewish advocates, who had assisted Beilis, and were duly sentenced for " inciting the people against the Government."

But no reprisals were able to check the storm of disgust awakened in liberal and radical Russia by the Beilis trial and the whole anti-Jewish policy of the reactionary parties. Nicholas II and his men did not succeed in stifling free speech entirely in Russia or in bringing about any unanimity of view, still less in directing European opinion.

In spite of outlawry and persecution Russian Jewry made economic progress in the last years of the nineteenth and in the twentieth century, as a result of the general improvement in Russia and the important part played by the Jews in the advance of Russian industry and export trade. To a great extent the Jews ceased to be middlemen between the landowners and the masses, a result of the abolition of bondservice; and at the same time, thanks to the development of railways, they found an occupation more profitable to the State and to themselves in providing a market at home and abroad for the products of even the most isolated Russian farms and of Jewish handicraft and home industry. Jewish handicraft advanced rapidly; by the beginning of this century it already supported half a million Jews. Even Jewish agriculture, of which more in another connection, made satisfactory progress. The whole structure of the Russian-Jewish people was changing. " From a people of middlemen there grew a nation differentiated into classes " (Lestschinsky). While assimilated Russian Jews began to play an increasingly important part in Russian culture and Russian politics, an independent Jewish-national, Yiddish-speaking civilisation was developing, with its own newspapers, literature, theatre and music, some of which was on a very high level. The Jews of Russia took the lead in the Jewish intellectual life of the world, as in the political and cultural aims of the Zionist movement. Then a blow fell upon them compared with which all that had gone before might be counted insignificant: the World War broke out.

.   .   .   .

The history of Antisemitism in Rumania is in many ways a reflection of what took place in Russia. At the outbreak of the World War these two countries were the only European States in which the Jews were practically without rights. It is true that the Berlin Congress of 1878 had imposed on Rumania the obligation of enacting the complete emancipation of the Jews, but successive governments omitted to do so, alleging that the Jews settled in the country, even if they had lived there for generations, were to be regarded as foreigners, who might be deported with impunity. It gives one an idea of the Rumanian régime when we learn that these " foreigners " were nevertheless compelled to serve in the army, where, of course, they still enjoyed no rights or protection, and that, in fact, the number of Jews thus serving was proportionally higher than that of the Christians. At the commencement of this century a fifth part of them, about 50,000, emigrated, chiefly to

America. Every kind of oppression, pogroms and wholesale deportations make up the history of the Rumanian Jews during the decades immediately preceding the World War. Here the leaders of Antisemitism were the " liberal " bourgeoisie, who feared the competition of the Jews, while the conservative landowners, who needed the Jews for the distribution of their products, were relatively pro-Jewish. Ignatiev and Plehve scarcely harried the Jews more cruelly than did the liberal leader and Prime Minister, Joan Bratianu. But even the landed nobility did not shrink from using the Jews as lightning-conductors, when the dissatisfaction of the impoverished peasants became threatening. As the Great Powers did not venture to intervene actively against violations of the law and Jewish persecution, the Rumanian Jews found themselves abandoned by all. Here there was no educated and intelligent middle class, as in Russia, to take the part of the oppressed, nor was there an industrial proletariat to feel its solidarity with the Jewish proletariat. The Rumanian Jews were deprived successively of one means of livelihood after another. An immense and naturally demoralising misery invaded them. But here, as in Russia, Jewish scholars continued their studies and Jewish poets their songs.

Xenophon, as a Swedish poet reminds us, was

> " . . . proud and glad to see Hellenes could endure
> And keep a cheerful heart and still aspire
> To nobler things than grief disconsolate,
> Nor would they like barbarians retire
> In frenzied terror 'neath the blows of fate."

Fortunately the Hellenes are not the only ones on whom this gift has been bestowed.

CHAPTER VI

ANTISEMITISM OUTSIDE GERMANY DURING AND AFTER THE WORLD WAR

THE WORLD WAR and the convulsions that followed in its train may perhaps be described as the greatest catastrophe that has befallen the Jewish people since the overthrow of the Jewish State. Scarcely any people was so severely hit by it. Nor did any nation, with the possible exception of the Belgian, receive the news of the outbreak of war with greater horror. This applies in particular to the Eastern Jews. For the Jews of Central and Western Europe had become so incorporated with the nations among which they lived, that when war broke out their Jewish consciousness was altogether suppressed by their German, French or English patriotism. The era of imperialism and militarism had transformed them with the rest. But the Jews of Russia, Poland, Rumania, who had so long been treated as the enemies of the State and were not assimilated to the same extent as their Western kinsfolk, could not feel the same patriotic devotion, even though many of them were infected by the prevailing war-like enthusiasm, and as a whole they loyally fulfilled their duty during the War. The ancient Jewish ideal, like that of the Quakers, is pacifist. Not manly strength and military heroism, but kindness, peace, mercy and philanthropy are the qualities most highly esteemed. During the years immediately preceding the War the economic situation of the Eastern Jews had improved. The concessions to constitutionalism which had been extorted from the autocracy seemed to many to herald the gradual transformation of

Russia into an enfranchised State on the European model. It was this development that was interrupted by the war. The Eastern Jews could look for no benefits from a victorious Russia, still less from a vanquished. And a war carried on within the frontiers of Russia would fall most heavily on them. That Jews were opposed to Jews in the War—the number of Jewish soldiers engaged is estimated at one and a quarter million, of whom about half were Russian Jews— enhanced the horror of the tragedy.

The Russian authorities distrusted their Jewish subjects, whom they regarded as pro-German and, from the fact that they spoke Yiddish and not infrequently German as well, predisposed to serve the Germans as spies and foragers. The very first year of the War was marked by the shooting of Jews accused on the vaguest grounds of espionage and by the brutal dispersal of West-Russian Jewish communities. The meeting between the homeless, desperate masses pouring eastward and the Jewish soldiers marching to the front has often been described. The cry of the former: " Brothers, look what they're doing to us," shows us the situation in a flash. In 1915, when the defeated and demoralised Russian army was retreating before the victorious Germans, it avenged itself on—the Jews. During the pogroms in the Governments of Vilna and Minsk thousands of Jewish women were ravished. Half a million Jews were deported from the Pale of Settlement to the interior of Russia in conditions so frightful as to arouse violent indignation among the Liberal opposition in the Duma. But the Duma majority was antisemitic and disregarded their protests. Yiddish and Hebrew newspapers were suppressed, Liberal papers were compelled to print a trumped-up account of the discovery of Jewish treason, and the reactionary organs agitated against the Jews in a way that puts one in mind of the methods that were afterwards to be so successfully adopted by the German National-Socialists: the Russian-Jewish surgeons were alleged to inoculate the soldiers with syphilis or to perform unnecessary amputations in order to render the army inefficient, and the like.

The revolution of March 1917, which brought about the fall of Tsarism, the complete emancipation of the Jews—the Tsar had already been obliged temporarily to abolish the Pale of Settlement, since a great part of it was in German occupation—and the transformation of Russia into a democratic republic, was hailed with rejoicing by the Russian Jews. Its overthrow in 1918 by the Bolsheviks, a number of whom were Jews, was on the other hand an unprecedented blow to most of them, since their great majority consisted of liberal, bourgeois radicals or social democrats. That, in spite of this, Bolshevism was depicted as Jewish by the counter-revolutionaries was only what one might expect, as it was the surest way of getting it detested and of stirring up nationalist passions to savage fury. It was at this time that the " Protocols of the Elders of Zion " became extraordinarily prominent as a factor in the agitation against the Jews. It needed no acuteness to see that Antisemitism was a ready means of producing a counter-revolutionary popular psychosis, and therefore in the summer of 1917, that is before the fall of Kerensky, the workers and soldiers' councils decided to take measures against it. In July 1918 Lenin outlawed all originators or instigators of pogroms. But this only confirmed the belief of the reactionaries that the Jews were the authors and leaders of the revolution. Thus the great final struggle between the Bolsheviks and their opponents in 1919–20 brought upon Russian Jewry a catastrophe of dimensions previously unknown. The desperate Bolshevist troops and robber bands, who looked on the Jews as hated bourgeois and, moreover, were themselves by no means free from anti-Jewish feelings, often started pogroms, which, however, were punished as far as possible by their leaders. But the White generals deliberately handed over the Jewish communities to the mercy of their soldiery. The orthodox Jewish masses of the Ukraine, to whom Bolshevism was a godless abomination, were put to the sword as—Bolsheviks. Their executioner, the hetman Petlyura, replied to a Jewish deputation which implored him to put a stop to the pogroms: " I beg you not to make trouble between me and the army ! " To save ammunition his soldiers often used only cold steel. Thus the Jews were literally butchered by the thousand. The troops went systematically to work, street by street, and the butchers, or ravishers as the case might be, distinguished themselves by a bestiality scarcely ever surpassed. It was considered a mercy to be killed outright instead of being gradually tortured to death. A father gave all he possessed that his son might " only " be shot. Parents were forced to witness the torturing of their children, children that of their parents. One's pen refuses to record the atrocities committed upon women. In many places practically every Jewess fell a victim to the brutal lusts and sadistic passions of the savage hordes. Denikin, Wrangel, Yudenitch, Krasnov and Koltchak acted similarly to Petlyura. In their armies also a systematic pogrom agitation was carried on, in which the " Protocols of the Elders of Zion " played an important part. Red and White armies swept backwards and forwards over the unhappy country, until at last the Bolsheviks were left the victors. During this period, from December 1918 to April 1921, at least 60,000 Jews were killed in pogroms, of which incomparably the greatest number and the cruellest took place in the Ukraine. Many times greater was the number of those who were wounded, maimed, permanently deprived of their means of livelihood, or shattered by the terror and anxiety to which they had been exposed.

The Bolshevik Government, which sees in Antisemitism one of the main tricks of reaction, has shown itself anxious to combat it by means of penalties as well as by systematic popular education. But Antisemitism still has much vitality among those who have been brought up in its traditions.

We shall return in another connection to the position of

the Jews in contemporary Russia and to their actual and pretended part in the Bolshevik movement.

.   .   .   .

In Poland Antisemitism began to spread as early as the first great Russian pogroms, when the Russian and Russified Lithuanian Jews poured into Congress Poland, and it was given a fresh impulse when, in the Duma election of 1912, the Jews of Warsaw voted for a Social Democrat and secured his election instead of his antisemitic opponent. No doubt they had offered their support to the patriotic cause, but the condition they attached thereto, that no Antisemite should be forced upon them, was significantly enough rejected. The " National Democratic Party," which was founded in 1897 and recruited from the same elements as the antisemitic middle-class parties of Austria and Germany, was opposed to the Jews as competitors in commerce and industry, as well as in the intellectual professions, the small Polonised Jewish upper class no less than the Yiddish-speaking Jewish masses. Many a Pole felt it was his patriotic duty to assist in the " Polonising " of commerce, which was still very largely in Jewish hands. The nationalist passions released by the World War and afterwards by the war with the Russian Bolsheviks did not fail to find another vent in the Jews. In Galicia the Antisemites celebrated the reunion of the province with Poland by great pogroms in Lemberg and several other towns. Both there and in Posen the Jews were charged with being attached to Austria or Germany, as the case might be. When in 1918 Poland took over Posen, practically the whole of its Jewish population removed to Germany. The antisemitic policy of Bolshevik Russia and the fact that a part of the younger generation of Polish Jews had been forced into Communism furnished welcome arguments to antisemitic and Russophobe agitators. The conflict with the Russians in 1919 was the occasion of sanguinary pogroms. General Haller's troops got out of hand and ran amuck among the defenceless Jewish population. Finally the situation of the Jews in Poland became so desperate that President Wilson, the British Government, and the French Socialist Party sent commissions of investigation to the country, which, of course, provided an additional argument to the national-democratic agitation against the Jews of Poland.

With Pilsudski's assumption of power in 1926 the situation of the Jews was ameliorated to the extent that the new régime was not directly hostile to Poland's national minorities and definitely dissociated itself from the national-democratic agitation. But the pauperisation of the Polish-Jewish masses proceeded and is proceeding rapidly. The position of the Jews there is far worse than before the War. Post-War inflation brought ruin to the Jewish middle class, and the formation of a class of Polish tradesmen and artisans, which had already begun before the World War, together with the rise of a powerful State capitalism and State-supported consumers' co-operative system, have deprived masses of Polish Jews of their means of subsistence. It is estimated that the State has taken over twenty to thirty per cent of formerly private commercial and industrial concerns, while the co-operative undertakings have displaced ten to fifteen per cent. The Jews, eighty per cent of whom were engaged in trade and industry and were now to a great extent deprived of their incomes, were not and are not taken into the service of the State or of the industries monopolised by the State, nor into that of the communes, the co-operative undertakings or the great industrial trusts. Polish-Jewish export trade and export industry suffered a blow of unprecedented severity when Russia closed its frontiers against them. In the universities what amounted to a *numerus clausus* was applied. No doubt the Polish people in themselves appear less susceptible to Antisemitism than the German; but the widespread unemployment among industrial workers, the distress among the peasants and the economic depression of the middle class have brought wind to the sails of the champions of " Poland for the Poles." This makes the Government inclined above all to rescue the latter and leave the Jews to their fate. Thus their distress is increasing at a terrible rate. As Jacob Lestschinsky pointed out at the Jewish World Conference at Geneva in August 1934, fifty-five per cent of the Jewish population in Warsaw, Lemberg, Vilna and other towns are unable to pay a tax of five zlotys (about 2s. 6d.) per annum. It cannot be said that the Polish Jews are intentionally subjected by the authorities to the same mental torture as is the case in Germany, but their material distress is far worse. The majority of Poles will not hear of any scheme for making the starving Jewish masses productive, for they consider that the soil of Poland should be reserved to the Polish people and that the number of Polish-Jewish artisans should rather be reduced in favour of the Poles. Actually the whole Polish-Jewish middle class is menaced with ruin. Millions of Polish Jews would be willing to emigrate, if only there were some country to receive them. The situation of the Jews in Lithuania and Latvia is similar.

That the Jews are able and willing to become efficient manual labourers and agriculturists has been proved by the young Eastern Jews in contemporary Palestine. But as neither that nor any other country can receive more than a part of Polish Jewry, the Polish-Jewish problem must be solved in Poland itself, or at least a *modus vivendi* must be found there. The problem, however, is rendered excessively difficult by the great numbers to be dealt with, 3,300,000 souls, about a seventh part of the whole population.

The Danish-Polish professor, Stanislas Rozniecki, of Copenhagen, in his book on the Jewish problem, characterises the demand of the Polish Jews for national rights as a " cultural luxury " and blames them for refusing to submit to the law of assimilation, an assertion which one of his critics, S. Faniecki, rightly styles naïve when one considers the immense force of the national idea, and declares to be

GA

based on an under-estimation of historical laws, which know nothing of free will in this connection. Moreover, it must be noted that the purely religious antagonism between the Roman Catholic population of Poland and the Jews not only has played but still plays a far more important part in the process of isolation than in the countries of Western Europe. For the idea of Poland as the specifically Christian country, whose sufferings, destruction and resurrection implied in a way an imitation of Christ, has in no small degree set its mark on popular conviction.

In Germany the Jews are found fault with for usurping and thus distorting the civilisation of the country, in Poland for isolating themselves from it. If the Polish Jews had become assimilated they would no doubt have been reproached for that. Whether the Jews become assimilated or not, they are equally to blame in the eyes of Antisemites. That is the way of Antisemitism.

Some sort of solution of the Polish-Jewish problem, since unemployment has decreased, seems, however, at present less impossible in Poland than in Germany. For one thing the Polish Jews are a power in spite of everything, thanks to their number and their representation in the Sejm[1]— compare the position of the Swedes in Finland—while the German Jews are powerless; and for another thing, as we have said, Polish Antisemitism is on the whole not so frenzied and savage as German. Nor does the Polish public appear so inclined, as was the German before Hitler's triumph, to forbear from opportunist motives from showing disapproval of anti-Jewish outrages. The antisemitic students' riots of 1931 were denounced by all leading Polish organs, except those of the National-Democrats, as a sign of want of civilisation and a disgrace to Poland. On this occasion one of the most prominent representatives of Polish-Jewish culture, the author, Sholom Asch, wrote: " In no circumstances must

---

[1] Since the above was written proportional representation has been abolished, as a result of which the Jews will be left with only a few seats.

we hold the whole Polish nation responsible for the doings of a section of the populace. During the recent sorrowful days we have heard deeply affecting words from responsible and saddened circles of the Polish community. These words lead us to hope that, in spite of their efforts, our enemies will not succeed in destroying the purely human bonds which in recent years have begun to unite Christians and Jews, bonds which are of vital importance to Poland, and that they will not succeed in raising artificial barriers between two peoples whom history has united in a common land and placed under the same destinies."

.   .   .   .

The Rumanian Jews, who even before the World War were treated and hated as aliens and like all Eastern Jews suspected of German sympathies, suffered almost unparalleled ill-usage in the course of the War. When Rumania became a belligerent all divisions of the army were ordered to form special Jewish units, to place them under the command of the sternest officers and to employ them in the most exposed positions. And this was done. By the treaty of 1920, which conferred great provinces upon Rumania and a Jewish population four times as great as before, the State was certainly obliged to grant the Jews equal rights, but Joan Bratianu, who came into power in 1923, contrived that the Jews in the newly acquired territories were excepted from this provision and deprived of their national status. The number of pogroms was legion. From the year 1922 there is not a single Rumanian town of any size that has not suffered from them. The " Christian League " led by Professor Cuza and the terrorist Iron Guard won for themselves a ghastly notoriety. Police and military often made common cause with the pogrom bands. When the prefect of Jassy took steps to suppress the terror he was murdered by an antisemitic student, who was afterwards acquitted by the court and hailed as a national hero (1925). Those who murdered Jews

from antisemitic motives could always count upon acquittal
or an extremely lenient sentence. The lead was taken by the
antisemitic students, whose hatred moreover was not infrequently turned against other national minorities, the
Magyars for instance. By means of the terror they practically
established a *numerus clausus* for Jews at the universities. As
in Poland the government of Rumania has intervened in
recent years against the extreme Right. In 1933 the Prime
Minister Duca dissolved the Iron Guard, but fell a victim
shortly afterwards to the murderous bullet of an Antisemite.

.   .   .   .

If Rumanian post-War Antisemitism is a direct continuation of pre-War and therefore of minor interest for the study
of the nature of the movement, that of Hungary on the other
hand shows us something new and instructive. The fact is
that before the World War, and even in the 1890's Hungarian
Antisemitism appeared to be played out; Liberalism and
assimilation had taken hold of practically all young educated
Jews in Hungary; the State and society no longer raised any
obstacles worth mentioning to the Jews' choice of a career or
to their complete absorption in the Hungarian nation. Of the
medical students in Budapest University during the years
1910–13 no less than 50 per cent were Jews, in its technical
college 40 per cent, of 6,743 advocates 3,049 were Jews, of
2,084 doctors 1,295 were Jews, of 1,214 journalists 516 Jews.
Jews were prominent as government officials, members of
parliament, municipal councillors, merchants, manufacturers, men of science, authors and artists. They adopted
Hungarian as their mother-tongue, Magyarised their names
to a great extent, merged themselves entirely in Hungarian
culture. They were not merely themselves Magyarised as
the Swedish Jews are Swedicised or the German Germanised,
but they were at the same time zealous pioneers of the
Magyars' language and civilisation. In the polyglot districts
the Jewish schools were often the only ones in which the

Hungarian language was used; a fact of some significance, since it led to their being attended also by Christian children. As a Magyarising factor the Jews were highly esteemed by those in power. The Jews are also very largely responsible for making Budapest a great capital, for creating Hungarian industry and commerce, for founding the leading theatres and bringing the Press up to a European level. Through their cultural contributions they had helped in great measure to confer on little Hungary the rank of a civilised State. Many of the country's highest nobility were of Jewish descent. Pogroms in Hungary, in Budapest—what an absurd idea !

The World War evoked among the Jews of Hungary a wild patriotic devotion. They willingly sacrificed life and fortune. Over 10,000 of the country's 500,000 Jews fell on the field of battle. The struggle against war-weariness was headed by a Jew, the Minister of Justice, Vilhelm Vázsonyi. Then the State collapsed. The Bolsheviks, among whom Béla Kun, Tibor Szamuely and several more were Jews, seized power (in March 1919) and held it for nearly five months. Their programme included the combating of all " capitalism," not excepting Jewish. (In this spirit they executed forty-four Jewish capitalists as counter-revolutionaries). Then " the awakening Hungarians " rose against the Soviet Republic, depicted as Jewish, and overthrew it with the help of Rumanian troops. A White terror ensued, which in extent and bestiality surpassed the Red. It was directed not only against the Bolshevist Jews but also against—the Jews; in fact, the whole struggle against the Hungarian Soviet Republic was given the aspect of a war of Magyar independence against the Jewish race. Horthy's bands harried the Jewish population very much as the White Russian armies had harried the Russian Jews. No Jew was any longer secure in life and limb, and when at last a relative calm supervened, the terror continued in a legitimate form. A law was passed providing that anyone who expressed dissatisfaction with the régime was subject to rigorous penalties for

" insulting the Hungarian nation." It is perhaps superfluous to mention that thousands of Jews were dismissed from their offices and that the universities adopted what amounted to a *numerus clausus*. No doubt this terrorist Antisemitism has now practically ceased, but in its place the struggle persists for the systematic exclusion of Jews from commerce and industry.

The victory of Magyar Antisemitism, prepared by the aversion aroused by masses of Jewish proletarian refugees from devastated Galicia, and won through a clever exploitation of Bolshevist misdeeds, foreshadowed in many ways the brilliant triumph of Hitlerite Antisemitism under the banner of a *Der Jud ist schuld* propaganda. Disjointed and tormented Hungary had at last found a scapegoat. It is hard to say how many Jews there were among the Bolsheviks, but that they comprised an infinitesimal fraction of the country's 500,000 Jews appears from the fact alone that the whole communist camp in Hungary, Jewish and non-Jewish, totalled at the most 5,000 men.[1] But as we know fear multiplies the vision: the appalling stories of " the Jews' " cruelties and crimes were accepted by the public with a readiness that was entirely uncritical. The Hungarians soon became convinced that the Jews were a people of extortioners, skulkers, traitors and Bolsheviks. The 10,000 who had fallen for Hungary in battle against her enemies were forgotten, and that ninety-nine per cent of the country's Jews were undoubtedly loyal and patriotic citizens made no difference. It is significant of the feeling in Magyar circles that the brothers Tharaud's description of the Hungarian Soviet Republic, influenced by those circles, bears the title, alike suggestive and misleading: *Quand Israël est roi* (1921).

.   .   .   .

In the Austrian half of the Habsburg monarchy the collapse was also accompanied by antisemitic excesses, though of less severity than was the case in Hungary, the only

[1] According to Oskar Jászi, *Magyariens Schuld, Ungarns Sühne* (1923), the number was about 5,000, but this figure appears to be somewhat exaggerated.

Habsburg country which had to undergo a period of Bolshevist terror. In Vienna, the home of over 200,000 of Austria's 250,000 Jews—nearly eleven per cent of the city's population—the wave of Antisemitism was rising even during the War, when the city was filled with Galician and other Eastern Jewish refugees. In 1918–19 the Austrian Jews had to enrol a defence force to protect themselves against National Socialist violence. Under the Republic the Christian Socialist and other antisemitic parties gained the majority. The universities became centres of hatred of the Jews. Christians as a rule broke off all private intercourse with their Jewish acquaintances. In the city of Vienna, it is true, the Socialists came into power in 1919 and remained in control, as we know, for many years, but in contrast to socialist parties in other countries they compromised with Antisemitism. Their most prominent leaders, Viktor Adler and after his death Otto Bauer and Julius Deutsch, were Jews indifferent to Judaism and do not seem to have opposed anti-Jewish feeling to any extent. The party studiously avoided even the appearance of being a " Jewish defence force." Its Press often contained anti-Jewish diatribes. During the time they held sway in Vienna the Jews were excluded from the city's administration, as they had been under the Christian Socialist régime. None the less the breaking up of the Austrian Socialist Party has involved among its results an intensification of Antisemitism, since a large proportion of those who support the victors are pronounced enemies of the Jews. True, no " Aryan clause " has been formally introduced, and the government is not antisemitic on principle, but the elbowing of Austrian Jews out of various walks of life is nevertheless actively going on.

On the other hand Antisemitism has rapidly lost ground in Czechoslovakia, even in the field of political economy. No doubt it is favoured by the German element in the population, especially by the students, but the Czechs as a whole have now turned away from it, and indeed often adopt an attitude of direct hostility to it. That the rulers themselves in Czechoslovakia have so resolutely sided against Antisemitism, which flourishes with the avowed or tacit approval of the authorities in the neighbouring States, is clearly to a great extent due to President Masaryk. Probably no other living statesman has taken the part of the persecuted Jews so warmly and eloquently, or branded Antisemitism with such indignation.

.   .   .   .

In other European countries Antisemitism is of no great importance for the moment. Greece however furnishes an exception to some extent; its Jews—who numbered about 120,000 or rather more than two per cent of the population —are admittedly well treated by the State, but in Salonika, which has been Greek since 1912, they are often exposed to persecution by the Greek population, who have been their competitors from of old.

The French Antisemites, Maurice Barrès, Léon Daudet, Georges Batault and others, have little influence on popular feeling in the France of our day. This state of things has not been changed by the great immigration of Russian Jews in the years immediately following the World War or that of German Jews in 1933. Doubtless the Jews, whose number in France may now be placed at about 200,000 with an approximately equal number in Algeria and the colonies, play an important part in industry, art and science, but instead of being regarded in the German fashion as enemies they are looked upon as fully qualified citizens, who, though of alien race, promote the economic welfare of the nation. It would scarcely occur to any Frenchman to treat Bergson, for instance, as the Germans have treated Einstein. Generally speaking little attention is paid in France to a man's origin. But we may well ask ourselves whether the French would have been so generously disposed if they had lost the War. It is significant that Batault in his pamphlet *Le Problème Juif*, published in 1921, attributes it to Jewish influence that harder terms of peace were not imposed on Germany—in which, by the way, he is undoubtedly right, in so far as a striking number of Jews in every country pleaded for more lenient terms.

The state of things is similar in Italy, where 45,000 Jews are now living, as in Sweden about 0·1 per cent of the total population. In November 1927 Mussolini declared to a meeting of foreign journalists, among whom were several Rumanians: " Fascism means unity, Antisemitism destruction and division. Fascist Antisemitism or antisemitic Fascism therefore implies a crass absurdity. To us in Italy it appears extremely ludicrous that the Antisemites of Germany should try to win their way through Fascism. And from other countries too, information reaches us that a Fascism of antisemitic shade is trying to strike root. We protest with all our energy against Fascism being compromised in this way. Antisemitism is a product of barbarism." Since that date Mussolini has consistently adhered to this point of view.

In England (and Ireland), where the Jews number about 320,000 or 0·7 per cent of the population, an antisemitic tendency asserted itself during and after the World War, partly due to a large proportion of English Jews being suspected of sympathising with the enemy on account of their German-Jewish extraction, and stimulated by the increased immigration of Eastern Jews. Even in society a certain degree of Antisemitism was observed, admirably described by Galsworthy in his play *Loyalties*. Maxse, Chesterton and Belloc wrote in no pro-semitic spirit. An extreme antisemitic group endeavoured on the German model to injure prominent Jewish politicians and to spread the wildest falsehoods about (the Freemasons and) imaginary Jewish plots against the non-Jewish world. " The Protocols of the Elders of Zion " were published in English and at first taken seriously by several journals of repute. But when in August 1922 this scurrilous pamphlet was exposed as a clumsy forgery and at the same time the methods of the English Antisemites were unmasked in a number of actions for libel, the tide of feeling turned and Antisemitism rapidly declined. It is by no means stamped out, as Mosley's agitation proves, but it cannot be termed important. In no country have the Hitlerite persecutions and the lying Nazi propaganda roused such a storm of abhorrence irrespective of party as precisely in England.

. . . .

In the United States again, which is now the home of the world's greatest Jewish centre, the World War tended to awaken nationalist hatred of foreigners in general and especially of the numerous German and East European Jews, who, as we have said, were supposed to harbour German sympathies. Yet it must be noted that here the government never allowed itself to be influenced, like those of Russia and Germany, by this popular feeling. In 1920 the " Protocols of the Elders of Zion " and a number of other extraordinarily malignant antisemitic pamphlets began to flood the country. Henry Ford, as we know one of the richest men in the world, financed the movement to a great extent and himself carried on in his widely circulated paper *The Dearborn Independent* a furious campaign against the Jews, who were made out to be a pack of dastardly Bolsheviks. A selection of the articles there printed, under the inspiration of the " Protocols of the Elders of Zion," were afterwards published in book form under the title of *The International Jew*. The notorious secret society, the Ku Klux Klan, agitated against Jews as well as against negroes and Catholics. A great sensation was produced in 1922 by a proposal to introduce a *numerus clausus* for students of alien race in Harvard University. It was defeated, of course, but served to show how the wind was blowing. The Jews of America however did not remain passive in the face of their detractors, and they were helped by many influential Christians, among them Wilson and Taft, who were revolted at the lying antisemitic propaganda. When Ford's organ accused a Jew, the lawyer Aron Sapiro, of belonging to an international Jewish conspiracy for subjugating and fleecing the farmers of the United States, Sapiro brought an action against Ford, and when the editor of *The Jewish Tribune* was charged with having betrayed secrets during the war to " the international Jewish conspiracy," he declared his intention of following Sapiro's example. Then Ford swung round. On June 30th, 1927, he approached the chairman of the American-Jewish Committee, Louis Marshall, declared that he had arrived at the conviction that the " Protocols of the Elders of Zion," which his paper had published, were a forgery, and said he deeply regretted his antisemitic past. His eyes had now been opened to the virtues of the Jewish race, the services of their ancestors to civilisation and human progress and to the Jews' industry and unselfish interest in all questions that concerned general welfare. He had not himself known of his paper's defamatory articles on the Jews and had been " deeply mortified " when he read them ! He now wished to make good by every means the injury he had done the Jews. With huge headlines the American Press gave publicity to his declaration, and the remaining copies of *The International Jew* were withdrawn and destroyed. The evil Ford had done could hardly be undone. *The International Jew* had been distributed wholesale in Rumania and the Ukraine, and by no means without result. But his defection from Antisemitism at least had this significance, that he no longer financed the movement. With the collapse at about the same time of the Ku Klux Klan there was an end of organised antisemitic propaganda in the United States. It had achieved no object, except possibly an indirect one: the decision of those in power to restrict the immigration of the non-Nordic peoples. American Antisemitism is still free from political colour—many prominent officials are Jews, and the fact arouses no opposition—but often expresses itself in social intercourse, as indeed is apparent from Ludwig Lewisohn's lifelike novels.

CHAPTER VII

GERMAN ANTISEMITISM DURING AND AFTER THE WORLD WAR

Every war involves a danger to the Jews, not only on account of their being blamed for defeat and of course for the war itself, if it is lost, but also because excited nationalist passions have a way of turning against all who in any respect appear alien. To this extent war involves a relapse into a primitive condition which is usually regarded as belonging to the distant past of European humanity, an epoch when, as philologists know, stranger and enemy were synonymous terms. (The Latin *hostis*, enemy, has the same root as *hospes*, guest, and is the same word as the Germanic *gastir*, guest.) But when the World War broke out the Jews of Germany were seized like the rest with patriotic enthusiasm. Besides the 50,000 conscripts, 10,000 volunteers flocked to the colours; before the end of the War the number of Jewish soldiers reached 100,000, of whom 80,000 served at the front. Those of them who still felt as Jews, enthusiastically seized the opportunity of proving their German patriotism. Nor was antisemitic agitation permitted during the first months of national rallying, when political parties, following the Kaiser's watchword, dropped all controversial questions. But with reverses Antisemitism broke out. The Jews were depicted as skulking from active service, and in November 1916 the War Ministry caused a statistical investigation to be made regarding the number of Jews at and behind the front, which was felt to be an egregious insult by the German Jews, who had lived in the belief that when the country was in danger they would be regarded as one with their fellow-citizens. This clear proof of distrust on the part of the government naturally resulted in a flaring up of Antisemitism all over the country, and it grew with the increase of Germany's difficulties during the war.

Whether the number of German-Jewish combatants, about 80,000, or of their dead, about 12,000, fell below the "normal" was disputed up to the time when owing to Hitler's victory it was made impossible for the Jews to discuss the question as equals. On the Jewish side it was energetically contested, with the support of abundant statistical material, that such was the case.[1] What is incontestable is that no fewer than 35,000 Jews were decorated, 1,500 of them with the Iron Cross of the first class, and that 23,000 were promoted, of whom 2,000 received commissions, in spite of the pronounced Antisemitism of the German corps of officers, and in spite of the Jews being less accustomed than most to the use of arms. The Antisemites refused to see the Jewish soldiers at the front. One of their popular songs said of the Jew: " *Ueberall grinst sein Gesicht, nur im Schützengraben nicht* " (" Everywhere his face is grinning, except only in the trenches ").

Another reason—or excuse—for the resuscitation of Antisemitism was the relatively important part played by the Jews in the November revolution of 1918. German Jewry as a whole was bourgeois-minded, but the minority who were not so had on an average more education than the classes who made the revolution, and in consequence were better fitted to express themselves in the spoken or written word and to organise. It is perhaps no exaggeration to say that the great majority of the German-Jewish privates and

[1] The percentage of difference to the detriment of the Jews, according to the estimate of the League of Jewish Front Soldiers 12·5 per cent instead of 13·42 per cent, is explained by the urban population, especially the educated classes, being to a large extent employed in civil-military service; by the Jews being less numerously represented in the younger conscription classes owing to the great decrease in their birth-rate, and so on. Of German-Jewish officers 16·1 per cent were killed; of all officers in the German army 14·74 per cent.

non-commissioned officers who were elected to the soldiers' councils and not infrequently took a leading part in them, belonged to the category of those who would have been officers if their promotion had not been hindered by Antisemitism. In other words they were intellectuals who in consequence of the animosity against the Jews had not been absorbed by the governing class and were therefore predisposed to become leaders of the proletariat. But in contrast to what was the case in Russia, where the Jews constituted and still constitute an educated *élite* among those strata of the population who are the support of the republic, in Germany the Jews as a rule made way for non-Jews when the work of the revolution was consolidated on a broad democratic basis. This applied not only to the soldiers we have been speaking of, but also to a host of Reichstag deputies of the radical Left. It was of special significance that many Jews were prominent in the establishment of the Soviet Republic in Bavaria and during its short period of existence: Landauer, Leviné, Levien, Mühsam, Toller, and above all Kurt Eisner, who was its prime minister. The agitation that was carried on against the last-named is scarcely to be matched for frenzy and Machiavellianism and contributed greatly to the intensification of Antisemitism all over Germany. In order to prove to the German people that the Imperial Government was to blame for the War and perhaps also to convince the Entente Powers that new Germany dissociated itself from the old régime and therefore ought to be given reasonable peace terms, he caused a number of dispatches to be published, which had been sent by the Bavarian Minister in Berlin after the outbreak of War. The dispatches which were couched in a warlike tone were published *in extenso*, the others merely summarised. That this method of publication, together with the exposure of Imperial Germany, aroused a storm of indignation, was only too natural, and it was equally to be expected that this feeling was enhanced by the prime minister being a Jew.

Eisner's mode of procedure was exploited not only against himself and his communist adherents, but against the whole of German Jewry. On February 21st, 1919, as he was on his way to the Landtag to resign his office, he was murdered by Count Arco-Walley, who by the way was a half-Jew. On May 1st the Bavarian Soviet Republic fell, and a violent antisemitic reaction set in. From that time forward Bavaria became one of the strongholds of Antisemitism in Germany.

Other material for agitation was supplied by the invasion of Eastern Jews, which began during the War, while the Jewish regions of Poland were in German occupation, and did not cease when these regions were evacuated after the peace. There was a talk of hundreds of thousands, nay, millions of Eastern Jews who were flooding the country, and of huge multitudes who had been naturalised by the " Jew-controlled " Weimar Republic. In the light of statistics the figures appear as follows. In the census year 1925, when the number of Jews in Germany undoubtedly reached its culminating point, 99,000 of Germany's 569,000 Jews were aliens. After that date the economic crisis and Antisemitism drove masses of Eastern Jews out of Germany. In 1933 the number of those living in Germany can hardly have exceeded 76,000. According to official Nazi figures 12,500 Eastern Jews were naturalised during the years 1919–33, a figure which, we may be sure, has not been put too low. Most of these had been domiciled in Germany for more than ten years and had German for their native tongue.

The Eastern Jews, perhaps, even among the Jews, the most calumniated national group in the world, who even in the most difficult circumstances have given clear proof of self-sacrifice, humanity and idealism,[1] but who include a mass of speculators, jobbers and swindlers, a result of their unhappy social structure, are judged one-sidedly from the inferior

---

[1] On account of their negligent exterior the orthodox Eastern Jews often impress the Westerner unsympathetically. But they ought not to be judged by their outward appearance. In their schools " importance is attached solely to inward culture, all else is without significance " (Ruppin).

elements which undoubtedly were most conspicuous and inclined to spread themselves in post-War Germany. The scandalous corruption of which they were guilty was certainly by no means confined to them, but was rather a sign of the times in the " Aryan," as well as the Jewish world; but while as a rule the non-Jewish swindles were quickly forgotten, the rascalities of the brothers Barmat, Sklarek and Kutisker were the object of a lasting and widespread interest, since the antisemitic papers and agitators knew how to make capital out of them. No small proportion of the German Jews were painfully disturbed at being lumped together with their Eastern kinsfolk, who differed considerably from them in appearance and manners. Ignorant of the existence of eminent characters among the Eastern Jews—men who as a rule keep in the background—they often looked at their East European co-religionists through the spectacles of their antisemitic neighbours. Thus they not infrequently dissociated themselves from them in a demonstrative way. But the Antisemites paid no attention to this, and doubtless their attitude would have been the same even if the German Jews in general had followed the advice of the extreme assimilationists in opposing the admittance to Germany of these largely impoverished and distressed kinsmen. Every Eastern Jewish swindler who was exposed, every Eastern Jewish politician who carried on Bolshevist propaganda (Rosa Luxemburg for instance), added to the general hatred with which the German Jews also were regarded. Many Jews who excited the special hatred of the Antisemites, Kurt Eisner for instance, were falsely described as " Galicians " or Eastern Jews, just as " Aryan " communists, such as Karl Liebknecht, were made out to be wholly or partly Jewish.

The Weimar Republic, the constitution of which had been drawn up by a German Jew, Hugo Preuss, was stigmatised as a " Jew Republic," its flag as a " Jewish standard." Here as everywhere the antisemitic agitation was not the end but the means, the end being the overthrow of the democratic parties through throwing suspicion on the government and the Republic by labelling them Jewish.

The unwritten law of Imperial Germany which denied an unbaptised Jew access to the permanent offices of the State, was now annulled. As will be shown in another connection, this by no means resulted in such offices being filled to any preponderant extent by Jews, but the unaccustomed sight of German-Jewish officials got on the nerves of many Germans. As Germany's misfortunes accumulated, so did nationalist feeling and hatred of the Jews increase. The latter grew more and more furious and hysterical. It was led by young men of the classes whose power had been broken by the November revolution and who had been hardest hit by the inflation which followed a few years later. The Jew was blamed both for Germany's misery and for that of the middle class. The Jew, that meant the Marxist, the parasite, the author of the World War and of defeat, the extortioner who by means of the Versailles Treaty and the golden International held Germany in his clutches and through the banks fleeced the debt-encumbered bourgeoisie and the peasant class. Un-German parliamentarism was his work; it was a tool in the hands of " Pan-Judah." Men battened on hatred of the Weimar Republic and on dreams of pogroms. Between 1923 and September 1932, 128 Jewish cemeteries and 50 synagogues were desecrated. No rumour was improbable enough to be refused belief, if only it added to anti-Jewish exasperation. " The Protocols of the Elders of Zion " secured an enormous circulation and general acceptance in youthful circles. The youths who in 1922 assassinated Germany's most prominent Jew, the Foreign Minister Walter Rathenau—they belonged to the Schutz- und Trutzbund, founded in 1919—were convinced that he was one of the three hundred Wise Men of Zion (!) and was entirely dominated by the idea of the destruction of Germany and the establishment of Jewish world-hegemony.

HA

Even in leading circles similar views were promulgated. Not even after Hitler's victory was greater toleration observed with regard to the grossest propaganda lies. In a Nazi pamphlet of semi-official character, *Die Juden*, written by Gottfried Feder and published in July 1933, we read that "the aspiration implanted in the blood of the Jews aimed at leading Germany into the arms of Bolshevism, which would enable them to plunder and enslave the whole nation." As in Hungary in 1919 no attention was paid to the fact that ninety-nine per cent of the country's Jews were anti-Bolsheviks.

The various "popular" (*völkische*) leagues, the Schutz- und Trutzbund, Stahlhelm, Jungdeutscher Orden, and so on, took an extraordinarily strong hold on young men, especially the students, who here as in other countries took the lead in ultra-nationalist movements. Most important of all, as we know, was the National Socialist German Labour Party founded by Hitler on February 25th, 1920, which carried fanatical Nationalism and embittered racial hatred to their highest pitch. Its flag was the swastika banner, which was believed, incorrectly, to be a specifically Aryan symbol; its watchword was "*Deutschland erwache, Juda verrecke!*" ("Germany, awake; perish Jewry.") In the party programme drawn up by Feder it was laid down that no one may become a German citizen who does not belong to the national community, which is only open to those who are of "German blood," therefore not to Jews (par. 4). The Jews are to be placed under the laws relating to foreigners (par. 5). Those who are not citizens cannot hold offices (par. 6), and are to be deported if the population cannot earn a livelihood in the country (par. 7). Non-Germans are not allowed to immigrate, and those who entered the country after August 2nd, 1914, are to be deported (par. 8). (These two paragraphs are of course aimed particularly at the Eastern Jews.) In order to strengthen the middle class the great department stores are to be communalised and let out at a low rent to small tradesmen (par. 16). (The great department stores were largely Jewish.) Speculators and usurers are to be punished with death " irrespective of religion or race " (par. 17). (According to the dogmas of National-Socialism the Jews are a nation of speculators and usurers.) Non-German journalists may not write in German newspapers, and non-Germans may not be financially interested in them (par. 23). Religious liberty is not to apply to such religions as tend to undermine the State or are in conflict with Germanic ideas of morality (par. 24). (Judaism does so conflict according to Nazi propaganda literature.) In the official commentary on the programme, again drawn up by Gottfried Feder, war is declared on " the world-enemy," who is declared to be identical with Capitalism, which overshadows the world, and " with its supporter, the Jew." It is true that neither in the programme nor in the commentaries is there any mention of the position of half- and quarter-Jews, but the belief in the worthlessness of Jewish blood (and the excellence of Nordic) is of course one of the corner-stones of the edifice of Nazi dogma.

Side by side with this extreme Antisemitism a more moderate variety had flourished from of old, and this too was greatly extended during and after the World War and was embraced in particular by the conservative, non-" popular " parties. Here there was no belief in the fables about Jewish plans of world-dominion or their enormous financial power, nor again in the German Jews' lack of patriotism or moral inferiority. The Jews, it was thought, were not inferior to but different from the Germans (*nicht minderwertig aber anderswertig*), which as a rule was explained by their civilisation being much more ancient than the German. The acuteness of the Jewish intellect and its fondness for logical extremes and fearless criticism, Jewish scepticism and melancholy disillusionment, Jewish pacifism, which contrasted so strongly with the heroic-military spirit of Potsdam, all this, it was thought, was hurtful to the German nation. The Jews, according to Oswald Spengler represented the dying pacifist " Magian " civilisation, the Germans the young " Faustian " civilisation thirsting for deeds. In some quarters it was even acknowledged that the Jews had made certain positive contributions to German cultural life, in the fields of science, art, literature, in their patronage of the arts and in their philanthropy. Indeed, some went so far as to consider the Jewish element a decided advantage, when it occurs in smaller proportions as in England or Scandinavia. (Compare Bismarck's words, quoted above, about the Jews as an " effervescent.") But in Germany the Jews were too numerous and too influential. It was said that the Jews, alien at heart to German ways of thinking, with a different vital rhythm and different ideals, misconstrued in good faith the traditions and " myths " of the German people and thus exercised on the whole a confusing and disturbing influence. For this reason it was regarded with disfavour in these circles that the Jews through the Press and literature should become a factor in the formation of opinion of great cultural importance (though this importance was much exaggerated by propaganda), and that papers of " European " outlook like the liberal *Berliner Tageblatt* and the *Frankfurter Zeitung* should be regarded abroad as representative of German instead of German-Jewish opinion. Logically perhaps this view should have led to a kind of *numerus clausus* for the Jews, that is, to their being forbidden to occupy more than a certain fixed number of offices, or of educational posts; but it should not have led to their total exclusion from the German national community, to the old highly cultivated Jewish families, which were generally regarded as *eingedeutscht*, being discriminated against, and to half- and quarter-Jews being treated as " full " Jews. Those men and women who subscribed in theory to this form of Antisemitism were however in practice for the most part antipathetic towards the Jews as such, and the division between the popular and the more conservative Antisemitism was not very clearly defined.

The consequence was that in the Weimar Republic the Jews were more and more isolated socially and economically. A sort of " re-ghettoising " set in, reminding one of that of the 1870's but now far more drastic. Society as a whole closed its doors to them. The students' clubs declared the Jews to be not *satisfaktionsfähig*, that is, incapable of being challenged to a duel, and introduced the " Aryan clause." The same course was taken by the sports clubs, the ramblers' associations, and so on. The " superior " summer boarding-houses declined Jewish guests, a thing which previously had only occurred exceptionally. To a great extent Jewish shops were avoided, factories refused to appoint Jewish engineers, Christian artisans to accept Jewish apprentices, Christian business men to engage Jewish clerks, Christian theatrical managers to include Jewish actors and singers in their casts. At the same time the Jews were being hit by all the economic misfortunes that fell upon Germany. Even before Hitler's accession to power 30,000 out of 115,000 German-Jewish wage-earners were unemployed, and 40,000 out of the 170,000 members of the Jewish community in Berlin were in receipt of relief. In the smaller towns, where everyone knew everyone else and the Jews therefore were particularly defenceless against Antisemitism, the economic boycott and psychic torture became altogether unbearable to many a Jew and a chief cause of the rapid decimating of the small Jewish communities and the wholesale flight to the great towns and industrial centres.

In the cultural domain also Antisemitism asserted itself vigorously. Various authors affirmed the opinion that the Jews were a branch of the human race differing specifically from the Germans, and that no community whatever ought to exist between them. The fight was carried on not only against living Jews but against the dead, where these continued through their writings to influence the German spirit. Wilhelm Stapel " proved " in his widely circulated *Antisemitismus* (1920) that Heine's "Lorelei" in contradistinction to Eichendorff's was a product not of German but of Jewish genius. "Whereas Eichendorff's rhymes have in them something of restraint, mystery, spaciousness, Heine's have something pointed, sharp, almost hoarse. . . . If one allows oneself to fall completely under the enervating influence of the sentence: *Ich weiss nicht was soll es bedeuten,* the words at once take possession of one's arms and force one to shrug one's shoulders and turn up the palms of one's hands in a typically Jewish gesture." As everything Jewish was regarded as poison, the assimilated Jews, who wished to be looked upon as full-blooded Germans, were necessarily considered the most dangerous of all, for which reason Hans Blüher and a number of other authors turned against them and against Jewish " mimicry " with special severity. While writers of Stapel's and Blüher's type as a rule preserved a courteous tone and occasionally expressed profound respect for Jews in whom they recognised noble qualities —such as the Zionist and philosopher Martin Buber, who was highly esteemed among religious German Christians— popular German writers like Theodor Fritsch gave expression to a savage, paranoic hatred of the Jews. Behind almost every event in the world's history they traced Jewish intrigues of the most Satanic character. Hitler's *Mein Kampf* is an offshoot of this tree.

Some of them drew the logical consequences of their German-national convictions and rejected Christianity itself as Jewish. They idealised an unhistorical picture of the Nordic past and the beliefs of the ancient Germans and were zealous for the renaissance of the Æsir religion. General Ludendorff was one of them. Charlemagne, who forced baptism on the Saxons and even had them cut down by the thousand when they resisted, was represented as the bane of the German nation. Others again confined themselves to rejecting the Old Testament. In order to maintain this obviously inconsistent point of view they were driven to confound the Old Testament with a maliciously distorted image of it, and to present Christ as an Aryan and his teaching as anti-Jewish, whereas in reality it is marked in the highest degree by Jewish cultural tradition and is filled to the brim with Jewish piety, Jewish sense of justice, Jewish charity and Jewish intensity.[1] (That Christ not only loved but also chastised his people, especially the powerful and worldly ones among them, is another genuinely Jewish trait.) As they conceived Judaism and the Jews to be detestable, they could not look upon Christ as a Jew. In the middle of the election campaign of 1920 they found an entirely unexpected ally in the celebrated Franz Delitzsch's son, Friedrich Delitzsch, professor of Assyriology, who in his book *Die grosse Täuschung*, just published, advanced the opinion that the Old Testament was without religious or ethical value, and that it ought to be debarred from schools and suitably replaced by a German Bible. Although theological scholars, Protestant as well as Catholic, were practically unanimous in rejecting the book, it eventually played an important part in antisemitic agitation and was succeeded by many more, which stopped at nothing in their abuse of the Old Testament and the Jewish people.

In the field of politics also the Jews were thrust aside or excluded. As early as 1919 the " national " parties decided not to admit Jews. And from tactical motives the non-antisemitic papers and parties removed many of their Jewish editors and Reichstag deputies.

Meanwhile National-Socialism was growing stronger and stronger. Its progress was marked by a violent antisemitic agitation, accompanied by outrages, students' riots and political assassinations. A considerable number of working men joined its ranks. " A man who has been out of work for

[1] " Not one word of Jesus Christ," says a famous Protestant theologian, Emil Schürer, " is thinkable unless one assumes as its antecedent the history of the Jews and the whole mental outlook of the Jewish people."

three years turns Communist; a man who has been so for five years turns Nazi," it was said, significantly enough. Heavy industry supported the movement financially in the hope of thus making it subserve its interests. That National-Socialism fell hardly on the Jews was no longer objected to by other leaders of industry, since, as a Danish inquirer, Albert Olsen, has recently pointed out, an intense German competition set in during the years 1931–33, when practically all the international cartels were shattered. " Certainly," he says, " the nationalist description of the Jew as a social parasite is a phrase lacking any foundation in reality," but when it came to competition the " Aryan " capitalist could take advantage of it.

Thus in Germany all political parties of any importance were opposed to the Jews except those which were not nationalist, that is, the Marxist Labour parties and the Catholic Centre party. Bourgeois Liberalism, which had formerly protected the Jews, was played out. Even before Hitler came into power, German Jewry, which was supposed to control the Weimar Republic, was an oppressed, baited and to a large extent ruined body. Victorious National-Socialism had only to complete the work.

When the Nazis assumed power in Germany, the Jews were handed over to them defenceless. The legal protection which the State now offered the Jews was often merely nominal. In a speech broadcast over the whole of Germany General Goering, Minister of the Interior and supreme chief of the German police, declared that the police would not protect Jewish department stores. This was a broad enough hint. The bloodhounds of racial animosity were let loose against defenceless German Jewry. The army of the Nazi Party, the Storm Detachment (S.A.) troops, which consisted in part of hot-headed elements and youths intoxicated by their power, drank deeply from the cup of sadism. Even before the Reichstag election of March 5th, 1933, Hitler's organ the *Völkischer Beobachter* had asserted that the Jews were planning a pogrom against national-minded Germans, and on March 16th the same paper declared that the Jews abroad intended to try to get rid of Hitler, for which reason " strong measures " were necessary. What effect this would have on young Nazis and on the S.A. troops is easy to understand. They had in truth been led astray and were so far not responsible for their cruel acts, which in some cases were undeniably the result of a kind of perverted idealism: they saw in the Jew not a human being but the incarnation of a detestable idea. Thus amid the cheers of the Nazis Germany was filled with ill-treated, despised, dishonoured and despairing Jewish men, weeping women and terror-stricken children. The papers were forbidden to mention Jewish suicides. And yet the Nazi leaders had moderated their original antisemitic plans, doubtless owing to the storm of indignation which their Jewish persecution had aroused abroad, especially in England, whose public opinion it was hoped to gain over, and partly out of consideration for the German-National Party, whose support was still indispensable to Hitler. Moreover the rapid annihilation of German Jewry, by a permanent effective boycott, for instance, would produce general confusion in economic life and unemployment for the Christian personnel of Jewish undertakings.

On February 28th, 1933, the day after the Reichstag fire, the so-called auxiliary police were called out in Prussia; these consisted of the Nazi Storm Detachments (S.A.) and the " black guards " (*Schutz-Staffeln*, S.S.), who immediately drove Jewish judges and advocates from the courts by force or threats, Jewish physicians from the hospitals, and so on. On March 31st the Prussian Minister of Justice ordered the presidents of the High Court to force all Jewish magistrates to apply for leave. In case of refusal they were ordered to deny them access to the courts. On April 7th all non-Aryan officials were dismissed except those who had been appointed before August 1st, 1914, had fought at the front

or had lost father or son in the war. Half-Jews and quarter-
Jews were also reckoned as non-Aryans (according to an
edict issued on April 11th). In a public interpretation of the
law Hitler explained that the Aryan clause did not apply
to Finns or Magyars, which meant in practice that it would
only apply to persons of Jewish birth. (The Reichswehr was
at first exempted from the Aryan clause, but this was applied
to it in 1934.) On June 23rd a law was promulgated by which
officials could be dismissed " for the simplification of the
administration or otherwise in the interest of the service."
By this means those Jews who were to have been retained in
their posts in spite of the Aryan clause were left at the mercy
of Nazi whim. On June 30th it was determined that a man
who married a non-Aryan could not be appointed to the
public service, and that an official who married a non-
Aryan woman was to be dismissed. In July it was laid down
that pensions payable to non-Aryans or their widows were to
be stopped. Only in peculiarly distressing cases might the
application of the law be mitigated. With this the exclusion
of the Jews from the civil service and from communal life
was completed.

Non-Aryan physicians were excluded on April 22nd from
panel practice. As five-sevenths of their clientèle were
estimated to be panel patients, this order meant the ruin of
most Jewish doctors. On June 2nd non-Aryan dentists and
dental mechanics suffered the same blow.

Former front-line soldiers or doctors who had served in
epidemic hospitals during the war were exempted from these
provisions. But as the Nazis carried on and still carry on
a vigorous and successful campaign against these doctors, as
against the lawyers who were permitted to practise, the
exemption is to a great extent illusory. An Aryan who dares
to consult a Jewish lawyer or doctor thereby defies the power
of Nazidom, and care is also taken that Jewish lawyers shall
not be given work in the offices of their Aryan colleagues.
A very clever Jewish physician may nevertheless occasionally

be consulted by Aryan patients, but no skill on the part of a lawyer is thought to outweigh the unpleasantness that his birth entails on his client.

During the summer of 1933 several orders were issued which deprived all non-Aryans engaged in the German film industry of their employment, and, as afterwards appeared, did not even allow foreign films in which Jewish men or women had taken part. On the other hand, as practically all the theatrical managers and artists engaged by the State or by municipalities had been dismissed, it was not considered necessary to pass special laws forbidding their engagement or appearance at private theatres, operas or concerts. Here the boycott was carried on by means of various kinds of pressure, such as an announcement by the authorities that they could not answer for the maintenance of order if a Jew were to appear—this actually occurred on March 20th when the world-famous Bruno Walter was to conduct an orchestra in Leipzig—or by threats that " the people " (that is, the S.A. troops) would take matters into their own hands, as Goebbels' organ expressed it on a subsequent occasion. On the other hand the Jews were allowed to have their own theatres and concerts, on condition that the stage and auditorium were closed to Aryans and that the performance was only mentioned in Jewish newspapers. Naturally non-Aryan painters and sculptors were excluded from German art exhibitions. On the other hand the names of those Jews whose generosity was called upon for the erection of the Berlin Künstlerhaus have not yet been erased from the marble tablet in that building. They amount to one-third of the donors.

The university professors have been dealt with in similar fashion. When the authorities no longer protected them from the Nazi students their fate was sealed, and this applies to practically all " non-Aryan " professors who according to the law of April 7th were not to come under the Aryan clause. A *numerus clausus* was introduced for " non-Aryan " students and schoolchildren: in no faculty, or school as the case might be, were they allowed to compose more than one and a half per cent. of the total number of students, though in this case half- and quarter-Jews and children of front-line soldiers were to be reckoned as "Aryans." As however the Jews are concentrated in the great towns, their children are for the most part deprived of the possibility of attending the State schools.

In journalism and literature the Aryan clause was put in force, not avowedly but in practice, namely "by the direct action of Nazi commissaries, Nazi cells, threats of boycott, police intervention, and as a result of yielding to the prevailing tendency." We will take one example out of many. With the permission of the Mosse concern a Nazi commissary, formerly editor of the *Völkischer Beobachter*, was appointed chief controller of the contents of the papers published by the concern. These papers were alternately suppressed and allowed by the police. Thus the management was forced to submit to what the Nazis decreed. The greater part of the Jewish staff was dismissed; the owners had to resign and emigrated. A similar fate befell the chief editor of the *Berliner Tageblatt*, and many more. The dismissed journalists were replaced by "Aryans." In like manner the item in the Nazi programme forbidding "non-Aryans" to publish books—except on Jewish subjects and addressed to Jews—has been realised, not by formal laws but by the actual influence which the Nazis have secured through the enforced conformity of all ideal and professional combinations or in other ways. At the time of writing a small number of "non-Aryans" are still allowed to carry on their work of journalists, university lecturers, orchestral conductors. But taking them all together they constitute an insignificant minority.

When the Nazis assumed power most of them probably had it in their heads that trade too was immediately to be cleansed of Jews. As the S.A. troops were in command of the streets it was obviously a risky proceeding in many places to visit Jewish shops, so that here and there the boycott against them began so to speak spontaneously, before it was proclaimed by the leaders. Clearly it would not do for the Government to appear to take the Jews' part by forbidding it. On the other hand it was evident, as we have said, that an effective and permanent boycott of Jewish trade would have involved a catastrophe for " Aryans " who were interested in it as part-owners, employees or creditors. The leaders therefore decided to let the hatred of the masses find a convenient outlet and at the same time to humiliate and injure German Jewry by proclaiming a general boycott on April 1st, 1933, against all Jewish shops, lawyers and doctors. Officially it was explained that the boycott was an act of self-defence against the anti-German atrocity and boycott propaganda in foreign countries, which was alleged to be the work of the Jews. Nominally it was not the Nazi State but the Nazi Party which ordered the boycott. But in practice the difference was of no account. The State gave its consent to this despoiling of hundreds of thousands of citizens, whose only crime was their Jewish birth. It was a blow in the face for Western ideas of justice.

The day of the boycott was preceded and followed by an anti-Jewish campaign of mendacity of vast proportions. Hitler's organ, which had conducted an uninterrupted drive against the Jews and incidentally had published on March 8th a forged letter to the effect that Tietz's department store had provided the Communist Party with money for its propaganda—the firm's *démenti* was only inserted in von Papen's organ—now wrote in a leading article on the fight against " the Jewish world-criminal " that " the same Jew who plunged the German people into the carnage of the World War and committed a further crime against it in the November revolution," was now once more about to stab Germany in the back. The appeal for the boycott, distributed in millions of copies, declared it to be World Jewry

that, being disappointed in its hope of turning Germany into
a " Soviet-Russian colony of criminals," had now set on foot
the anti-German agitation according to " a gigantic pre-
arranged plan," encouraged thereto by the German Jews.
(The last-named had done the very reverse !) They were
acting " according to the programme announced by the
Jewish Zionist leader Theodor Herzl at a great Jewish
Congress at Basle in the year 1897 ":

> " As soon as a non-Jewish State dares to do injury to us
> Jews we must be in such a position as to be able to stir up its
> neighbours to make war on it. To do this we must avail our-
> selves of public opinion. We must influence this public opinion
> in advance through what is called the eighth great Power—
> the Press. With very few exceptions, which need not be taken
> into consideration, the whole of the world's Press is in our
> hands."

This last quotation is taken from the notorious forgery,
" The Protocols of the Elders of Zion." As Herzl's name was
made use of, the Zionist Federation of Germany sent a plain
refutation to all important German papers, including the
news agencies. It was inserted only in a single paper. But the
false quotation from Herzl was printed in a great number of
German papers under glaring headlines. Thus the German
Jews were defenceless against the propaganda of lies and
persecution.

On March 31st the German Jews were distinguished in
mediæval fashion by the yellow badge, which, it is true, was
not attached to their clothes but to their places of business
and to the name-plates of lawyers and physicians. In addition to this large placards were employed to the same end,
stating that the person concerned was a Jew. On the day of
the boycott the Government caused the Bureau of Accounts
to announce that those who bought in Jewish shops in a
certain town of Saxony—the day before that fixed for the
boycott !—would be arrested by the S.S. troops and stamped

on the face with the words: "We traitors have bought from Jews."

On April 1st S.A. men were posted at the doors of Jewish shops. The effect was what had been intended. On the one hand practically nobody ventured to break the blockade, on the other the public was informed which shops, lawyers and doctors were Jewish and could act accordingly in future. In agreement with a decree of the Minister of Propaganda, Goebbels, on the evening of March 31st—that it was issued by a minister of the Reich proves that no further trouble was taken to maintain the fiction of the Government's neutral attitude to the blockade ordered by the Nazi Party—the boycott was broken off on the evening of April 1st, to be resumed on April 5th if by that date the foreign anti-German "atrocity campaign," which was alleged to have declined thanks to the announcement of the boycott, had not ceased altogether. This meant the definite calling-off of the official boycott and implied a veiled defeat. For on the one hand it was evident that the German Jews had no possibility of influencing the foreign Press, and on the other the organised attack on the defenceless Jewish minority, including the anti-Jewish agitation of the Nazi leaders in speeches, broadcasts and in print, had produced a storm of disgust in all foreign countries, especially in England, and notably among Conservatives.

But the anti-Jewish agitation and the "quiet" boycott continued. Of the former we will here quote only one example which throws a peculiar light on the methods of the Hitler-Goebbels propaganda. In the *Völkischer Beobachter* of April 2nd there was printed in full-faced type a quotation from a note addressed to France on February 6th, 1920, by "the Jewish Foreign Minister" Rathenau. It said among other things: "Annihilate Germany in the full sense of the word, kill off its population, people its country with others! It is not sufficient to split up the Empire into small States. If you wish to dishonour a neighbouring nation, annihilate it, so that even its memory is wiped out. . . . Annihilate the very memory of the nation, in annihilating the German people." Here the passage quoted in the paper ended. Its continuation, of which, of course, nothing was said, reads thus: " Are you aware of this? Is it your will? Is it the mission of France? Good. What is left for us to lose, including our lives, is scarcely worth the trouble. Your armies are ready. March! But if it is not your will, then, men and women of France, make peace! But peace cannot be based on dishonour and injustice, but only on that of which you have hitherto been the mouthpiece: the idea of humanity and of the rights of man." Thus the appeal of the fervent German patriot Rathenau to the great humane traditions of the French people had been given an implication directly contrary to its real meaning; a typical case which may be said to sum up the treatment of the Jews in the Germany of our time.

To a great extent the Jews were deprived of their positions in commerce in the same way as in the Press. This applies in the first place to all positions of trust, in the chambers of industry and commerce for instance, but also to a great many private undertakings. Jewish directors of banks and companies, managers, engineers and so on, were forced to resign; the great department stores and other important Jewish concerns were " Aryanised "; many thousands of clerks, agents, travellers, typists and stenographers were dismissed. Their places were taken by " Aryans," especially those of Nazi leanings.

Leonhard Tietz's immense department store in Cologne— to take a concrete example—was given another name, Westdeutscher Kaufhof A.G.; its staff on July 1st, 1934, was (according to the *Jüdische Rundschau* of August 10th) entirely Aryan except for 3.85 per cent.; of its six directors four were then " Aryans," and of the eight members of the board of management five. Its chief, Dr. A. L. Tietz, who was then stated to hold only 7.5 per cent. of the shares in his former undertaking and who had emigrated to Amsterdam, was still tolerated as a member of the board. But on August 31st the *Frankfurter Zeitung* announced that the remaining Jewish directors and members of the board had resigned. The mode of procedure may be regarded as typical.

A number of Jewish concerns had to be liquidated. Exceptions were only made in the largely international tobacco and fur trades, since to bring these into line would have involved the transference of these very profitable branches to foreign countries. In the same way an exception was made of the cosmopolitan spa Wiesbaden. The A.E.G. (Allgemeine Elektricitätgesellschaft), the creation of Emil Rathenau, published an official certificate that it was now an " Aryan " enterprise. In certain Nazi circles it was proposed that " Aryan " shops should be provided with signs bearing the words " *Deutsches Geschäft.*" This would have meant the practical continuation of the boycott and possibly the total annihilation of Jewish tradesmen. This, however, was negatived by the Reich Finance Minister. The fact was that a few weeks before Christmas 1933 he had exempted trade from the Aryan clause, giving as his reason that the ruin of Jewish undertakings would involve unemployment for their Christian staff. In many parts of Germany, however, and especially in Franconia, where the notorious Julius Streicher is supreme chief of the Nazis, an attempt is being made to annul this decision in practice by all kinds of threats of reprisals. A large proportion of the Jewish traders, shopkeepers, artisans and manufacturers are definitely ruined, especially those established in the country and in the small towns. Whether the rest will be able to continue their existence is still an open question. The fact that they are excluded from the so-called German Labour Front, which includes all employers and employed, except officials, as well as the owners of entailed estates, is enough to render their position extremely insecure, since on principle only

IA

those who are enrolled in the Labour Front are admissible to any undertaking.

During the first months of the Hitler régime, when anybody could ill-treat or kill Jews with impunity, tens of thousands of them emigrated to foreign countries, and nearly half their number to France. In the autumn of 1933 their total probably exceeded 50,000,[1] but emigration still continues, though at a slower rate. Of the exiles a strikingly large proportion were intellectuals, who were now deprived of any chance of subsistence in Germany. Seven hundred and fifty were teachers in colleges, most of them " non-Aryans." The most famous of them, Albert Einstein, had already been driven out by the Antisemites, who had designs on his life. A great number of the dismissed or expelled men of science, authors and artists were illustrious. Practically speaking, they had passed for Germans all over the world and had regarded themselves as such. They had helped in a conspicuous way to add lustre to the German name. The agitation carried on against them by the German Press, particularly its official section, and the assurances that " to the Jews science is only a business," " a means of destroying the civilisation of the world," may perhaps have strengthened the Nazis in their conviction but increased the abhorrence of foreigners.

What is characteristic of the Nazi persecutions is their combination of order and terror. Individual outrages have no doubt been numerous, but they have seldom had the character of pogroms. Instead of these the method of legislation has been chosen, cold and systematic. Jewish descent has been legally placed in the same category as simple crime and dishonourable acts. " On account of their descent people have been judicially degraded to a state of pariahs, a thing which can hardly have occurred since the days of slavery.

[1] According to what James MacDonald, chief of the bureau appointed by the League of Nations for dealing with German refugees, informed the Swedish Press on January 9th, 1934, the Jews comprised about 75 per cent of the total number of refugees, and 98 per cent of the funds subscribed for them was derived from Jews.

That a moral degradation accompanies the judicial is perfectly natural in our age, when equality before the law is theoretically taken for granted." Most people can scarcely have realised what this means to German Jewry, to the persecuted schoolchildren who are usually treated as scum by their fellows and their teachers, the " half-Aryans " who are told that their " Aryan " father or mother is guilty of " race-pollution," the ruined men and women who have no prospects, who go in fear for their subsistence and that of their children and, surrounded as they are by malicious enemies, are even denied the respect that is usually accorded to those in misfortune. One of my friends, a pure " Aryan," who paid a visit to Germany, said to me on his return: " When I realised what is implied by the vilification of the Jews and their expulsion from society, I was unable to sleep. If they had killed them all it would not have moved me so much."

The following episode may be cited as typical of the Jews' position after Hitler's assumption of power. An official of the Jewish congregation of Breslau, Dr. Rechnitz, had inserted in the congregation's paper, of which he was the editor, an appeal to Jewish employers to engage non-Aryans who had been dismissed on account of their race. The author of the appeal was himself unemployed. The article was made the subject of a prosecution, since it contained two criminal assertions: First, that the Jews' economic and cultural successes often gave rise to hatred among their German compatriots, and secondly, that the German Jews were martyrs who were handed over defenceless to their adversaries. The prosecutor considered that Rechnitz and the author of the article were perhaps guilty of no crime in the " obsolete " view of the Roman law, but that they deserved sentence nevertheless, since they had attributed false motives to the Jewish policy of the Nazis and insinuated that the German Government did not protect the lives, honour and property of the German Jews as zealously as those of German citizens, an insinuation which was entirely unjustified (!) and might injure the prestige of Germany. The Court agreed with this opinion and sentenced the accused to thirteen months' imprisonment, which was not to include the two and a half months they had been kept in " protective " custody and the concentration camp. As a reason for the leniency of the sentence it was alleged that the accused had not been guilty of any political delinquency and that the criminal article might be the result of " a certain mental distress." Rechnitz declared that, if he was sentenced for having injured his country and was thus deprived of his honour, it was comparatively indifferent to him whether his imprisonment were long or short. It may be added that in 1914 Rechnitz served as a volunteer, was very severely wounded, returned to the front, was promoted officer, won both Iron Crosses, and after the war wrote the history of his regiment.

But it would be unjust to identify the whole German people with the party which officially represents it. Swedes who have lately visited Germany bear witness that in wide circles, especially among Conservatives, Hitler's anti-Jewish policy is regarded as unwise and unjust, and the Jews are looked upon as a predominantly loyal, useful and estimable element of the population. The complaints of Nazi papers, even in Streicher's Franconia, that in spite of all " education " large sections of the population are not antisemitic, deal with Jewish shops and consult " alien " doctors, that the Jews know how to " coax " people into sympathising with them, tell their own tale. The Jewish legislation of the Nazis is not yet defined in detail. At the time of writing the conflict regarding the Aryan clause in the Church is not yet concluded, and the rulers are evidently not agreed about the future marriage law, which perhaps will forbid mixed marriages as " race-treason " or as downright " race-pollution." The great question is, however, whether the Nazis will succeed by means of the education department and the regulated Press in Nazifying the younger generation or not. If they can manage to inspire young people with the idea that it is racial treason to employ a Jew, then of course the further existence of Jews in Germany will be rendered impossible in any circumstances.

Obviously the victims of the Nazi revolution most deserving of pity are the Christian half- and quarter-Jews, who are almost all entirely strange to everything Jewish but have now been suddenly thrust out of the national community as members of an alien race. No official figures are available regarding their number. According to private information, to which I have had access, without however being able to check its correctness, the half- and quarter-Jews together may amount to between 600,000 and 700,000. Among them was the former leader of the Stahlhelm, Lieutenant-Colonel Düsterberg, a man regarded all over Germany as the ideal type of a Prussian officer, and in 1932 the antisemitic German-National Party's candidate for the presidency. In the same year, however, Goebbels' organ disclosed the fact, of which he himself seems not to have been aware, that he had a Jewish grandfather. But it is scarcely an exaggeration to say that the majority even of " full " Jews did not feel as Jews to any extent worth mentioning, although as a rule they considered it discreditable to leave the community in which they were born. Their education was wholly German, as was their intellectual outlook. Arnold Zweig in his recently published book *Bilanz der deutschen Judenheit* (1934) has emphasised this point. Nine-tenths of them, he says, were nothing but Germans with a Jewish component, which might show itself either as a religious or a family or a racial bias, but which adapted itself without difficulty to their feeling for Germany as their homeland. They were distinguished—I am still quoting Zweig and experience leads me to agree with him—by their devotion to German culture and by a love of German ways so strong as to make them unjust to everything non-German, Jewish customs included. " Jews have spread Germanism over the whole earth, have overrated it, nay, worshipped it." The German-Jewish lady in Strasbourg, an emigrant, who praised " our officers " (i.e. the German officers) at the expense of the French, and her sister in misfortune, who indignantly exclaimed: " A German woman does not make up her face," are both typical. No wonder German-Jewish emigrants to France are often distrusted as a Germanising element, or that the Eastern Jewish pioneers in Palestine, who have brought the land under cultivation and built towns amid hardships and dangers, are angry with new-comers from Germany, who despise everything that is not in agreement with German habits and practices.

To a minority of German Jewry their Jewishness was not merely a component but something central. They were not merely " German citizens of the Jewish faith " but affirmed their Jewishness without reservation. That did not make them any worse citizens. They are to be envied in so far as they suffer for what they hold sacred. Their number, especially that of the Zionists, has greatly increased, since it is obvious that discrimination against the Jews, coupled with the repeal of their emancipation, was bound to bring proud men and women back to Judaism, that is, if the new age had endowed them with the power of unlearning. After the day's boycott of April 1st, 1933, when the whole of German Jewry was branded and ejected, the *Jüdische Rundschau*, the organ of the German Zionists, made a now famous appeal to the Jews of Germany: " *Tragt ihn mit Stolz, den gelben Fleck !* " (" Wear the yellow badge with pride ! "). Judaism, which in the whole of Western Europe, and especially in Germany, was on the road to destruction owing to the indifference of its members, now acquired a new glory, lofty and intense.

The blow that has fallen upon German Jewry obviously involves rich possibilities of Jewish self-examination and rebirth. For this reason the greatest Jewish poet of our generation, the lately deceased Chayim Bialik, described Hitler as a scourge of God who checked the Jews on the road that led to self-abandonment and death.

CHAPTER VIII

RACIAL ANTISEMITISM

Acoording to the Bible's historical information, which is probably in the main correct and has been confirmed or revised on important points by modern research, the Jewish people originated in ancient Palestine through a mingling mainly of the following nations and tribes: (1) "The descendants of Terah." According to the Bible, Terah was the father of "the Hebrew" Abraham, who migrated from Southern Babylonia to Canaan about 2200 B.C. and, like the Babylonians, probably belonged ethnologically to the very mixed Arab-Iranian branch of the Mediterranean race. (2) The Hittites, a warrior people which at the period mentioned formed the upper class in Asia Minor and Canaan. Judging from sculptures which have been preserved their type resembled the Armenian. Their official language is considered to have been Indo-European as regards its original structure, but the popular tongue, the so-called Hittite, was certainly neither Semitic nor Aryan, from which it has been assumed that a people speaking an Indo-European language subdued and became merged with a number of tribes settled in these regions. The Jewish type to be found in comic papers, with a "Jew nose" and short legs, is thought to be traceable to this Near-Eastern racial component. (3) The Egyptians, a Hamite people, with whom, according to the Bible, the Israelites often intermarried. The fact that a negroid element occasionally, though rarely, occurs among the Jews is thought to be mainly due to this.[1] (4) The tribes of Israel, that is, Bedouins of Arab type who began to penetrate into Palestine about 1400 B.C. or perhaps two centuries later. The " refined Oriental " type which occurs especially among the Sephardim or Spanish Jews, of whom more presently, is regarded as mainly derived from this element. (5) The so-called Canaanites, who in their turn arose through the coalescence of an original Amorite population, probably closely related to the Babylonians (see below), and immigrating Babylonians, Hittites and Egyptians. (6) The Philistines, after whom Palestine is named, a people probably belonging to the Ægean civilisation and allied to the Greeks, therefore a Mediterranean people.

The assertions which we often find even in objective anthropological works regarding the appearance of the peoples here enumerated, the shape of their skulls, the colour of their skins, and so on, generally rest on an uncertain foundation.[2] From the fact that Hebrew is closely related to Arabic the erroneous conclusion has been drawn that the " genuine " Jews must have been of Arab type. The Bedouin racial component is only one of many.

During the Hellenic period and under the Roman domination the Jews intermarried with Greeks and Romans, and their mission brought them then and later a number of proselytes of various peoples and races: Celts, Germans, etc. To what extent the Khazars who were converted to Judaism during the eighth century A.D. were absorbed in the Jewish heritage is a disputed question.

When the Jewish State was destroyed its population dispersed in two currents: one northerly (Syria, Babylonia

[1] The Hamitic (Ethiopian) race finds favour even in the sight of Hans Günther. He describes them as outwardly and inwardly an aristocratic race, handsome, warlike, frank and proud, a race of rulers which composed and still to some extent composes the governing element in North Africa.

[2] This also applies in some measure to the account of the Jews' racial composition which forms the introduction to Arthur Ruppin's *Soziologie der Juden* (Engl. trans. *The Jews in the Modern World*), and which I have here followed in part. The article by Ernst Kahn in the fourth volume of the *Jüdisches Lexikon*, col. 1243 ff., appears to me to give a summary in the main correct.

and Persia), and one westerly (Egypt, North Africa, Spain), which were only to be reunited a millennium later in Poland. In the course of centuries the northerly current received a number of foreign tributaries, above all through proselytes. The blond element, which according to some inquirers did not occur among the Jews of Palestine, is thought to be due to Kurds on the northern border of Babylonia and later to Slavs. For the latter had absorbed some Nordic blood, which was thus indirectly transmitted to the Jews. The westerly current absorbed blood from a multitude of Mediterranean and Oriental proselytes. Thus the distinction originated between Oriental-Sephardic, that is, " Spanish " or " Portuguese " Jews, who are now most numerous in the Levant, and Ashkenazic or German and Polish Jews. For the former Spain supplied a centre of in-breeding (1000–1492), for the latter Poland (1100–1500). Among the former the Bedouin-Mediterranean racial component has been intensified, among the latter the Near-Eastern. In 1700 about fifty per cent of all Jews were Ashkenazim, in 1930 ninety-two per cent. It is thus the Ashkenazic type of Jew which predominates and to this type the future clearly belongs. Of Sephardic Jews only five per cent are blond, of Ashkenazic ten to fifteen per cent.

The old disputed question, whether the Jews have preserved their racial purity in the Dispersion, can according to Ruppin be answered in this way: that in classical antiquity and for a few succeeding centuries they absorbed a good deal of foreign blood, but this was derived in the main only from peoples who had been the vehicles of one or other of the strongest original racial components of the Jews, the Near Asiatic-Dinaric and the Mediterranean-Oriental. Thus the majority of present-day Jews would be racially pretty much the same as their forefathers in Palestine, even if some of their ancestors do not lead back to the Holy Land. But apart from the mixture of race which has resulted from assimilation in our day, the Ashkenazic Jews especially are more differentiated than formerly, since they are no longer concentrated in Pales of Isolation (in Eastern Europe), as had been the case in many previous centuries, but are scattered over the whole world. Factors of environment bring about an approximation of type between Jews and non-Jews in the same country, a differentiation to which the linguistic corresponds. As regards type the Jews of Nearer Asia are scarcely distinguishable from the surrounding non-Jewish population, and the same applies, though perhaps in a less degree, to the Jews in Southern Europe. On the other hand the difference between them and the people of Northern Europe is great, and for this reason this is the very field in which the real or supposed differences between them and the people among whom they live have become the subject of lively discussion. That the Jews in spite of their variety of type have preserved certain traits in common may be due in the first place to the fact that during the millennium preceding Jewish emancipation they seldom married outside their own kin.

Now as to the actual term, racial Antisemitism, it must be stressed at the outset that this dates from only about seventy-five years ago and that the term is a misnomer, inasmuch as modern anthropologists, even the antisemitic ones, are now agreed that the Jews, against whom racial Antisemitism is exclusively aimed, are not a pure race but, like the Germans for example, a people of extremely mixed race, though not possessing a common language and territory. Furthermore science has entirely abandoned the hypothesis commonly accepted in the nineteenth century, that since the Indo-European languages, as discovered by A. W. Schlegel in 1808, formed one linguistic family, the ancient peoples who spoke these tongues also belonged to one and the same Indo-European or, to use the terminology now current in Germany, " Aryan " race. (The Persians and Indians in their earliest writings described themselves as belonging to the stock of the " Aryans," that is, the noble.)

Everything points to different races having been intermixed at a very early stage and to different peoples having adopted the speech of others alien to them in race, as has been the case in more recent times, for instance—with the English-speaking negroes of the United States. If we are to retain the terms Aryan or Semitic as applied to peoples, we must therefore be quite clear that they really denote peoples of Aryan or Semitic speech and certainly not ethnographically homogeneous groups. In other words, *the terms Aryan and Semitic belong to philology, not to ethnology,* and for that matter the same is true of the designations Germanic, Slavonic and Romance. The Nazi term Aryan, therefore, together with the hypothesis on which it rests, belongs to a bygone phase in the history of science. Max Müller, who himself at one time believed in an Aryan race, has expressed the matter thus: " To me an ethnologist who talks about ' Aryan race,' ' Aryan blood,' ' Aryan eyes and hair,' is as great a sinner as a philologist who talks about a dolichocephalic dictionary or a brachycephalic grammar. It is worse than the, Babylonian confusion, nay it is even a downright fraud." The term Aryan is thus far too vague to be used scientifically without quotation marks. Whether any Aryan primitive people really existed is extremely doubtful. Robert Hartmann has described it as an invention of the learned. If it did exist it was probably of very mixed race. But racial hatred, like its complement, the deification of what one considered to be one's own race, refused to be influenced by scientific research, especially when it formed an ingredient in aggressive Nationalism, as was the case, for instance, with Panslavism and Antisemitism.

The term racial Antisemitism is at the same time misleading in another respect. " The popular view that antagonism to the Jews, 'Antisemitism,' is a racial antagonism, and has anything to do with race, is entirely erroneous," says one of the greatest historians of our time, Edward Meyer. Naturally we find that the Jew often differs from the mass of the people and therefore makes an alien impression, especially in Northern Europe on account of his dissimilar racial composition. But if innate, instinctive racial hatred were a fact, mixed marriages between non-Jews and assimilated Jews would scarcely be so common as they are even in antisemitic countries. In the United States, as we know, marriages between blacks and whites are very uncommon. And that hatred of the negroes is so much stronger in the Southern States than in the Northern gives us a hint of what is concealed behind the protective disguise of racial Antisemitism: in the Southern States, where negro slavery was an institution up to 1865, a contempt of the black pariah people still survives, and their great numbers make them a source of fear at elections. But no hatred is felt for the Indians, who have never been slaves and who are not to be feared, and marriage between reds and whites is not considered degrading. In old Turkey there was no hatred of the Jews, but there was of the Armenians, on whom discontent and resentment were vented on occasion, as in Russia they were vented on the Jews. On the other hand a pronounced Antisemitism existed, and exists, among the Greeks, although the Jews, their rivals in trade, do not differ very widely from them ethnographically. Nations are not guided by their " racial instincts " but by their interests, real or imagined, sometimes also by their emotions. Real or assumed racial antagonism or kinship only plays a subordinate part. As a rule it is merely an excuse.

Julius Goldstein cites the following example among many. During the war, when it was expected in Italy that Rumania would throw in her lot with the Central Powers, the paper *Popolo d'Italia* wrote: " Leave off calling the Rumanians our sister nation ! They are no Romans, though they adorn themselves with that noble name. They are composed of a jumble of extremely barbaric peoples who were subdued by the Romans, and of Slavs, Petchenegs, Khazars, Avars, Tatars, Mongols, Huns, Turks, Greeks, so it is easy to understand

what a rabble they are. The Rumanian is to this day a barbarian and an inferior individual who to the amusement of the
French tries to play the Parisian and is fond of fishing in
troubled waters, if only there is no danger involved, for danger
is what he tries to avoid as far as possible." After Rumania had
gone over to the side of the Entente Powers the same paper
wrote: " The Rumanians have shown once more in a glorious
way that they are worthy sons of the ancient Romans, from
whom like ourselves they are descended. It is thus our nearest
brothers who now with the courage and resolution for which
they are distinguished have joined in the conflict of the Latin
races against the Germanic; in other words, the fight for
liberty, civilisation and justice against Prussian tyranny, arbitrariness, barbarism, egoism. . . . Nothing else was to be
expected of a nation which has the honour to belong to the
Latin race which once dominated the world."

Racial Antisemitism, as we have said, is a recent phenomenon. Its father is the French diplomat and author Joseph
Arthur de Gobineau. With the support of linguistic and
historical, not of anthropological, arguments he sought to
assert in a four-volume work, *Essai sur l'inégalité des races
humaines*, published in 1853-54 (Engl. trans. " The In-
equality of Human Races," 1915), that of all races the white
was the only civilising one, and that of this race the
" Aryans," whom like Chamberlain and others of his
followers he regarded as a primitive people, were the most
excellent; so that, broadly speaking, a nation was noble in
proportion to its Aryan racial component. (However,
Gobineau did not regard racial admixture as objectionable.
He even thought a small dose of negro blood advantageous
as a stimulant to the artistic imagination.) Of all white
races he considered the Germanic the most Aryan and
therefore the noblest. The blond, tall, civilising " Aryan "
was contrasted with the sordid, selfish, swarthy, undersized
" Semite," a parasite on civilisation. Gobineau was an
aristocrat and a clerical of the first water, feudal in his
entire outlook, orthodox and a believer in the Bible. His

object was not so much to glorify the " Aryans " as to promote Conservatism and Catholicism. The nobility, whose blood according to Gobineau was the purest—Count Boulainvilliers had already (1722) represented the French aristocrats to be the descendants of Frankish conquerors ruling over the Celtic and Latin plebeians—ought to hold sway in mediæval fashion. He called the idea of fatherland a Canaanitish monstrosity, forced upon the Aryans by the Semites. He did not wish to glorify Germany at the expense of France. He regarded the Germans as less Germanic than the French, a view, by the way, which may be so far correct in that the people of the north-eastern third of France and half of Belgium may be racially more Nordic than those of South Germany. But as the inhabitants of Germany considered themselves the Germans *par excellence*, while the French felt injured by his glorification of what was German, and moreover, like other Latin peoples, laid more stress on cultural community than on racial contrasts, Germany and not France became the stronghold of Gobineauism. For in Germany there had been since the beginning of the nineteenth century a tendency to glorify all things German, according to which the Germans stood out as physically and morally superior to all others, including the reputedly corrupt " Welsch " peoples, not to speak of the Jews. For these reasons Gobineauism here found the soil prepared for it, but not in France. The French would not hear of it. Renan explained in a letter to Gobineau that race is only of significance at an early stage, and the politically minded French anthropologists, de Lapouge for instance, did not rely upon it.

Gobineau found his most noteworthy adherents in Bayreuth, which became the centre of the Germanic cult and Antisemitism. As early as 1851, that is, before Gobineau appeared as the champion of the " Aryan " race, Wagner, in his pamphlet *Ueber das Judentum in der Musik*, aimed especially at the composers Mendelssohn and Meyerbeer, had described the Jews as an artistically impotent people, parasites on the infirmity of German culture. That he nevertheless acknowledged at a later date their " great gifts of heart and spirit," and in 1882 engaged Hermann Levi to conduct the first performance of *Parsifal*, is proof of the relatively moderate nature of the Antisemitism of that day.

In his music dramas Wagner has completed the work of Gobineau in a way the latter can scarcely have imagined —to say nothing of the many German Jews who were Wagner enthusiasts. The glorious, godlike Aryan race, which according to Gobineau was destined to supply the ferment among the nations and to die out through being merged in them, is met with again in the *Götterdämmerung* and the other Wagnerian music dramas, where ideal Germanic figures personify in their conflict and destruction what appeared to the poet-musician as the opposite of Jewry, the German nature in its tragic greatness. The ancient Germanic pantheon and the heroes of German romantic chivalry, radically transformed outwardly and inwardly so as to symbolise ideal forces, now became a living reality to great sections of the German people. The tide of German Nationalism rose rapidly and with it that of Antisemitism, which now in a new way took possession of leaders of culture in Wagner's land. Thus the way was prepared for the Wotan enthusiasm of the Nazis, for Rosenberg and Hitler. The suggestive power of Wagner's music and the wild exultation with which its conductor was greeted were a foretaste of the excitement and devotion witnessed at Hitler's mass meetings. It was no fortuity that the most prominent representative of German racial Antisemitism belonged to the Bayreuth circle and was connected in the most intimate way with the master himself. This was Wagner's son-in-law, Houston Stewart Chamberlain, the son of an English admiral and a German mother.

Chamberlain's great work, *Die Grundlagen des 19 Jahrhunderts* (" The Foundations of the Nineteenth Century,"

Engl. trans. 1911), which marked an epoch in the history of racial Antisemitism and of Pan-Germanism, appeared in 1899 and was a brilliant success on account of the author's extraordinary gift of style and wide reading, but still more on account of its tendency. It has been strikingly said that, if Gobineau's work was a mournful requiem for the splendour of the dying Aryans, Chamberlain's was a joyous song of triumph for the glory of the Germans. *Die Grundlagen* found readers by the hundred thousand and has contributed as no other book to disseminate the views of the Jews' worthlessness and of the superiority of the German people and their historical mission. William II was among its most devoted admirers; he read it aloud to his sons and personally assisted in great measure to increase its circulation in leading circles. It ought to be found in all advanced schools, he considered. Admittedly the work is now regarded as worthless from a scientific point of view; it abounds in the grossest casuistries, blunders and contradictions. But the semblance of scientific truth which, in spite of his total deficiency as an anthropologist, this æsthetically gifted amateur lent to Antisemitism and Pan-Germanism, and the mentality he and his followers, such as Ammon, Driesman, Woltmann, Rosenberg, helped to create and spread in Germany, were not affected by this. The anthropological authority of Nazi Germany, Hans Günther, who considers *Die Grundlagen* scientifically impossible, rightly insists that it was nevertheless Chamberlain who brought the racial problem into the field of actuality.

According to Chamberlain it is the tall, blond, long-skulled Germans who have created everything of value, while the Jews, racially the result of " an incestuous crime against nature," are represented as base-minded, material, culturally sterile, miserable middlemen and cheap-jacks in the intellectual field.

The real history of the world only begins according to Chamberlain with the great migrations of the Germanic peoples which were the prelude to the Middle Ages, " the moment when the German grasps the heritage of the ancients with a hand overcharged with force. China, India, Babylon, Judæa, Persia, Greece and Rome are to us merely pro-legomena. . . . Only disgraceful mental indolence or shame-less falsification of history can see in the Germans' entrance into world-history anything but the rescue of dying humanity from the clutches of the eternally bestial." In accordance with the then prevailing, now abandoned, view of dolichoce-phalism as a sure distinguishing mark of race and of the cultural superiority of the long-skulls—the population of highly civilised South Germany and a number of German leaders of culture are short-skulled—he declares that the Germanic long-skull bears witness to the painful yearning of the race for light,[1] and " proves " that all manner of great historical personages must have been long-skulled. That they must also have been blond goes without saying ! His thesis of the ethical and religious superiority of the Aryan and particularly the Germanic peoples over the Semitic is " proved " as a rule by means of tendentiously chosen quotations, usually from the sacred writings and heroic songs of ancient peoples, by extremely subjective interpretations of " portraits " preserved from the earliest times, many of which as we know resemble the attempts of little children, or by the use of various disputable historical, philological or anthropological hypotheses, which are made to pass as facts if they suit his purpose. If a person is noble, he is an Aryan as a matter of course; if he is the reverse, he is a Semite; if he is a mixture of good and evil, the good in him is derived from Aryans and the evil from Semites. On occasion the author appeals to what is known as the layman's common sense against the conclusions of science. It is obvious that by such methods one can prove pretty nearly anything.

[1] . . . " den länglichen Schlägel, den ein ewig schlagendes, von Sehnsucht gequältes Gehirn aus der Kreislinie des tierischen Wohlbehagens nach vorn hinaushämmert."

KA

When Chamberlain is otherwise at a loss to explain the existence of important civilisations and their leading personages before the entrance of the Germans into the world's history, he postulates great prehistoric Germanic migrations from which he " proves " that all the great ones of mankind were Germans, in Hellas, in Babylon, in Egypt, in China, in the Aztecs' Mexico, in the Incas' Peru—a fantastic Rudbeckianism which, like the philosophical outlook of the great Swede's quasi-scientific poem, is inspired by a glowing affection for his own race and at the same time by a bitter hatred or contempt of what is outside it. One may well ask why the Germans, who, according to Chamberlain, founded brilliant civilisations in Southern Europe, Asia and America, waited until the Middle Ages before doing so in their own native country. Chamberlain however provides no answer to this question. Nor did these Germans of Chamberlain's create a civilisation that bore the stamp of their own spirit, as was done by the Greeks, the Romans, the English. No, " they burst in triumphantly, scattering, like Japanese jugglers in a variety show, the many-coloured balls of civilisation over the barbarians seated in the pit—and then vanish without a trace, after the manner of good fairies when they have showered bounties on their favourites." The author here quoted, Fritz Kahn, rightly says that, if the Mongols had conquered Europe, a yellow Chamberlain would have been able to prove in the same light and airy way that all the great European leaders of culture since Attila's time were descended from the Huns—the undersized Kant, the broad-skulled, rough-haired Beethoven and the rest—and that a " Semitic " Chamberlain living at the height of Babylonian civilisation, before it had yet received its great contributions from Persians and Europeans, would in the same way have been able to make out his case for the Semites in general and the Babylonians in particular as the only promoters of culture and civilisation.

Faced by the choice of denying the genius of David,

Solomon, the Prophets, Jesus and Paul, or of declaring them to be descended from Germans, therefore not Jews in an ethnological sense, Chamberlain decided on the latter alternative. They were no Jews, but blond, long-skulled Aryan Amorites ! In 1892 Felix von Luschan had advanced a theory that the Jewish people had come into existence in Palestine through an intermingling of Hittites, Semitic peoples and Amorites, which last he believed to be Indo-Europeans. No more was required. After giving a caricatured description of the first and second of these Jewish racial components, Chamberlain pictures the Amorites as a people from the North, " tall, blond, blue-eyed men with a fair complexion," and exclaims : " We seem to see a different nature, when among the countless physiognomies of the Egyptian monuments we suddenly catch sight of this frank and forceful face, beaming with intelligence. As when we meet the eye of genius in the midst of the ordinary human crowd, so here we cannot resist the appeal of these features among the rabble of Babylonians, Hebrews, Hittites, Nubians and whatever their names may be. Homo europæus! How could you stray into this company ? Yes, as an eye, beholding the divine beyond, you appeal to me." The method is typical of Chamberlain and his antisemitic followers, but not of them alone. Constantin Brunner has illustrated this by a typical quotation from the time of the World War, more precisely from an article in the *Daily Graphic* in which Lord Headley gave his countrymen the results of his studies in physiognomy. Almost all the German leaders from the Kaiser down to the subordinate generals have a Satanic expression. The German ambassador to the United States, Count Bernsdorff, has a devilishly cruel and hard cast of countenance, fitted to serve as a model for his Satanic majesty; Hindenburg's is bestial and has something of the wild boar about it, suitable for Beelzebub ! The Kaiser's and Falkenhayn's faces speak of will-power, cruelty and harshness; both might serve as types of the Prince of

Darkness. Bülow and Mackensen represent the cat-like type; their diabolical expressions bear witness to ferocity and treachery. . . . If we then turn our eyes to the British generals and admirals and to the chiefs of the Allied forces, it is like coming out of subterranean caves into heaven. . . . According to the same paper all German geniuses are non-Germans.

It may be added, by the way, that in 1907 von Luschan stated that he had abandoned his hypothesis of the Amorites' Aryan affinities; that they are now generally regarded as racially akin to the Babylonians, that is, as typical " Semites," and that a scientific expedition sent to Egypt just before the World War established the fact that the fair complexions and blue eyes in the tomb paintings, which some have taken to represent Amorites, were a first coat and were painted over in dark colours that have since crumbled away. Eduard Meyer, the great specialist in the prehistory of Nearer Asia, on the authority of the same paintings as Chamberlain relied on, has described the Amorites as " frequently corpulent, with a markedly hooked nose, uniformly black hair and a reddish yellow beard." " Their resemblance to the Babylonians is complete," he says, " except that their nose and consequently what we should call their pronounced Semitic profile is more strongly marked."

Among the representatives of racial Antisemitism in our day Hans Günther deserves special mention, partly because in contrast to Gobineau, Chamberlain and Rosenberg he is really well-read in racial biology, and partly because he has played and still plays a leading part in Nazi race-ideology and race-policy. As early as 1930, when the Nazis came into power in Thuringia, he was appointed in spite of the University's protests professor of ethnology in Jena, and since Hitler's victory the racial-political ideas he represents have become so to speak officially recognised. The publication *National-sozialismus und Rasse*, written by Dr. Rudolf and issued by the National-Socialist Party, is mainly based on Günther's *Rassenkunde des deutschen Volkes.*

Günther, as is well known, is one of the leaders of the "Nordic" movement, whose motto is "*Wiedervernordung*" or, more usually, "*Aufnordung*," that is to say, strengthening of the Nordic racial component in the German people. Only on one condition, he thinks, can the threatened downfall of the German people be changed into a rise: "if its Nordic blood, which all Indo-Germanic peoples have to thank for their greatness as witnessed by history, is restored to its former power and Nordic man again becomes prolific and takes the lead."

This movement made a great appeal to post-War Germany. Chamberlain's racial chauvinism was no longer tenable, since science had demonstrated that there was no such thing as an "Aryan," "Semitic" or "Germanic" race; but the mentality itself survived. "Nordic" men, who, as Eugen Fischer had shown in 1910, were being numerically out-flanked by others, are according to the Nazi faith just as superior to all other races as ever were Gobineau's Aryans and Chamberlain's Germans, and in the dream of Germany as the leader of the Nordic peoples, the "blond International," we undoubtedly see the survival of the old aggressive Pan-Germanism. That Günther theoretically refrains from branding any race as inferior, seeing that no objective criterion exists, is of no practical importance, since he not only exalts Nordic man to the skies but also paints most other races in dark colours, imparting a semblance of scientific exactitude ("race-psychology") to his own emotionally swayed fallacies, which moreover are strongly coloured by politics.

According to German racial doctrine—I here follow Günther and Rudolf—the German people consists in the main of seven more or less intermingled races which occur all over Europe, each with its own unalterable spiritual qualities. The tall, long-skulled, blond Nordic race—the term originated with the Russian anthropologist Deniker in 1898 or 1899—occurs in its greatest purity in Scandinavia.

It formed the dominating racial component in the ancient Germans, but among the Germans of our day only four to six per cent are pure Nordics. Nordic man is and has always been the real civiliser. It is he above all who created the ancient civilisations of India, Persia, Hellas, Rome, the Italian Renaissance, as well as the present civilisation of Europe and its offshoots overseas. The leaders have almost always been Nordics. The genuine Romans and the genuine Hellenes belonged to the blond Nordic race. This race is further distinguished by heroism, combativeness, contempt for death, boundless self-sacrifice, pride, self-consciousness, frank and unfaltering loyalty, a clear and foreseeing intelligence, a sense of reality and justice, statesmanship, an instinct for research, a seeking for truth, depth of feeling, sensitive cordiality, a sense of duty, sexual discipline, passion for creative activity, immunity from the spirit of the mob, et cetera. In certain cases these merits may degenerate into extravagance; frivolity, envy, a reckless waste of national forces, impaired racial consciousness and resultant intermingling with alien races have brought about the ruin of Nordic empires and civilisations. The western (Mediterranean) race: short-statured, long-skulled, dark-complexioned, lively and alert, is specially common in western and southern Germany. Günther denies to this type any profundity of talent, creativeness or strength of mind, and pictures it as a kind of animated Frenchman. The eastern (Alpine) race, which includes, for instance, Beethoven, is dark-haired, short-skulled, thick-set, clumsy, petty-minded, lacking in nobility, boldness, self-sacrifice and creativeness, earth-bound, unwarlike. It is specially numerous in the industrial districts, in Saxony, Upper Silesia, the Rhineland, South Germany. In the eyes of the State Alpine man has a certain value as an industrious and peaceable worker. But, especially if he has some Nordic blood in his veins, the sense of his own inferiority causes him to hate Nordic man. Marriages between members of these two races turn out badly. Wherever in Germany Nordic man is hated, an Alpine element is to be found. (This characterisation is typical. Evidently, as Albert Olsen has pointed out, what lies behind it is the idea that the Marxian proletariat, which has proved immune from the Nazi gospel, is destined by nature herself to be kept under by the ruling race and to serve its purposes. According to Rudolf blonds are strikingly numerous, precisely among S.A. men, and a Nazi mentality is proof that the person in question has Nordic blood.) The East-Baltic race, to which the majority of Russians belong (as well as Strindberg and Archbishop Söderblom), is numerous in those parts of Germany once held by the Slavs. East-Baltic man is described as widely different from Nordic: ugly, gloomy-minded, reserved, suspicious, industrious but weak-willed and, therefore, wherever the rule of the State is firm, a quiet and peaceful subject. But behind his calm exterior lurk restlessness, discontent and a powerful imagination, qualities which, especially as they are often combined with brutality and cunning, predispose the East-Baltic to Bolshevism. An artistic sense in the Nordic, constructive spirit is foreign to him, but he possesses musical gifts. The Sudetic race differs only slightly from the East-Baltic. Both these races are suspected to be vehicles of " Asiatic " blood. The Dalic race, whose existence by the way is questioned by many anthropologists, named after the Swedish province of Dalecarlia (Dalarna), where it is stated to be of frequent occurrence—also called the Falic (Fälisch) after Westphalia, where again it is said to be numerously represented—is described as a " heavier " variant of the Nordic. If Günther describes Nordic man as an idealised Viking, he pictures the Dalic as an idealised yeoman: blond, tall, heavy, bound to the soil, upright, stern, serious, patient, loyal. The strength of a Luther, a Bismarck and other Lower Saxons, their defiance and love of freedom, are referred to their Dalic element. The prototype of this race is Hindenburg, whose axiomatic acknowledgement of Germany's obligation to carry out the undertakings imposed on her by the victorious Powers was disapproved by the Nazis. Typical of the political tendency of this "science," and its fondness for free-and-easy generalisation is Rudolf's assertion, indirectly aimed at Hindenburg's policy, that while Nordic man— meaning the Nazis!—is in the habit of testing treaties to which he is a party and afterwards rejecting them if they are mendacious or forced upon him, Dalic man, disastrously for his own people, considers himself bound by Germanic fidelity to observe them, and further that the Dalic race is only adapted for peaceful times and normal conditions. Finally we have the Dinaric race: dark-complexioned men, often with aquiline nose, particularly numerous in the alpine districts of Germany and Austria, as well as in the whole of south-eastern Germany and in the Balkan peninsula. Their affinity to the Near-Eastern type is obvious. The Dinaric has a passionate love of his native district, is an excellent soldier and defends it bravely, as witness the Tyrolese in 1809 and the Montenegrins and Albanians on various occasions. In Carinthia, according to Günther, the Dinaric Germans were the only ones who in 1918 took up arms in defence of their native land. The Dinarics are good-natured, though of a hasty temper, good judges of human nature with an eye for the ridiculous, they are sentimental, musical (Haydn, Mozart, Chopin, Verdi, Wagner), and good men of business. In Vorarlberg they are considered the equals of the Jews in this last respect. Rudolf hastens to add that the Dinaric with a Nordic streak is not at all like this. Rather is he inclined to despise all worldly interests.

Even so brief a survey as this may have afforded an insight into the tendency and method of this "racial science." Starting from certain primitive pure races, of which nobody knows anything definite and whose very existence is uncertain, you attribute to them according to your sympathies and antipathies certain qualities, which are assumed to be unalterable, and proceed to explain all individual traits and cultural phenomena as manifestations thereof. Everything in politics is made to depend on race. Whatever is anti-Nazi is anti-Nordic and is laid to the charge of a racially "less desirable" element, Alpine, East-Baltic or Jewish, which, apart from the Jews whom Günther does not include in the German people, number about forty millions. Günther illustrates his loose statements by a number of portraits, including some of famous men, which are usually furnished quite arbitrarily with vague captions, such as "Nordic-Alpine," "Nordic-Alpine-Dinaric," "predominantly Nordic" or the like—a mode of procedure which for scientific probity worthily matches the text of his *Rassenkunde*. It is a fact that in Scandinavia and Holland, precisely those countries where Nordic people predominate, the population favours democratic and pacifist ideals. It is a fact that great parts of Germany where the non-Nordic type predominates, Franconia, Swabia, Thuringia, have taken and still take the lead in German cultural life. But Günther's racial romanticism takes no account of such things.

After these general reflections we will pass to an examination of Günther's Antisemitism, as it appears in his great book *Rassenkunde des jüdischen Volkes* (1930), which is an extension and adaptation of a similarly entitled appendix to his *Rassenkunde des deutschen Volkes*. The author has here omitted a number of his former gross charges and errors, and has sought in some measure to moderate the expression of his animosity. But his knowledge of the Jewish people's psyche has been largely derived from antisemitic lampoons, which give one a picture of their victims no less untrue than the war-time attacks on the Germans. He often supports his assertions by quotations from Jewish writers, for the most part unknown, who are in no way representative of the Jewish psyche. What should we say of an author who, on the strength of quotations from some obscure communist organ, "proved" that the Swedes are Communists? He naïvely accepts falsified quotations from the Talmud as characteristic of Jewish mentality, speaks of the (naturally non-existent) " commandment " to hate non-Jews, and actually makes uncritical use of Theodor Fritsch's libellous *Handbuch der Judenfrage* as an authority ! He believes in the fable of a Jewish International with power over international finance and control of the world's Press, whereby the non-Jewish peoples are impregnated with the heterogeneous Jewish spirit. He therefore regards Antisemitism as natural and necessary. He believes that the Jews are so different in nature from other people that they have a smell of their own; an old idea, by the way, which seems to be dear to promoters of popular animosity. During the World War the same thing was said of the Germans. It is true he admits that a number of Jews have emancipated themselves from the " command-ment of hatred " in question, but asserts that what he con-siders the racially-determined antipathy between Jews and non-Jews is mutual, and quotes as evidence a Jewish writer whom one may look for in vain in Jewish books of reference. In spite of all this, however, he does not seem altogether unwilling to do the Jews justice. He even acknowledges that many Jews have " a certain " feeling of solidarity with their native land and the people among whom they live, that many an educated German Jew has become rooted in German culture, and that individual German Jews have succeeded in being at the same time Germans and Jews, nay, in becoming German patriots. If the Jews are to be thrust out of the national community, as he recommends, and Jews and non-Jews cease to concern themselves with one another's affairs, " the foundations of Antisemitism would be for the most part destroyed." The non-Zionist section of Jewry, he considers, will die out through the falling of the birth-rate— though not so rapidly as to render it no longer necessary to prevent the intrusion of Jewish blood into the non-Jewish hereditary stock. Günther sums up his view of the Jews' ethnographic future in these words: " Zionism or downfall."

Günther gives the following significant description of the

two racial components, the Near-Eastern and the Oriental, which according to him are the chief determinants of Jewish mentality. The Oriental component: this race has issued from the desert and is spiritually disposed to reconvert settled country into desert. It is distinguished by measured dignity, insensibility, religious intolerance, a passionate delight in persecution, sombre, glowing earnestness, occasionally blazing up in sudden impetuosity, dignified self-control with sudden outbursts of sexual sensuality, alternations of inert, often idle dreaminess and intense activity. A faculty of observation not profound but acute, tenacious will-power, cunning and calculation, a cold pitilessness and an inordinate vindictiveness are controlled or held in check by a sober intelligence. Its pronounced combativeness is always made subservient to calculation: the bandit raid, coming as a surprise when success seems assured, is characteristic of the Oriental nature.

The Near-Eastern component: commercial talent, a supple intelligence, a convincing manner of speech, a pronounced faculty, amounting to zeal, to merge oneself in a foreign intellectual atmosphere with the calculated object of exploiting people, a power of interpreting and propounding the intellectual treasures of others, a propensity for the art of the theatre and above all for music, a proneness to cold, calculated and voluptuous cruelty, lack of constructive political capacity, but on the other hand a tendency and capacity for forming religious communities and more or less secret, semi-religious, semi-political combinations. Furthermore a wavering between unbridled sensuality and the mortification of the flesh, an association of religion with sexuality, a disposition to exaltation, a tendency to violent lamentations and outbursts of joy, to expressionism in art, a desire to control the masses by inflammatory agitation, great power of imagination, et cetera.

It is perhaps hardly necessary to add that when Jews or other Orientals have made a significant contribution to civilisation, this is not attributed to their Oriental or Near-Eastern component, but to their Nordic. The Sumerians, who founded the Babylonian civilisation, were " perhaps " Nordics, at least in their upper classes, as were the Philistines and the great statesmen and prophets of the Bible. Naturally this also applies to Christ. Unfortunately Günther does not inform us how Christ's gospel of peace and love, addressed to the whole of mankind, is to be harmonised with what the Nazi doctrine tells us of Nordic man's anti-universalist and anti-pacifist leanings. Nor does he furnish any proof that the races above described, which within historical times nowhere occur unmixed, nay, whose existence as pure races is, as we have said, problematical, had precisely those qualities which the author ascribes to them. Nor is it possible to furnish such proof. " If, which God forbid," says Friedrich Hertz, whose criticism of Günther's racial theory I have here followed in the main, " a Jewish Günther should one day arise, he would be able by the same methods to take revenge on the whole of civilisation on behalf of Jewry."

The mode of procedure of Günther's racial psychology in the above-mentioned cases is easily exposed: he draws the Orientals with the Bedouins as his model, and for the Asia Minor stock, which he places particularly low, he takes as a prototype the Armenians, whereby, clinging of course to his hypothesis of the unalterability of racial characters, he avails himself of conventional lay-figures such as might be employed by a popular writer for the stage. Moreover, especially when dealing with the Asia Minor type, he has added a number of traits of present-day political significance, which are meant to explain psychologically and in accordance with anti-semitic dogma certain traits regarded by him as Jewish, which did not make their appearance before the last century. But his characteristics by no means tally with a number of peoples which according to Günther are predominantly Oriental or Near-Asiatic, not even with the Arabs and Armenians. The latter were originally a simple race of mountaineers like the Scots or the Swiss, who have also turned to trade in later times. Even the ancient Assyrians were no traders, but warriors, farmers and founders of States. This applies moreover to most Near-Asiatic peoples in ancient times and to some extent at the present day—the Turks for instance. He has himself been conscious of this and has tried to draw a distinction between a more settled-agrarian and a more mercantile-nomadic Near-Asiatic type, but this twofold partition is naturally arbitrary and should properly be replaced, as Hertz has pointed out, by a sub-division on a larger scale. But in so doing Günther may be held to have acknowledged indirectly that the Near-Asiatic race is far from possessing any single " race-soul."

There is scarcely a statement in Günther's characterisation of the Near-Asiatic and Oriental racial souls which cannot be questioned or confuted. A few examples merely. No one who is acquainted with the way in which biblical and post-biblical literature judges the orgiastic fertility cults of contemporary " Aryan " and " Semitic " peoples—for the cult of the phallus also occurred in the North—or their obscene myths, can possibly regard " the connection between sanctuary and brothel," as Günther puts it, as anything Jewish. As we know, Plato, in the Symposium, expresses surprise that the Asiatics looked upon the pæderasty prevailing among the Hellenes as abominable. Were not the " Aryan " Persians just as intolerant in religion as any " Semitic " people ? Where can we find a more pronounced ritualism or a grosser *do-ut-des* religion—I offer sacrifice in order that the god may repay me—than in the sacred books of the ancient Aryans, the Veda, and Avesta ? Far from transforming Sicily and Spain into deserts, the Moors cultivated those countries in an exemplary way. With the fall of their rule, agriculture and horticulture declined. As is well known, the descendants of the Bedouins often become typical peasants (fellahin). And as to the art of agitating and rousing the passions of the mob, who have surpassed

Hitler and his men, who according to Günther appear to lack the Near-Asiatic racial component " alien to Europe " ?

Günther's idea that mental qualities are a product of the race and that it is possible scientifically to plot a person's soul as if it were a mosaic of traits inherited from different races, continually tempts him to the boldest guesses, which he afterwards adduces as if they were scientifically-proved facts. I take one example from among many. Like Chamberlain, Günther regards fidelity as a special characteristic of the ancient Teutons and therefore of Nordic man. Now everyone who is acquainted with history knows that breaches of faith were extremely common among the Teutons as among all other uncivilised peoples, a consequence, not of any inferior racial qualities, but of their stage of culture. Roman literature abounds in complaints of the Teutons' bad faith. Velleius Paterculus characterises them as " extremely cunning and a race that seems born to lying." Ammianus speaks of " the perfidious nation of the Goths," and Procopius calls them " the most faithless people in the world," and so on. The earliest history of the Franks, Icelandic literature, in fact the whole history of the age of chivalry, are full of breaches of faith. The high estimation in which loyalty was held in feudal times has been strikingly compared by Hertz with the over-refined worship of nature in the rococo period. History can also tell us of the unswerving fidelity of Teuton warriors to their lords. But not only of Teutons. The idea that the bodyguard must never desert its chief or survive him if he falls is to be met with among the most varied peoples, the Kaffirs, the Japanese, the Gauls, the Iberians, and many more. But wherever in history Günther comes across a manifestation of this spirit, he supposes at once that he has stumbled upon a " Nordic " racial trait. In the words of Ittai to David (2 Sam. xv. 21) he sees an example of Nordic bodyguard fidelity ! He entirely disregards the fact that different peoples at the same stage of civilisation have similar social institutions and social ideals: when the laws of

Hammurabi show certain similarities to those of the ancient Franks, he puts this down to the influence of the Nordic racial spirit !

Günther regards mixed marriages between Jews and Occidentals as harmful. In his opinion the races are far too different in their composition. The offspring, " according to all historical experience," will suffer from this. Unfortunately we are not told to what historical experiences the author refers. Furthermore, according to Günther, the Jews are greatly to be feared as promoters of what he calls " the modern spirit." But it remains to be proved that this is a specifically Jewish creation and not a universal phenomenon, which only bears the outward impress of the general social, technical and intellectual culture of our age. Outside the frontiers of Naziland one may, to say the least of it, regard the assertion that expressionism is a product of the Near-Asiatic racial soul with scepticism. In general we may doubtless regard it rather as a manifestation, or a variety, of romantic subjectivism with roots in pietism, the baroque and the gothic. Capitalism is also considered by Günther to be a Jewish ingredient in " the modern spirit "—in which connection, however, he apparently tries to distinguish between a Nordic capitalism, of which he approves, and a non-Nordic, which he regards as objectionable. In " the modern spirit " he includes those views which have a disintegrating effect on family life and for which, according to him, the Jews in particular carry on propaganda. The enormous importance of the Old Testament as a factor of influence in the very opposite sense is, of course, not insisted upon. In reality it is the ideal of humanitarian and democratic Liberalism that Günther is specially anxious to define as Jewish and unworthy of Nordic man. But this ideal is an outgrowth of the age of enlightenment, in the shaping of whose culture the Jews, as we know, had an extremely small share.

It has been strikingly said that what Günther really

criticises as " the modern spirit " is the same as the extollers of " the good old times," which as we know never existed, have regarded in all ages as characteristic of the younger generation: licentiousness, acquisitiveness, faithlessness, egoism. History tells us that these vices have always flourished—in certain periods, such as the first centuries of the Germanic migrations, probably more than now. To represent them as being peculiarly a manifestation of the Near-Asiatic spirit is a downright outrage on historical truth.

It can scarcely be called presumptuous if we say that Günther's " racial psychology " has nothing to do with science. To this and to its predecessors in the same field we may apply without reservation the words which Chamberlain, in one of his lucid intervals, wrote of the partial treatment of history he had encountered in the schools of different countries: " While their own contributions are always thrust into the foreground, those of others are passed over in silence or disguised; certain matters are always placed in the clearest light, others again in the deepest shadow; the result is a total image which in many points is only distinguishable by the most subtle eye from unadulterated falsehood."

.   .   .   .

Nowhere outside the borders of Germany has the Nazi racial doctrine found acceptance, not even in the countries whose population, in contradistinction to the German, is Nordic with relatively little admixture, Scandinavia, Holland, England, where, according to Günther, " the genuine Teutons " are to be found. Precisely in these countries harmonious relations prevail between the Jewish and non-Jewish populations, especially in Holland, where the percentage of Jews is far greater than in Germany—in itself an indirect evidence of the improbability of the Nazi racial ideology being correct. It seems as though these particular nations, in the security of their self-consciousness, were to a great extent unsusceptible to the preaching of racial chauvinism. Professed anthropologists also have everywhere refused to recognise this racial doctrine as scientific. This also applied to the majority of German specialists, until Hitler seized power and destroyed the freedom of scholarship. But even those who thought that psychic qualities are probably connected with race considered it impossible in the present state of knowledge to establish this relationship, since practically the whole of mankind with the exception of a few primitive tribes is the result of a number of prehistoric and later mixtures of race, of which as a rule we know nothing. Most modern anthropologists will doubtless agree with the well-known investigator of heredity, Fritz Lenz, that the sum of mankind's inheritance is largely common to all and that it is impossible to settle the racial constituents of any particular individual. It is hard to characterise a person, even oneself, harder still to characterise whole nations. To characterise races, to say nothing of factitious ones, as is done by Günther, is impossible, if one wishes to avoid being landed in sheer arbitrariness.

To what extent race, upbringing, and environment may determine human qualities is a matter on which opinions are divided. Some deny the importance of race, others ascribe to it a decisive influence. Meanwhile it is certain that nations—not to speak of races—appear in the most varying lights at different periods, even when they have undergone no fresh racial admixtures. What changes, for instance, Puritanism brought about in what is called the English popular character ! How different does the German of 1800 appear from the German of 1900 ! Who would have guessed a century and a half ago that the Jews were destined to take a great part in modern intellectual life and to rank high in the world of sport ? (In the last Olympic Games the Jews won as many events as the English. Of the eight world's championships in boxing the Jews hold five.) What a difference in the Teutons of to-day and of two thousand years ago ! How falsely would a Roman Günther of the time

LA

Augustus have characterised the Germanic " race-soul " !

Now as touching the Jews, they are already, according to Günther, racially akin to the Germans: through their Asia Minor racial component with the Dinaric Germans, through their Mediterranean-Oriental with the Western Germans, and they are also the vehicles of the blood of all other European races, including that of the Nordic race. Günther estimates the Alpine and East-Baltic element in the Ashkenazic Jews as approximately the same as in the Germans. His assertion that the Jews are " alien to Europe," on account of the difference in their racial composition, does not, therefore, appear convincing. According to a greater authority than Günther, Fritz Lenz, Jews and Germans are, on the contrary, " very similar as regards essential aptitudes, and this is especially true if by Germans one means men of preponderantly Nordic race."[1] From a purely ethnological point of view there may often be greater kinship between a German Jew and a Nordic German than between the latter and an Alpine German, and many a German Nazi may be less Nordic than many a German Jew whom he has driven into exile.

In such circumstances it cannot surprise us if we often see antisemitic Germans praising the achievements of Jews, of course in ignorance of their authors' origin. Gundolf's work, *Shakespeare und der deutsche Geist*, was lauded to the skies by the *Deutsche Tageszeitung* (July 1, 1911) as a masterpiece of the German intellect, " filled with deep reverence for everything great and beautiful and with a rare nobility of soul." How different his judgment would have been if the reviewer had known of Gundolf's Jewish birth ! Alfred Messel's celebrated Wertheim building in Berlin was praised in the first edition of Heinrich Class's (pseudonym Einhart) *Deutsche Geschichte* (1914) as a symbol of the rebirth of genuine German architecture—this was deleted in the later

---

[1] I am not aware whether, since Hitler's triumph and the standardisation of opinion in Germany, Lenz has withdrawn this statement.

edition, when evidently the author had been informed of Messel's birth—and indeed this building was praised as lately as 1931 in a Nazi periodical, *Der Freiheitskampf*, for originating a new, genuinely German style, recalling the aspiring Gothic, and this was contrasted with " horizontalism," which was described as a manifestation of " desert taste " and as un-German, levelling internationalism. The well-known weekly, *Fridericus* (1930, No. 3), describes the inventor of the radio amplification tube, Robert von Lieben, another Jew, as a German genius, exploited by the Jewish Telefunken Company. And so on. How painful would be the situation of the Nazis if all poetry, books, and inventions were anonymous !

Since the German Jews as a whole wished above all to be Germans, and only in the second or third place Jews, of which more below, they have often yielded to the temptation of apologetically making light of the actual differences between German and Jewish or described them as passing away thanks to assimilation. He who writes these lines views the Jewish question from an entirely different angle. I do not wish to deny the differences which exist, nor would I efface them, if that were in my power. But without denying the, perhaps disputable, significance of race in forming intellectual qualities or the complicated character of Antisemitism, I have tried to show that the hypothesis of racial Antisemitism, that there are clefts between races which cannot be bridged, is baseless, and that the whole ideology of racial Antisemitism lacks scientific foundation. And indeed the world's most eminent anthropologists seem now to agree that, especially as regards moral qualities and intelligence, the differences are greater within each race than between the races; further, that no race is inferior in itself and that the whole of mankind forms a single species. But naturally the tendency of German science is now all in the opposite direction, since it has to work under governmental pressure. The main thing is to deny all intellectual community between the "fellow-countryman" and the "alien" in all branches of culture and to make out that the influence of the Jews is radically evil.

An eminent German mathematician, Ludwig Bieberbach, has recently endeavoured to show—in *Forschungen und Fortschritte*, June 20th, 1934—that this also applies to mathematics. The Jewish mathematicians belong to the " S-type " (" Strahltyp "), the narrowly rational, abstract logical category, which proceeds from certain definite ideas and adapts them to reality. The German mathematicians on the other hand belong to the intuitive " J-type"; their starting-point is the contemplation of reality, they experience it and try to form an image of it. Bieberbach praises the antisemitic students of Göttingen University, who " manfully " defended themselves against the Jewish professor of mathematics, Emil Landau. According to the same authority the French mathematicians, significantly enough, also belong to the S-type.

The views of racial philosophy represented by victorious Nazidom are directed not only against the Jews but also, when consistently followed out, against everything and everybody declared to be racially alien. They are opposed to the whole tradition of Western civilisation, which hitherto has never belied its syncretic and œcumenical character. In practice it will doubtless prove impossible to scale off all " racial aliens." For it is a true saying that all culture stands on ground that is not its own and that only barbarism was once native to the soil. But the tendency is remarkable and alarming.

CHAPTER IX

"THE PROTOCOLS OF THE ELDERS OF ZION"—"THE GREATEST FORGERY OF THE CENTURY"

THE SO-CALLED " Protocols of the Elders of Zion " are among the most politically significant and symptomatically interesting documents in the history of Antisemitism. They are significant in that they were the chief means employed after the World War to promote savage hatred of the Jews in Eastern Europe and Germany. It is no exaggeration to say that they cost the lives of many thousands of innocent persons and that more blood and tears cling to their pages than to those of any other mendacious document in the world's history. They are symptomatically interesting from the fact that this gross fabrication in spite of its absurdities was taken seriously in such wide circles. Even in England and America there were those who allowed themselves to be influenced by it. The *Morning Post* devoted no less than sixty columns to the Protocols when they appeared in English in 1920. *The Times* called for an investigation, and they made a strong impression on American opinion, above all as a result of Ford's book *The International Jew*, which was inspired by them, and of which we have spoken above. The very fact that people could believe for a moment in the fabled existence of a powerful Jewish secret world-conspiracy, which had for its object the destruction of the Christian States and the foundation of a Jewish world-monarchy on their ruins, shows the truth of Shaw's saying that our age is just as credulous as the Middle Ages, though its credulity finds other objects. Everyone who knows anything of Jewish history during the last few centuries must be aware that the Jewish people is a weak and divided people that can be subjected to almost any treatment with impunity, and that the talk of its control of the money market and the Press is nonsense. Moreover, the slightest reflection ought surely to have told any person in his senses that the very idea of the policy of the Great Powers being directed by a secret body of Jews operating in conjunction with the Freemasons and working the statesmen like marionettes had nothing to do with reality. And yet—all the time from May 1920, when the Protocols were reviewed in *The Times*, till August 1921, when they were exposed as a fabrication, the possibility of their genuineness was widely reckoned with. They were translated into nearly all living languages, including Chinese and Arabic, and were spread in huge editions over the whole world. Vast quantities were showered especially over Eastern Europe. Alfred Rosenberg, whom we now know as one of the leading German statesmen, for a long time the Nazi Party's expert in foreign affairs and appointed a kind of *Lebensanschauung* minister by Hitler, launched the book in Germany with brilliant results. This was done through a book called *Die Protokolle der Weisen von Zion und die jüdische Weltpolitik* (1923), wherein, two years after their exposure, he sought to prove the genuineness of the Protocols and furnished them with a commentary. In Germany, by the way, two translations appeared, one in 1919 by Gottfried zur Beek (pseudonym for Ludendorff's coadjutor, Major Müller von Hausen), the other by the already mentioned Antisemite, Theodor Fritsch. They were both reissued after Hitler's victory in 1933, the first in its 14th, the second in its 13th edition (66th to 75th thousand).

The Protocols were first published as a supplementary chapter to an extended edition (1905) of a Russian pamphlet by Serge Nilus, originally printed in 1901 or 1903, with the title: " The Great in the Little. Near is the coming of Antichrist and the Kingdom of the Devil on Earth." Of this edition, which significantly enough was a product of the Imperial printing office at Tsarskoie Selo, only one copy seems to have been preserved. It is in the possession of the British Museum, which acquired it in 1906. The edition of 1905 bears the title: " The Great in the Little, or Antichrist as an Imminent Possibility. The Confessions of an Orthodox Believer." The Protocols were evidently intended to serve as evidence for the thesis announced in the title. This pamphlet, which under the title of " He is at the Door " (he=Antichrist), together with the Protocols, was reissued in 1911, 1912 and 1917, is of a mystical apocalyptic character, full of visions, omens, prophecies, especially those of the holy thaumaturge Seraphim of Sarov; mystical symbols, which are alleged to be due to the hosts of Antichrist, are here interpreted. Orthodox Russia and the absolute autocracy are represented to be the last bulwark against Antichrist. In one chapter of the enlarged edition it is asserted that the end of the world is at hand, that Antichrist will soon come to establish the dominion of the Devil over the whole earth, and that he, Antichrist, will be of the tribe of Dan and will be acknowledged by the Jews as the Messiah. It is to be noted that the early editions of the book contain nothing about the Protocols. The words " Wise Men of Zion " however do occur once apropos of the Jewish plan (to be mentioned below) of 929 B.C. for the conquest of the world; and from this seed it is not unlikely that the Protocols afterwards grew. Protocols, by the way, is to some extent a misnomer, since they consist of a single statement laid before the assembled wise men of Zion by the leader of the secret Jewish world-government at twenty-four separate meetings with the object of initiating them, first into the methods adopted by this government in alliance with the Freemasons for inciting the Goyim (non-Jews) against one another and ruining them economically, politically and morally, and then into the system of government it proposes to establish in the future Jewish World-State.

As the Protocols made their triumphal progress through the world disjoined from the untranslated book "The Great in the Little" or "He is at the Door," it is necessary to point out that they formed an integral part of this most crudely superstitious pamphlet. Immediately after the ninth chapter, in which Nilus relates how at Kiev he saw a comet which revealed to him that Tsar Alexander III would soon be snatched away by death, the Protocols begin as chapter the tenth.

The spokesman of the secret Jewish world-government believes only in the right of force. Humane and liberal ideas have been launched by the Jews merely in order to accomplish the downfall of the non-Jewish States. The Jews were the first to spread abroad the watchword " Liberty, Equality, Fraternity," and in the name of these ideas the " brutishly unintelligent " non-Jewish nations follow the banners of the Jewish leaders. " The heads of the Goyim are fuddled by spirituous liquors, and their young men have been rendered dull by classicism (!) and early licentiousness, into which they have been enticed by our agents—tutors, lackeys, governesses in rich families, shop-assistants and others." The introduction of the intuitive method in education has served as an excellent means of corrupting non-Jewish youth. " Its chief task consists in transforming the non-Jews into a herd of mentally indolent, obedient animals, who are unable to understand a thing until they are shown a picture, but after that blindly believe in it." It is noted with satisfaction that " in France one of our best agents, Bourgeois, has already publicly announced a new programme of intuitive education," The successes of Darwinism, Marxism and Nietzscheanism were also arranged by the Jews. " Thanks to the Press we have got the gold into our hands, though we had to go through torrents of blood and tears to get it." But the result has been splendid. " To-day I am able to inform you," we read in the third Protocol, " that we are only a few steps from the goal. There only remains a little way to go, and we shall be ready to close the circle of the Symbolical Serpent (see below). When this circle is complete, all the realms of Europe will be held within it as in the grip of a vice." For it should be explained that under the guidance of the secret Jewish world-government the people have destroyed the aristocracy, their natural defenders and helpers, whose own interests were indissolubly bound up with the welfare of the lower classes, whereas " we are interested in the opposite—in the degeneration of the Goyim." The organisation of society demands the division of mankind into classes and orders. In order to prevent non-Jews from seeing this, the Jews have hindered them from getting a correct insight into social science.

Thanks to the fact that the Jews have gold " wholly " in their power, they intend, when the social discontent encouraged by them has reached its climax, to arrange a general economic crisis and on one and the same day throw the working masses of Europe on to the streets. The workers will then be delighted to shed the blood of those whom in their ignorance they have envied from childhood. But the Jews, knowing of course the time fixed for the revolution, will already have seen to their own safety. " Remember the French Revolution, which we have designated ' the Great Revolution '; the secret of its bringing about is well known to us, for it was exclusively the work of our hands (!). Since then we have led the nations from one disappointment to another, so that in the end they will submit to the king of the blood of Zion whom we shall give to the world."

A detailed description is given of the infernal work carried on by the Jews for twenty centuries in inciting various nations, classes, religious confessions and races against one another. And the result: *per me reges regnant*, through me the kings reign. If any country should oppose the Jews, its neighbours are to be forced to make war on it; but if they refuse, the Jews will reply by a general war. (This passage is taken by those who believe in the genuineness of the Protocols to prove that the Jews planned and brought about the World War, for which reason the translations made after 1914 usually give " World War " in place of " general war," which is the reading of the Russian original.)

To provide for the contingency of the Jews' intrigues being prematurely exposed and of the nations taking up arms against them, they have taken care that the capitals of Western Europe be furnished with underground railways, so that if the worst comes to the worst they may be blown up with all their institutions and muniments.

Since only autocracy can save the non-Jews, the Jews endeavour everywhere to promote constitutionalism and liberalism; but when the Jews have seized power, absolutism must be introduced, for " the constitution, as is well known to you, is nothing but a school of party strife, dissension, quarrelling, differences of opinion, political hatred." In order to discredit this system the Jews must therefore contrive that persons shall be elected as presidents, " whose past contains some obscure and shady affair, some ' Panama,' " after which the Jews will increase the nations' confusion and despair to such an extent that in order to regain peace, law and order they will submit to an absolute Jewish world-monarch of the seed of David, whom they will accept as a deliverer and saviour. After this the nations, having first been deprived by the Jews of all belief in God, will be converted to the Jewish religion, and the Jews, in alliance with their creatures, the Freemasons, will rule over the whole earth. Should any try to oppose them, the Jews will know how to remove these persons in such a way that no one will guess they have been murdered.

To these Protocols Nilus has added a number of explanations. We are told that the Protocols are signed by representatives of Zion of the thirty-third, that is the highest, degree, and are extracts from a complete book of protocols from the first Zionist Congress, which was held at Basle in 1897, but that the plan itself for the Jewish conquest of the world was conceived as early as 929 B.C., that is nearly three thousand years ago, by Solomon and other wise men of Zion. These men had determined to conquer the world " through the craft of the Symbolical Serpent." We must here pass over the detailed interpretation of this symbolical image—a serpent striving to coil itself around the earth till its head meets its tail. Suffice it to say that its head represents the secret Jewish world-government, the composition of which is unknown not only to the Goyim but also to the rank and file of the Jews; that its body is the Jewish people, and that the serpent's head will not reach Zion, in other words encircle the earth, until the Jews have destroyed the Great Powers economically and morally. This object is to be attained chiefly through Jewish women, who pass themselves off as French, Italian or Spanish. The graphic representation of the progress of the Symbolical Serpent shows the Jewish world-conquest as taking place in seven stages: the first in 429 B.C., when after the death of Pericles the Jews began to undermine the greatness of Greece, and so on, until the seventh, when Alexander II was murdered. Nilus informs us that the indications on the drawing point to Moscow, Kiev and Odessa, and that Constantinople is indicated as the eighth and last stage before Jerusalem. He imputes to Judaism the most infamous opinions and " proves " his assertions by referring to the " Talmudic " books Jihal 67, Sauh 58, Hopaim 14, and so on. These books have never existed, and their names are not Hebrew. But the careful references together with the fictitious names are naturally designed to give a semblance of authenticity to the antisemitic falsehoods.

Such are the contents of what has become the chief among the canonical books of modern Antisemitism, has provided it to a certain extent with its theoretical basis, and is looked upon by millions of people as a bible, which, according to the German courts of law, is what the Protocols were to Walter Rathenau's assassins.

Now let us see how the Protocols came into being. Their editor, Serge Nilus, an otherwise unknown official in the chancery of the Synod at Moscow, gives two divergent accounts of how they came into his hands. (He is called " professor " in various antisemitic pamphlets, but is not to be found in any Russian book of reference.) According to the edition of 1911 Nilus's correspondent came across them in the Zionist head office, " which is situated in French territory." (It never has been so situated.) According to the edition of 1917, usually known as the " pogrom edition " from the use it was put to, he acquired the manuscript—it has now disappeared !—in 1901 from Alexis Nikolajevich Souchotin, who died some years later as vice-governor of the Government of Stavropol. This person, according to Nilus, received it in his turn from a lady living abroad, whose name he does not remember, and she in her turn came by it in a mysterious way, presumably by theft. That the meetings of the wise men of Zion are identical with the first Zionist Congress is asserted by Nilus for the first time in the edition of 1911. Here Nilus claims to have received definite information that the Protocols are derived from that Congress—it must then have held twenty-four secret meetings besides the official ones during the three days for which it was assembled !—and that it is Theodor Herzl's speech which is reported in the document. Herzl, it should be said, was, according to Nilus, " the prince of the exile." (That the last exilarch, prince of the exile, died in 1063, does not trouble Nilus, who evidently believes that the office continued to be held, though in secret.) Other editors give quite different versions of how the manuscript came into Nilus's hands, one proof among many of their way of dealing with the truth. C. Butmi, one of the founders of the " Black

Hundreds" (*see* above, p. 86), who had included the Protocols as early as 1907 in his provocative pamphlet *The Enemies of the Human Race*, declared that they came from the secret archives of "Zion," not from the Zionists but from a Masonic organisation working for Jewry. Theodor Fritsch declared frankly that the Russian secret police found the manuscript in 1901 during a domiciliary visit to a Jew's house, that it was written in Hebrew and that the translation was confided to the orientalist (!) Professor Nilus. According to Gottfried zur Beek, Nicholas II received information of the secret meetings at Basle in 1897 and despatched thither a secret agent, who managed to bribe a Jew closely associated with the freemasons, who was to bring the Protocols from Basle to Frankfort-on-Main. On the way there, in a little town where the Jew passed the night, the Russian and his assistants then copied the twenty-four protocols, which were written in French, after which they were published by Nilus in Russian. According to the Polish editor the manuscript was simply stolen from Herzl's room, and so on.

If Nilus really had the manuscript in his hands as early as 1901, it seems curious that he postponed the printing of the Protocols for so many years, especially as he assures us that they made such an overwhelming impression on him " as can only be exercised on the human mind by a divine power, like the miracle of a man born blind who recovers his sight." And this was a matter which concerned the welfare of the whole of mankind ! Whether Nilus himself was the author or, what is more probable, some official or officials of the Russian secret police or of its branch in Paris, must here be left open.

One need not be a specialist in historical research or have any extensive knowledge of matters Jewish to see through the fraudulent nature of the Protocols after a cursory glance. To begin with, the expression " Wise Men of Zion " makes one more than suspicious. For this is unknown in Jewish linguistic usage. It has evidently been coined in order that its mysterious sound may have a suggestive effect on ignorant, anti-Jewish masses—or on the mystically-inclined Tsar. The expression *per me reges regnant* (Proverbs, viii. 15) is a quotation from the Vulgate, the translation of the Church of Rome. Why should a Jew make use of it ? He quotes in his mother-tongue or in Hebrew. There are allusions to the presidential election of Loubet, who was implicated in the Panama scandals, and to Léon Bourgeois' educational reforms, which are much later in date than 1897. (The faithful Antisemite sees precisely in these facts a proof of how the secret Jewish world-government had determined long beforehand to arrange the presidential election and the educational reforms in question !) Anyone who has the slightest knowledge of Jewish religion must be aware that the methods recommended by the " Wise Men of Zion," as well as the whole idea of a political Jewish world dominion, are entirely foreign to Jewish ways of thinking. Benjamin Segel, in his exhaustive book, *Die Protokolle der Weisen von Zion, kritisch beleuchtet,* points out page by page one absurdity after another. A mere fraction of what he brought to light would have sufficed to make any impartial tribunal brand the Protocols as a miserable forgery. But even before Segel's book saw the light the whole edifice of lies collapsed.

One day in the year 1921 a Tsarist officer who had belonged to the Ochrana and was expelled from Russia came to *The Times* correspondent in Constantinople, Philip Graves, and offered for sale a literary curiosity, a much-worn French novel with the title-page missing. To do the distressed Russian a good turn Graves bought it. He began to read. He came upon the words " *per me reges regnant.*" It struck him that he had read them not long before in—" The Protocols of the Elders of Zion." He took down the Protocols and began comparing. Whole sentences, whole paragraphs, nay, whole pages were practically identical. He sent the French novel to the library of the British Museum for identification. It was found to be a lampoon against Napoleon III and his domestic and foreign policy: *Dialogue aux Enfers entre Machiavel et Montesquieu ou la politique de Machiavel au XIX siècle, par un contemporain.* The first edition, which is anonymous, was published in 1864; the second, which was printed in Brussels and gives the author's name, bears the date 1858. The author, whose name was Maurice Joly, had to serve fifteen months' imprisonment on account of this production. Machiavelli utters the thoughts that Joly in his savage hatred attributed to Napoleon—or at least he wished to convince his readers that Napoleon thought in this way— while Montesquieu says pretty much what Joly himself would have liked to tell Napoleon to his face. It is mainly Machiavelli's words that the author of the Protocols has put into the mouth of the representative of the Jewish world-government. For according to the Protocols the Jews fully admit that their policy is a scoundrelly one. In several passages the plagiary has misunderstood the text, which has given rise to absurd blunders.

The legal defence department of the Basle Jewish community published in 1933 a comparison, paragraph by paragraph, of the Protocols (in the editions of Beek and Fritsch) and corresponding parts of Joly's book. The identical or "adjusted" texts—they are printed in parallel columns—occupy 42 folio pages. For instance, when Joly makes Montesquieu say to Napoleon: " *Now I understand the apology for the god Vishnu. You have a hundred arms like the Indian idol, and every one of your fingers touches a spring,*" the Protocols give these words to the spokesman of the Elders of Zion: " *Our kingdom is to be an apology for the god Vishnu. With a hundred hands we shall enclose the mainsprings of the social machinery.*" And so on.

On August 16th, 17th and 18th, 1921, in three long articles in *The Times*, Graves gave the facts as to the alleged authenticity of the Protocols. The articles were afterwards published as a pamphlet under the title: *The Truth about the Protocols. A Literary Forgery.* The articles produced an enormous

sensation all over the world and to all intents and purposes
shattered the power of Antisemitism in England. Other
exposures followed, particularly in Segel's book, mentioned
above. From these it appeared that the Protocols, the first
edition of which was a very small one, were not originally
concocted in order to incite the masses against the Jews, but
to frighten the Tsar into complying with the demands of
the extreme Right and to throw suspicion on his moderate-
liberal Prime Minister Witte as a Freemason and an agent of
international Jewry. The year 1905, as we know, opened
with the " Bloody Sunday " in St. Petersburg. The revolutionary movements were getting too strong for the weak and
vacillating Tsar, who therefore, under Witte's guidance,
was induced to make various constitutional concessions,
which the extreme Right regarded as the beginning of the
end. Those passages of the Protocols which are not
plagiarised show how the author or authors took pains to
make every constitutional concession appear insane and
the struggle for autocracy a sacred duty.

The exposures of Graves and others came as a hard
blow to the fanatical Antisemites. Someone hit upon a
way out. Joly was of course a baptised Jew, whose name was
Moses Joël ! He had written his *Dialogue* with the object of
undermining the monarchical principle and preparing the
way for Jewish world dominion. He was naturally a Communist and had been shot as a *communard* in 1871. He was
undoubtedly acquainted with the Jewish plans of world-
conquest. The verbal agreement between his book and the
Protocols was therefore perfectly natural ! In Germany
Count Reventlow, Theodor Fritsch's crony, also voiced this
opinion. Perhaps they had never read Joly's book. For it
turns out that Joly was not only a monarchist but—an
Antisemite. In November 1924 his autobiography was discovered in Paris: he was descended from a strictly Catholic
family of government officials.

Since Graves's exposures several Russian sources of the

forgery have been discovered. Thus the last six protocols, which deal with the economic system to be introduced by the Jews when their king rules over the earth, are plagiarised from a pamphlet aimed at Witte and written in the late 1890's; and so on.

The actual germ of " The Protocols of the Wise Elders of Zion " is undoubtedly contained in a trashy adventure story published under the pseudonym of Sir John Retcliffe, alias one Hermann Goedsche, a Prussian postal official dismissed for forgery, who turned out cheap literature on a large scale. The novel in question, *Gaeta, Düppel, Biarritz*, which was published in 1868, contained a chapter headed " In the Jewish cemetery of Prague." Here the author describes how on the Feast of Tabernacles in 1860 he chanced secretly to overhear the princes of the twelve tribes of Israel—that the ten tribes have been lost since the year 722 B.C. is a small matter—who assemble here by night at the tomb of the holy rabbi Simeon ben Jehuda as a " cabalistic Sanhedrin " every hundred years. The twelve, who come from the great cities of Europe, Amsterdam, Toledo, Worms, Lisbon, Constantinople, etc., collect around the eldest of their number and discuss—in Chaldean !—in solemn phrases the progress of the Jewish plan of world-conquest and what diabolical measures they ought next to adopt in order to lay the world at their feet as masters of the Press and of gold. This chapter was afterwards published separately in several editions and also (1886) in a condensed form: the statements of the twelve leaders are here reduced to one and put into the mouth of a rabbi. This " speech," by the way, is even to be found in Swedish, both as an appendix to the Finland edition of the Protocols, and in a pamphlet published in Stockholm in 1933, called *Fyra Zions protokoll, ej förut utgivna på svenska* (Four Protocols of Zion, not previously published in Swedish.) The Swedish editor assures us that Retcliffe " had to pay with his life for having disclosed their contents." (It may be stated in parenthesis that Goedsche

MA

died on November 8th, 1878, thus ten years after the appearance of the novel in question.) It is significant that this "address of the rabbi" is cited as a proof of the genuineness of " The Protocols of the Elders of Zion." After Hitler's triumph the chapter was published once more, this time by the fanatical Antisemite, Johann von Leers, who in his preface did not indeed vouch for the historical authenticity of the address, but described it as a masterpiece and as a warning, unfortunately not heeded in time, to the non-Jewish peoples to beware of the Jews, who in post-War Germany had established just such a dominion as was foretold by Goedsche's princes. This chapter was translated into Russian as early as 1872, and when republished in 1903 (by Kruszevan) had an important share in exciting passions before the Kishinev pogrom. Had the Protocols existed at that date, they would certainly have been used instead.

It was only during the restless and sanguinary years immediately following the World War that the Protocols began to play such an extraordinary part in antisemitic agitation, being introduced to Western Europe by exiled Russian officers. The Bolshevik revolution, of course, was regarded as Jewish and therefore as a proof of the authenticity of the Protocols.

It is significant that both in Germany and in Eastern Europe the Protocols continued, and still continue, to play an immensely important part in antisemitic agitation, although there can now be no doubt of their spuriousness. As has been justly remarked, it is as though the exposure of the swindle has itself lent them a new *élan* and authority. No doubt they are now rejected by many Antisemites; in fact they have opened the eyes of a great number to the real nature of Antisemitism and turned them away from it. Others again acknowledge that they are spurious, or at least not demonstrably genuine, but consider this of minor importance, since in any case they give a correct description of the Jews and their aspirations ! But a great body of leading Antisemites, especially in Germany, still insist on their genuineness and endeavour by means of various devices to convince the public of it. In the edition published by Gottfried zur Beek in 1933, a facsimile letter from the British Museum has been inserted, dated 23.6.1928, which certifies, what nobody has doubted, that the library possesses a copy of the 1905 edition of the Protocols. The intention is of course to suggest to the reader that the library has officially confirmed their genuineness.

Theodor Fritsch adopted another method. At a commemoration, on July 27th, 1929, of the twenty-fifth anniversary of Herzl's death, the chief rabbi of Sweden, Dr. Marcus Ehrenpreis, who had himself taken part in the first Zionist Congress, delivered a speech which was reported in a Swedish-Jewish review. He said amongst other things:

" Herzl left us at the age of forty-four. He had worn out his strength in his work for Israel. But after all it was perhaps no misfortune that he died young. For eight years he had worked for Israel—years full of blessing to such an extent as to be richer than periods of our history. His work tended towards a goal which he had set up in advance.

" Herzl had no links with religion, but his was a deeply religious nature. If a prophet is a ' foreteller,' one who sees coming events and uses his gift of words to proclaim them to others—then Herzl was to some extent a present-day prophet. Just as Deutero-Isaiah decades in advance saw the victorious might of Cyrus, so did Herzl, twenty years before we experienced the convulsions of the World War, foresee them and prepare us for what was to come. He foresaw the break-up of Turkey, he foresaw that England was to take charge of Palestine. ' We are on the threshold of decisive historic events,' he said twenty years before the World War; ' and these events open up new possibilities for the Jewish people.' When he closed his eyes he could die convinced that his work would survive.

" To-day, twenty-five years after his death, we are able to survey the results of his efforts. It is rarely that a generation can see the fruits of its own work. This can be said of our generation. Herzl formulated the programme of the Basle Congress: 'Our object is a Jewish homeland in Palestine guaranteed by international law.' Twenty-five years later Jewish Palestine stands under the guarantee and protection of the Powers. Fifty Powers have given England a mandate to exercise suzerainty in Palestine and have acknowledged the Jews' historical connection with the country. ' This day have we rolled away the reproach of Egypt from off you.' "

This passage was reprinted in an antisemitic paper in Stockholm, and in his 1933 edition of the Protocols Fritsch inserted a duly attested certificate from a public translator of the correctness of the translation. At the same time he declared in his preface that in this speech Dr. Ehrenpreis had acknowledged the genuineness of the Protocols. Had he not explained that Herzl had a goal set up in advance? It is true that the speaker's words made it clear that the goal was a Jewish Palestine under the guarantee of international law, but that did not trouble Fritsch. Dr. Ehrenpreis has instituted proceedings against the publishers—Fritsch himself died in 1933—and against the Swiss papers which gave circulation to these lies. At the time of writing the case has not been decided.

It is significant, by the way, that the same publishers, the Hammer-Verlag, issued in 1934 a new edition of Ford's *The International Jew*, in spite of the author having withdrawn his book as mendacious and prohibited its circulation, and that the editor assures us in his introduction that Ehrenpreis has " emphasised the genuineness of the Protocols."

It is possible, probable even, that some of those who still stand up for the genuineness of the Protocols do so in good faith. The grotesque view that the Bolshevik revolution was a " Jewish " revolution and a link in a secret Jewish plan of world-conquest has with them become a fixed idea, and on that account the Protocols appear to them prophetic and genuine. They are not aware that the ideas discussed in them are diametrically opposed to the Jewish religion, since they have been inspired with the most preposterous conceptions of this religion, above all through distorted and falsified quotations from the Talmud.

The history of the Protocols, like the Dreyfus affair, gives one a profound insight not only into the nature of Antisemitism, vulgar or otherwise, but also into the generally insecure position of the Jews of the Dispersion. What is most disconcerting from the latter point of view is naturally the fact that a forgery of this kind was not immediately rejected as an absurdity by European opinion, but in many places, as has been shown above, was taken quite seriously. The antisemitic national psychosis they gave rise to in Eastern Europe and Germany was obviously of the same nature as that which was formerly evoked by the fables of Jewish ritual murders and torturing of the Host. Where there exists a will to hate, there the most fantastic charges will be readily accepted, provided they fan the flame of hatred, as indeed was demonstrated by the propaganda on both sides during the World War. But we must nevertheless regard it as a monstrous thing that the Prussian Minister of Education, Rust, has ordered that the Protocols (in Rosenberg's annotated version above referred to), together with Hitler's *Mein Kampf* and several other works of vulgar Antisemitism,[1] are to be compulsory reading in the Prussian schools, an attempt to poison the minds of children, which throws a lightning flash on the position of German Jews, particularly the Jewish children, and at the same time on the mentality of the Nazi rulers.

The portraying of the Jews as the incarnation of evil is a sort of diabolism in a new form, a secularised diabolism so to speak, but not on that account any less preposterous than its mediæval prototype. It is only to the outward view that times, that is human beings, undergo any radical change.

Note. Since these pages were written the Protocols have

They are: Rosenberg's *Der Mythos des 20 Jahrhunderts*, Günther's *Rassenkunde des jüdischen Volkes* and Theodor Fritsch's *Handbuch der Judenfrage*.

once more attracted the world's attention, this time owing to the action brought by the national organisation of the Jewish congregations in Switzerland and the Jewish congregation of Berne against the committee of the Swiss Nazi Party on account of its having published a Swiss edition of the Protocols. A number of well-known persons in and outside Switzerland, among them many (anti-Bolshevist) Russian exiles, have been heard as witnesses. There can henceforth scarcely be any doubt that the Protocols are the work of the Russian Ochrana and probably of its branch in Paris. The well-known politician Vladimir Burzev, who gave evidence, declared that Nilus, whom he described as a cross between a fanatic and a forger, knew the Protocols to be spurious, although he made use of them; but that the Tsar, on being informed that they were a forgery, prohibited their employment, which however did not prevent their being hawked about.

The Nazi expert, a leading Antisemite from Germany, Lieut.-Col. Fleischhauer, tried to make out that the resolutions mentioned in the Protocols were not adopted by the Zionist Congress at Basle in 1897, but by a secret general assembly of the Jewish Bne-Brith Order held at the same place and time. Joly, he said, was a Jew and identical with the Joe Levy who figures in Herzl's Zionist novel *Alt-Neuland*.[1] One has only to omit the letter *e* in Joe and the letters *ev* in Levy and one has the name Joly. The omitted letters evidently had a secret significance, only known to the Jews, and so on.

The pronouncements of the Court's expert, the author Loosli, and the plaintiffs' expert, Professor Baumgarten, both, be it said, " Aryans," annihilated not only the plea that the Protocols were genuine, but also the allegation that they were an expression of the Jewish spirit and of Jewish aspirations.

[1] It has long been known that in Joe Levy Herzl drew a portrait of his friend Joseph Cowen.

Judgment was given on May 19th, 1935. It was declared that the Protocols were forgeries and plagiarisms and of such a nature as to come under the head of obscene literature according to the laws of the Canton of Berne. The defendants were sentenced to fines. The president of the Court concluded his judgment with these words: " I am convinced that the Protocols are obscene literature and more than that, namely, ridiculous nonsense."

CHAPTER X

HITLER'S *MEIN KAMPF*

IN A WELL-KNOWN CHAPTER of *Mein Kampf*[1] Hitler expounds with almost staggering frankness his views on the methods proper to political propaganda. It must be addressed, he says, only to the masses. Its intellectual level must be adjusted to the comprehension of the most limited capacities among those to whom it appeals. The greater the multitude it seeks to reach, the lower must be its purely intellectual level. The important thing is to understand the emotional imagination of the masses, to find the way to attracting their attention and so to reaching their hearts. Hitler blames the German war propaganda for not throwing the whole guilt of the War on the enemy. This ought to have been done, even if it conflicted with the actual facts. Above all nothing good about your opponent ! " What would one say for instance of a poster intended to advertise a new soap, which at the same time described other soaps as good ? " In other words: by appealing to the most primitive instincts of the masses and deluding them into confusing your adversary with a repulsive and malicious image of him, you are to fill them with a savage hatred which will serve as a tool in the hands of the political leaders. And in fact Hitler has acted in conformity with this principle. Inspired by maniacal hatred of the Jews his bands marched under the swastika banners and overthrew the Weimar Republic, " the Jew Republic." It had actually been possible to persuade the masses that the Reich was controlled by diabolical Jews and

[1] Engl. trans. (abridged), *My Struggle*, London (1933), ch. vi.

that Hitler's struggle was a noble war of liberation from them.

Since *Mein Kampf* is an integral part of Nazi propaganda and Hitler, as we have seen, expressly recommends the use of lies in the service of propaganda, we have reason to ask whether Hitler himself believes in the antisemitic absurdities and vulgar abuse with which *Mein Kampf* abounds. Unfortunately it is impossible to answer this question. In anti-Nazi circles in Germany however the opinion seems to prevail that Hitler, in contrast to such men as Goebbels, really believes like one possessed in his antisemitic Munchausen stories.

Hitler gives anti-German war propaganda the testimonial that it was psychologically correct to exhibit the Germans as barbarians and Huns. It may therefore be of interest to quote some specimens of its utterances, especially as these showed a great similarity to those of Antisemitism; in doing this however it must be noted that malicious blackening of other nations was by no means more common in the Entente countries than in Germany. The caricatures of the enemy are terribly distorted and mendacious. According to a post-War school-book for children of ten to twelve years, written by Rector Miraquet and Professor Pergameni, and awarded a prize by the Royal Belgian Academy, the Germans are a nation governed by perverse racial instincts, greedy for plunder, rapine and murder, hypocritical, servile, cunning, cruel, malicious, ungrateful for generous hospitality, morbidly desirous of world-dominion, without magnanimity and incapable of understanding the heroism and unselfishness of an adversary. Wherever a German may settle, he remains German in heart and soul, in habits and customs. " Relatively honourable among themselves, like the members of a band of robbers . . . towards non-Germans they are without faith, law or honour." The Russian anthropologist Menshikov " proved " that the Germans belong to one of the lowest races of mankind, and that the shape of their skulls approximates to that of Neanderthal man. One of the most

eminent of French historians, Gabriel Hanotaux, declares
that nearly all the treasures of German culture are borrowed; that there is nothing left of Goethe's originality if we
abstract what he has borrowed from Shakespeare, Voltaire
and Rousseau, and that it was unnecessary for Kant to
burden with his heavy books a world which, since it possessed the Gospels, Plato and Descartes, had no need of
them. " The Germans will continue," in Hanotaux's
opinion, " to imitate and counterfeit Western civilisation."
The Italian dramatist Zacconi, who had translated several
of the best German works, declared: " To-day every child
knows that the German soul is full of barbarism. I knew it in
expounding the greatest thinkers of that people. The German
soul is always fundamentally cruel, sordid, immoral."
Rudyard Kipling declared bluntly that the German race
must be exterminated altogether. One could continue such
quotations almost indefinitely. Constantin Brunner, from
whom the above have been taken, has collected a veritable
anthology. And the result of this anti-German propaganda?
I confine myself to quoting the letter of a German-American
in the *Kölnische Zeitung*: " Here such a savage hatred prevails
of everything German that one cannot help being surprised
that it has not broken out before. . . . It is therefore not to be
wondered at that Germans here commit suicide from despair.
We are truly in a difficult situation. We do not fight with
weapons, nor are we attacked with swords, but with what is
still worse: with slanders and hatred." It must however be
acknowledged that Hitler and Co. have far outstripped their
foreign instructors. A brief abstract of the antisemitic
sections of *Mein Kampf*—and Antisemitism is one of the
leading ideas of the book—can give but a feeble idea of this.

It was only in antisemitic Vienna that Hitler turned
Antisemite. Here he became imbued with the conviction
that the Jews were not a religious community but an alien
people, though most of them would not hear of this; that
they controlled the socialist Press; that Marxism was Jewry;

that Jews were specialists in the white slave traffic and in the dissemination of obscene literature. He began, so he tells us, to study Marxism. He asked himself whether its founders really understood its implications. If they did so —and Hitler thinks that was the case—" the originators of this national malady," he says, " must have been real devils, for only the brain of a monster and not of a human being could have conceived the ingenious plan of an organisation the activity and final result of which must lead to the collapse of human civilisation and thus to the destruction of the world." Proceeding from the premises that Marxism is " Jewish " and, if victorious, must lead to a catastrophe for mankind, Hitler declares: " So I now believe that I am acting in the spirit of the Almighty Creator; in defending myself against the Jews, I am fighting the battle of the Lord." Not only Socialism is to be crushed, however, but modern democracy in its entirety. " Only the Jew can praise an institution that is as dirty and false as himself."

Then the War broke out. That the German Jews in common with the rest of the population took up arms in defence of their country, that Jewish volunteers flocked to the colours with the rest, that one of the noblest and undoubtedly the most brilliant of the leaders of German Labour, Ludwig Frank, a Jew, went to the front as a volunteer immediately on the outbreak of war and fell a few days later, a splendid example to thousands of Germans, especially Socialists—of all this Hitler must have been well aware. In his version however these events appear as follows: " Marxism, whose final goal is always the annihilation of all non-Jewish national States, saw to its horror how in July 1914 the German workers, whom it believed it had in its toils, roused themselves and took their places in the service of their country in hourly increasing numbers. In a few days the mists of this infernal national imposture were completely dispelled, and the mob of Jewish leaders was suddenly left forlorn." But it recovered itself and " pretended quite insolently that it shared in the national awakening." And Hitler deeply regrets that steps were not taken at once " against all this swindling pack of Jewish poisoners of the people," whose number he estimates at the end of his book at between twelve and fifteen thousand. They ought to have been given short shrift " without paying the slightest attention to their shrieks and wails, were they never so loud." The opportunity was lost. The best of the Germans fell at the front. And behind the front " these scoundrelly perjurers organised the revolution," while at the same time " the Jew " was robbing the nation, crushing it in his grasp and inciting against " the Prussians." William II had held out the hand of reconciliation to the Marxists, " little thinking that rogues have no honour. While still holding the imperial hand in theirs, with the other they were already groping for the dagger. With Jews no bargaining is possible; for them there is nothing but the stern alternative." After this it is scarcely necessary to say who in Hitler's opinion is to blame for Germany's defeat, nor what race is the only civilising one.

The Jew is the opposite of the " Aryan." He lacks not only all power of political construction and civilising capacity, but also all idealism. " If the Jews were alone in the world they would either drown in dirt and offal or would try to cheat and exterminate one another in furious conflict, unless, that is, the total absence of devotion which is shown in their cowardice should here again turn the struggle into a farce." The Jew is not even a nomad; he is merely a parasite on the bodies of other nations, and " where he appears, the nation which acts as his host will die out sooner or later." He is also entirely taken up with this world, and, as we learn from this great authority on the records of the Jewish religion, " a complete stranger to the belief in a life after this."

Language is to the Jew simply a means of concealing his

thoughts. Whatever language he may use, he expresses merely the nature of his own people. When his object is achieved and all non-Jewish peoples have become his slaves, a world-language will probably be introduced, so that he may be able to control them the more easily.

How the whole existence of the Jewish people is based on a continuous lie is best shown by the " Protocols of the Elders of Zion." That the *Frankfurter Zeitung* considers them spurious is the best proof of their genuineness. " With a sureness that is almost terrifying they expose the nature and activity of the Jewish people and lay bare the inner connection as well as the final aims." After describing the history of Jewry since the Dispersion as one long series of attempted extortions, the author tells us how by an assumption of idealism, love of liberty, philanthropy, patriotism and interest in the needs of the working classes the Jew has with diabolical cunning secured mastery over Germany, its Freemasons, its Press, capital and working class, while in secret he only looks after his own interests and those of his race. " No doubt he palms off his women now and again on influential Christians, but on principle he keeps his masculine stock pure. He poisons the blood of the others but preserves his own. He hardly ever marries a Christian woman, but lets the Christians marry Jewesses.[1] In any case the bastards turn out to the advantage of the Jewish side. A number of the higher nobility in particular have thus been completely destroyed. The Jew knows this very well and therefore systematically carries on this kind of

[1] In Germany during 1927 there were 53·94 mixed marriages to 100 full Jewish. Everywhere it seems that more Jews than Jewesses contracted mixed marriages. In Prussia, where the vast majority of German Jews are domiciled, of Jewish marriages in 1927, 26.0 per cent men and 16·59 per cent Jewesses married Christians. The corresponding figures for the whole of Germany were 25·80 per cent and 16·12 per cent. In Hamburg a total of 1,001 mixed marriages existed in 1925: 601 were Jews, 400 Jewesses (A. Ruppin: *The Jews in the Modern World*, pp. 319 ff.). Since the above was written the *Jahrbuch der Stadt Berlin*, 1934, has been published. From this it appears that in Berlin, where about one-third of the Jews of Germany were living in the year in question, 2,271 Jews or Jewesses contracted marriages during the year 1933, and of these 463 men and 204 women married non-Jews.

disarming of the circles from which his racial opponents draw their spiritual leaders."

A contempt for manual labourers is in particular a work of the Jews. " The romanticising of our life, which was really a Judaising of it," first brought this about. The Jew gets the worker " ostensibly to make an assault on capital and in this way is able the more easily to get him to fight for the very same thing." The object is the destruction of the national economy, in order that international finance may triumph on its grave; the corruption of the personality and of the race, in order that the inferior Jew may be left in sole control. The Jew's " infamy may assume such gigantic proportions that no one need be surprised if among our people the personification of the Devil as the symbol of all evil takes the living form of a Jew."

As regards the Zionists, they are by no means aiming at " a Jewish State in Palestine in order to settle there; they only desire to have an autonomous centre of agitation for their international deception of the world, one which is exempt from interference by other States: a refuge for convicted rascals and a training school for budding swindlers."

The Jews see victory already approaching and are therefore becoming more and more insolent. " The black-haired Jewish youth lies in wait for hours, with Satanic joy reflected in his face, for the unsuspecting girl, whom he defiles with his blood and thus steals from her own people. By all means in his power he tries to destroy the ethnological foundations of the nation he intends to subjugate. Just as he himself systematically ruins women and girls, so he does not even shrink from tearing down the blood-barriers of others to the greatest possible extent. It was the Jew and no one else who contrived that the negroes were brought to the Rhine " (alluding to the French occupation of the Ruhr), " always with the same secret motive and the same clear object: to destroy the hated white race by means of the necessarily resulting bastardising, to cast it down from its present cultural and political level and to make himself its master. For a racially pure nation, conscious of its own blood, can never be subjugated by the Jew. As long as the world lasts he will only be able to rule over bastards."

The Jew works systematically for political and economic world-dominion. " Thanks to his international influence he weaves a net of enemies around those nations which fiercely oppose this attack from within "—Hitler evidently refers to pre-War, aggressive Russia and Germany—"incites them to war and finally, if necessary, plants the flag of revolution on the battlefields." He tries to undermine art, literature, morality, religion. When the last great revolution is at hand, he throws off the mask and appears as a " thorough-going Jew and tyrant. . . . The most terrible example of this is furnished by Russia, where with a truly fanatical savagery he has killed thirty millions of people, sometimes with inhuman tortures, or let them starve to death in order to secure for a lot of Jewish penmen and stock-exchange bandits the mastery over a great nation." But if the parasite kills his victim, he himself dies, too, sooner or later. The collapse of the Soviet system—Hitler of course believes Russia to be ruled by Jews—will not therefore be long delayed.

Jewish world-finance desires the annihilation of Germany, as of Japan. During the War the Jewish financial and Marxist Press carried on an agitation against Germany, until one State after another, against its own interests, joined the side of the Entente. Germany's insane foreign policy after the peace was undoubtedly in agreement with the desires of the Jewish rulers of the country and a part of their effort to destroy Germany and found a Jewish world-dominion. If they succeed in Bolshevising Germany as well as Russia, the whole world will sink into the arms of this octopus. Thus the fate of the whole world depends on that of Germany. The Jews cleverly adapt their methods to the varying conditions of different countries, but as a rule in their fight against Germany they proceed along the line of pacifist ideology. The destruction of Germany however is in the interest neither of the English nor of the Italians, but it is in that of the French. " This nation, which is lapsing more and more into mongrelisation, constitutes in its alliance with Jewish efforts for world-dominion a lurking danger to the continuance of the white race in Europe. For the pestilential infection they spread on the Rhine, in the heart of Europe, through negro blood, was equally a manifestation of the sadistically perverse vindictiveness entertained by this chauvinistic hereditary enemy of our people, and of the Jews' coldly calculated plan of beginning the bastardising of the European continent at the centre, and by infecting the human material of the white race with inferior blood depriving it of the very basis of an independent existence."

The Aryan peoples, related in blood and in culture, who hitherto have been tearing each other to pieces, must have it made clear to them that it is the Jew who is the enemy of mankind and " the real originator of all suffering." For we are to understand that the secret Jewish world-government holds " the European States in its hand as will-less tools." But above all it is necessary to render him innocuous in Germany. The fight against him must serve as a signal to light the way of the Aryan nations towards a better future.

Such, briefly summarised, is Hitler's idea, largely inspired by Rosenberg's writings, of the Jews' nature and aspirations, reproduced as far as possible in his own inflammatory terms. Millions of otherwise normal Germans believe in this insanity—using the word in its literal sense—and Hitler's *Mein Kampf* has become the canonical book of Nazi Germany, in the spirit of which its youth is to be brought up.

On the other hand Hitler has not been particularly

fortunate hitherto in his endeavours to implant his hatred of the Jews in other nations. Witness the notorious fiasco suffered by his envoy Rosenberg in London, immediately after the Nazis had seized power. It is scarcely an exaggeration to say that he was there treated in an unprecedented manner, less like the representative of a friendly nation than as an exposed criminal. But an antisemitic agitation, directed and in part financed from Berlin, is still being carried on in the United States, Rumania and elsewhere. It remains to be seen whether it will be more successful than the revolutionary agitation organised by Moscow throughout the world when the Bolsheviks seized power in Russia.

Hitler deals in crude generalisations, adapted to the comprehension of the masses. He writes almost always " the Jew," not " the Jews." The Jewish patrician families of Central and Western Europe, who in culture, refinement, and humanity are perhaps among the highest in modern civilisation, the Jewish dock labourers of Salonika, the idealist agricultural youth of Palestine, the Eastern Jewish proletariat, and the Eastern Jewish aristocracy of learning— all these are to him just one undifferentiated unity—" the Jew," the impostor, the Bolshevik, the dastard, the enemy of mankind. Probably he has himself fallen a victim to the same kind of propaganda as his own. He tells us in *Mein Kampf* how surprised he and his comrades were during the War when they were confronted for the first time with English (Scottish) troops and discovered that these were far from being cowardly shopkeepers. If he had really got to know the Jewish people, his astonishment would have been no less. Perhaps he would have come to hate it, as the Italian Zacconi, already referred to, that distinguished connoisseur of the greatest and noblest minds of Germany, who under the pressure of war-psychosis was seized with hatred of that country; or as the half-Englishman Houston Stewart Chamberlain, who during the war called England, his

NA

former country, " a nest of receivers of stolen goods, hypocrites, liars, and card-sharpers." But then the image he drew would have borne witness not only to the blinding force of hate but also to its keenness of sight, in the same way as a malicious caricature may bring to light essential though distorted features in the person attacked. But of this there is no trace in *Mein Kampf*. Of the Jewish people, its thinkers and poets, its workers and dreamers, its misery and its ideal aspirations, its great masses, its few elect, Adolf Hitler knows —nothing.

CHAPTER XI

JEWISH INFLUENCE IN THE GERMANY OF THE WEIMAR CONSTITUTION

IT IS, as we know, a Nazi dogma that the Jews controlled the German Republic, until Hitler succeeded in breaking their power. The inner conflicts which occupied Germany during this period are described as a war of German patriots against the governing Jews and the republican parties who are represented as their tools. But even in quarters where the violent methods of the Nazis are disapproved of and their general mendacity is seen through, some credence has been given to the story that the Jews, who in the census year 1925 comprised 0·9 per cent of the population of the Reich, more or less controlled the political, economic, and cultural life of Germany during the fifteen years or so preceding the Nazi victory, and this has been regarded, if not as a defence, at least as an explanation of the Jewish persecutions of 1933.

The facts to be given below are intended to illustrate the truth or otherwise of these assertions. On the other hand they are not intended in any way as a confutation of the view that there really existed a Jewish question in Germany during the period of the Weimar Constitution and that the Jews' choice of professions and callings was in many respects unfortunate. The writer has often insisted, both before and after Hitler's victory, that such was the case, and has dwelt on the causes that brought about this situation, so tragical both from a human and a Jewish point of view.

The happiest period, economically speaking, of the German-Jewish middle class was the Wilhelmine era, the years between 1871 and 1918. It shared in the general boom that followed the Franco-Prussian war and the achievement of German unity. The Jews then occupied far more numerous and more prominent positions in industry and communal life than was the case after 1918. The inflation and the progressive concentration of industry brought ruin upon them.

Politically the new constitution changed the Jews' position to this extent, that the principle obtaining under the Empire of not admitting any unbaptised Jew to high office in the administration was abolished, which, however, as will be shown later, did not lead to any "Judaising" of German officialdom.

There was not and never has been any risk of the Jews strengthening their position numerically in republican Germany. The birth-rate of the German Jews fell considerably below that of the German " Aryans," as is fully shown by Felix Theilhaber's investigations. In 1871 the Jews numbered 1·2 per cent of the population of Germany; in 1925, as we have seen, only 0·9 per cent. Even before the Nazis' success the birth-rate of the German Jews was so low that their approaching disappearance was a common topic. Besides this they were losing great numbers through baptism and mixed marriages, the children of which as a rule became Christians or had no religion. It was calculated that by the year 1970 the number of German Jews would not exceed 270,000. As the Jews are mainly concentrated in the great cities—a consequence of their, by no means free, choice of occupation—it might have been expected that the numbers of town Jews at least would have kept pace with those of their non-Jewish fellow-citizens. This, however, was not the case. In the year 1870 5·5 per cent of the population of Berlin was Jewish, in 1925 only 4·3 per cent. In 1866 4·5 per cent of the population of Hamburg was Jewish, in 1925 only 1·75 per cent, and so on.

The Jews' choice of occupation in Germany was a consequence of historical factors and traditions and especially of Antisemitism, which could readily make any Jew who chose a branch formerly in the hands of non-Jews appear a usurper. Although as a result of progressive assimilation a gradual transfer was taking place from mercantile to non-mercantile occupations, trade was still the Jews' chief source of livelihood. In 1925 no less than 58·37 per cent of the Jews of Prussia followed mercantile occupations. Industry and handicrafts claimed 25·85 per cent. The corresponding figures for the non-Jewish population were 11·99 and 40·94 per cent. An investigation of the executives of the largest German industrial concerns, undertaken by Sombart in 1927, gave as a result that of 808 managing directors 108 were Jewish, that is 13·3 per cent, and of 2,092 members of boards 511 were Jewish, that is 24·4 per cent. Thus the Jews exercised great influence in the mercantile and semi-mercantile field, though without its being possible to talk of any "Judaising." It was regarded as the Jews' special domain and therefore gave rise to less bad blood. As already mentioned, the Jews were specially hard-hit by the crisis and by the concentration of trade and industry in great companies at the expense of the many private firms, for which reason the period of the Weimar Republic represented a serious decline for them. They lost ground particularly in those branches where their position was relatively strong, such as the grain and ready-made clothes trades. Between 1913 and 1930 the non-Jewish metal firms were increased by 6·5 per cent, while the Jewish decreased by 13·3 per cent. Between April 1st, 1928, and April 1st, 1930, non-Jewish private banks were reduced by 8·6 per cent, Jewish by 19·7 per cent; on April 1st, 1928, 10·9 per cent of the directors of German banking companies were Jews, two years later 7·1 per cent. The number of Jewish employees rose, that of independent Jewish undertakings decreased, a result of the progressive proletarisation of the Jewish middle class. There is astounding exaggeration in the antisemitic assertions that the Jews occupied half, nay, three-quarters of the higher official posts in the Republic, assertions which are usually illustrated by quotations, attributed to some well-known Jew, to the effect that now " we Jews " are masters, or by fabricated lists of names. In the twenty Cabinets that held office from the inauguration of the Republic until January 30th, 1933, there were altogether two Jewish Ministers, Preuss and Rathenau, and four of Jewish descent. That is to say, out of about 250 Ministers all except six were pure " Aryans." Out of about 500 higher officials in the Ministries of the Reich, including Secretaries of State and members of Government boards, there were before Hitler's victory at most fifteen Jews or men of Jewish birth. The number of Jewish Secretaries of State in the administration between 1918 and 1933 was just two. Out of about 300 higher officials in the Prussian Ministries some ten were Jews or of Jewish birth. In the other States of the Reich their number was still smaller. Out of Prussia's twelve *Oberpräsidenten*, thirty-five *Regierungspräsidenten*, and over four hundred *Landräte*, until the reform of the administration in 1932 there was not a single Jew. (After this date the figures have not been accessible to me.) Of the ten members of the general board of the Reichsbank it is true that two were Jews (Max Warburg and Oscar Wassermann) and one man of Jewish descent (Franz von Mendelssohn), but no Jew sat on its board of management, nor on that of the Prussian State Bank.

Of all Government officials in Germany (in 1925) 0·16 per cent were Jews; of the higher officials 0·29 per cent; of the intermediate and lower officials 0·17 per cent. In the administration and the judicial system they were relatively numerous, 1·67 per cent and 0·34 per cent respectively. But according to the German Ambassador to the United States, Dr. Luther (in the *New York Times*, May 25th, 1933), nearly 50 per cent of the Governmental office-holders were Jews, and according to a statement of Hitler's (in an interview in the New York *Staats Zeitung*, June 8th, 1933) they amounted to 62 per cent.

Between 1895 and 1925 the number of "Aryan" officials in Prussia was multiplied by seven, that of the Jewish by three. But according to Hitler's statement to Lord Rothermere (*Deutsche Allgemeine Zeitung*, July 11th, 1933) the number of German-Jewish officials had increased twentyfold since the war. He added, by the way, that only three German Ministers had direct connections with the Press and that in all three cases the intermediary was a Jew. The true state of the case was that almost every Reich and Prussian Ministry had a Press agent—acknowledged or otherwise—and of these precisely two were Jews. The Foreign Office had a special Press Department, on the staff of which there was one solitary Jew. Its chief was never a Jew. It looks as though the Nazi leaders themselves believed in the stories current of the "Judaising" of the State; a number of statements by Hitler and others point to this.

Among students at the colleges and universities the Jews comprised in 1886–87 rather more than 9·6 per cent, in 1911 8 per cent, in 1930 5·08 per cent, and in 1932–33 4·71 per cent. Relatively speaking, therefore, their number was constantly decreasing. Of all those who took the school-leaving certificate not quite 4 per cent were Jews. Unfortunately the census of 1925 gives no guidance for fixing the number of Christian "non-Aryan" masters in the colleges, and figures for the Jewish are only available for Prussia and Saxony. Here the latter amounted to 4·7 per cent. In South Germany their number was considerably lower. The number of Christian non-Aryan masters certainly did not exceed that of the Jewish. There cannot justly be any question of a "Judaising" of the colleges, since the number of "non-Aryans" did not amount to 10 per cent, nor of any "systematic intrusion into the German colleges," which before the Nazis' triumph were well able to protect themselves against non-qualified candidates for professorship. But erroneous ideas about the Jews "sticking together" and their enormous influence, combined with antisemitic agitation, gave rise to all sorts of stories circulating in the academic world about non-qualified Jews being appointed to professorships by the Government of the " Jew Republic " in defiance of all right and justice. If any Jewish scholar was unfairly promoted to a professorship, this was certainly not due to his being a Jew. On the contrary, the usual course of events seems to have been that, in order to avoid a suspicion of favouring those of their own race, the Jews worked against one another, and that the Government and the weak bureaucracy did not venture to oppose the anti-semitic opinion of the students, especially as the majority of the professors themselves were by no means inclined to make a stand against it. This applied not only to promotions. It is perfectly true that Jewish scholars, writers, poets, met with pronounced hostility even in institutions founded and conducted by Jews, and that " every blond Cheruscan was more benevolently criticised—even by a Jew—than his black-haired colleague " (Arnold Zweig).

During the Wilhelmine period, when a great many careers were closed to unbaptised Jews, these, as we know, flocked to the legal and medical professions, for which they were well adapted, and this tradition was maintained during the period of the Weimar Constitution. Jewish advocates and physicians were naturally most numerous in Prussia, where two-thirds of the Jews of Germany were domiciled and where Jews were also relatively most numerous: 1·06 per cent of the population. No less than 26·6 per cent of Prussia's advocates, 15·71 per cent of its officially appointed physicians and 15·51 per cent of other medical men were Jews. (Independent Jewish dentists amounted to 15·79 per cent, chemists to 5·80 per cent.)

No official figures are available for Berlin, where 30 per cent of all the Jews in Germany lived, constituting 4·29 per cent of the population. In his great speech in the provisional session of the Reichstag at the Kroll Opera House on June 8th, 1933, the editor-in-chief of the Government organ,

Alfred Rosenberg, stated that 74 per cent of the advocates in the capital were Jews and 80 to 90 per cent of its hospital physicians. These figures were, to put it mildly, exaggerated. According to later private statistics, which Rosenberg, disregarding those he had given previously, inserted in the *Völkischer Beobachter* of August 20th, 50·2 per cent of Berlin's advocates were Jews and 47·9 per cent of its physicians. The figures for physicians appointed to hospitals, which were evidently lower than 47·9 per cent, were not given. Even if these figures should be exaggerated, it is obvious that there was a striking disproportion between the numbers of the Jewish population and those of the Jewish physicians or lawyers—a circumstance which was duly exploited in propaganda. But in other parts of Germany, not excepting the great cities, the proportions were essentially different. According to Nazi statistics, the figures of which however are described as too high in Jewish quarters, 17·9 per cent of Germany's physicians were Jews and 27 per cent of its lawyers. The extent of their practice before Hitler's victory clearly showed that they were by no means felt to be so alien to the German people ("*volksfremd*") as is now asserted.

According to the census of 1925 the Jews comprised 3·17 per cent of musicians and those employed in the theatres, 4 per cent of those engaged in the film industry and 7·29 per cent of all artists, authors and unattached scholars. More detailed information is available for Prussia. Of all Prussian authors the Jews comprised 10·09 per cent; of editors 5·52 per cent; of painters and sculptors 3·30 per cent; of actors 6·81 per cent; of theatrical producers 10·96 per cent; of musicians 1·63 per cent; of singers 7·90 per cent. The rapid growth of Antisemitism after 1925 brought about in these fields as in others a pronounced decline in the number of Jews, especially as regards newspaper editors and actors in the provincial theatres; but unfortunately we have no statistical material to show this. Most of these were domiciled in the great cities, where the Jews are concentrated. Apart from a few exceptional cases the Jewish theatrical managers were not connected with municipal, but with private theatres.

As we know, it was part of the Nazi method to make out that the Jews were masters of the German Press and in particular to style the papers of the Left a "Jew Press." The latter suggestion had a semblance of justification inasmuch as several very well-known liberal papers were largely owned by Jews, and that many prominent journalists, most of them liberal, were of Jewish birth. The Mosse concern and the still more important Ullstein company were in the front rank. The former owned the *Berliner Tageblatt*, founded in 1871, which, under Theodor Wolff, became after the November revolution the chief organ of the German Democratic Party; the latter acquired after 1913 the *Vossische Zeitung*, and in 1914 Georg Bernhard became its editor-in-chief. The third great paper of the same category was the *Frankfurter Zeitung*, founded a few years after 1848. This paper in common with those of the syndicates just mentioned advocated reconciliation with France, the policy whose foremost representative was Stresemann. This more than anything else earned them the bitter hatred of the Nazis and associated parties. Under Stresemann they enjoyed a certain prosperity. Afterwards their influence declined, though they were still to be reckoned with in some of the great towns. They made little impression on opinion in the country districts. The socialist papers on the other hand were not owned by Jews, but a relatively large number of Jewish writers were among their contributors: Eduard Bernstein, Hilferding, Stampfer and others. This so-called Jew Press was in practice Jewish to the extent that it was not antisemitic. But as a rule it was entirely uninterested in contemporary Jewish questions, which was also notably the case with the *Berliner Tageblatt* and the *Frankfurter Zeitung*. For this reason alone therefore the expression "Jew Press" is a gross misnomer; to say nothing of the fact that the great majority of the owners and journalists of the " Jew Press " were " Aryans."

According to the *Handbuch der deutschen Tagespresse*, in the year 1932 not ten of the eighty-five most important German papers were edited by Jews, and out of 4·703 political papers in Germany only 12 were Democratic, 125 Socialist, 49 Communist and 192 leaned to the Left without any special party colour. Thus only 8·3 per cent of all German papers could be described as organs of the Left. In 1913 they were 16·4 per cent; four years later 19·6 per cent; in 1926 11·2 per cent, and four years later 8·5 per cent, figures which throw a curious light on the talk of progressive " Judaising." Against these 8·3 per cent there were 40·7 per cent papers of the Right, including those of the Centre. The remaining " non-political " papers were also actually conservative for the most part, occupying an intermediate position between the German People's Party and the German-National People's Party. It is true that if we consider circulation figures—in 1932 the circulation of all German papers was about 29 millions a day—we find a decided modification in favour of the papers of the Left, since they accounted for 28 per cent, while the figures for the Right and Centre were 48 per cent and for the " neutral " papers 24 per cent. What percentage of the so-called Jew Press was Jewish cannot be statistically determined. But if we divide the total number of persons employed on the German Press by the number of Jews so employed, we shall find here, as in other fields where the German Antisemites have complained of " *Ueberfremdung*," that the talk of the Jews' numerical superiority was recklessly exaggerated.

On the other hand it is true that one concern did exercise a dominating influence on the Press of the Weimar Republic, namely, that of Hugenberg. This, which was formed before the War was over, was strongly German-National and was financed by heavy industry, which was practically pure

" Aryan." Those banks which were under Jewish management remained, practically speaking, uninterested in the political Press. Ever since the period immediately succeeding the Versailles treaty the Hugenberg syndicate controlled directly or indirectly more than half the papers in Germany. In the moulding of opinion it was far more important than either Ullstein or Mosse. And yet Germany (and Austria) was the country where the Jews were most prominent in the Press.

Many of the organs described as " Jew papers " and a number of German-Jewish authors, such as Jacob Wassermann, Lion Feuchtwanger, Emil Ludwig, Arnold Zweig, Franz Werfel, Joseph Roth, Leonhard Frank, Ernst Toller, Alfred Döblin, the Austrians Stefan Zweig and Arthur Schnitzler, were very widely read abroad, just as the French-Jewish authors Marcel Proust[1], Henri Bernstein, Pierre Benoit[1] and André Maurois in translation were among the most widely read authors in Germany. The Antisemites saw in this a proof of how the Jews through their control of the Press knew how to push their own people at the expense of everyone else. Outside Germany however the matter is explained in an entirely different and more natural way. It specially vexed the German Antisemites that what they regarded as a product of the mentality of Jewish publicists was looked upon abroad as German. To judge however from the verdict of foreign countries on the spirit of the " Aryanised " third Reich, this transposition cannot be said to have redounded to the disadvantage of German prestige.

In political as in municipal life the Jews were forced more and more into the background. In the Reichstag elected in July 1932, which contained 608 members, there was all told one Jew of Mosaic confession and thirteen who did not belong to the Jewish religion. In the Prussian Landtag, elected in April of the same year, which contained 432 members, the corresponding figures were two and two. In the other Landtags there were practically no Jews.

[1] According to the Alliance Israélite Universelle, Pierre Benoît is an "Aryan" and Marcel Proust was a "half-Aryan."

The above figures show therefore that the influence of the Jews, so far as it can be deduced from the statistical material, was not as a rule proportional to their number but decidedly greater, but that they did not outstrip the " Aryans " in any field. Conditions in Berlin were exceptional—as also in Vienna—and were indeed cleverly exploited in propaganda. Antisemitism was represented to be a struggle in defence of Germanism threatened by the Jews. Whether some change in the Jews' choice of occupation, above all a diminution in the number of physicians and lawyers, might have mitigated Antisemitism, seems uncertain, for the hate-psychosis which possessed them did not allow the Nazis to attach much importance to facts. When, for instance, it was shown by criminal statistics that German Jews committed fewer outrages on morality than their non-Jewish fellow-citizens, this was explained away in the Nazi Party's official work on the Jews, Gottfried Feder's *Die Juden*, by saying that the Jews' wealth enabled them to avoid coming into court by paying compensation. As we have suggested above, Hitler was probably in good faith when he stated that the Jews held 62 per cent of official posts. That the correct figure was 0·16 per cent—or rather something less than this, taking into account the further exclusion of the Jews since the census year 1925—was therefore a fact without importance. If the Jewish officials had been fewer, Hitler and millions with him would have believed just as firmly in the 62 per cent—a living illustration of Hans Andersen's story of the feather which grew into a hen. Proclaimed at hundreds of political meetings, and continually worked up in the antisemitic Press, the fable of the Jews' supremacy in the Weimar Republic became not merely an election lie of the greatest importance to Nazi propaganda but also an article of faith to millions of Germans, especially among students. And the necessity of breaking this alleged power of the Jews was often urged as an excuse to foreigners. But it is obvious that, since the Nazis proceeded from the assumption that the Jews are the incarnation of all evil, their actual aim was, and is, the total extinction of the Jews in German cultural life.

Large sections of the German people demanded in their distress a new god in place of the one who seemed to have abandoned them—a god who was to rescue them from their misfortunes and whom they longed to serve with passionate devotion. His name is *Blut und Rasse*—the blood and the race. But at the same time they adopted a belief in a new devil. The Jews, who dwelt among them but were of a different race and a different blood, became their Evil One. And as in days long past, the days of trials for witchcraft for instance, they believed the devil was lying in wait on every hand and thought they could trace his machinations and his power in everything.

.   .   .   .

The cultural contributions made by German Jews—and Austrian, who cannot be kept apart from them—during the four generations which have elapsed since the beginning of their emancipation and assimilation, are too numerous to be recited within the limits of this volume. A mere statement in catalogue form would occupy many pages, even if it were confined to the most famous names in the spheres of industry, technology and inventions, in the sciences and in medicine, in jurisprudence and political science, in scholarship and music, literature and the plastic arts. German-Jewish physicians are particularly numerous, and many of them may be described without exaggeration as benefactors of humanity.

Of Germany's forty-four Nobel Prizemen (up to 1933) seven were Jews, namely, the medical research workers Ehrlich and Meyerhof and the scientists Wallach, Willstätter, Haber, Einstein, and Franck, to whom may be added the half-Jews von Bäyer, Heyse, Hertz, and Warburg. Three Jewish Nobel Prizemen from Austria, Bárány, Landsteiner and Fried, belonged to the German sphere of culture.

It is evident that the Jews' share in German cultural life would have been considerably greater both before and during the years of the Weimar Republic, if they had not been shackled by Antisemitism. This applies to their outward career—as is witnessed by the biography of almost every famous Jew—but also to the attitude of German public opinion towards them. None the less they owe a profound debt of gratitude to German culture. On the other hand no impartial observer can deny that their influence on that culture was in a high degree productive, even if their contributions, like those of the German " Aryans," were not always beneficial.

It has already been pointed out that these Jewish men and women regarded Jewish qualities, apart from exceptional cases, as factors of minor, or often of no importance. And outside Germany they were everywhere looked upon as Germans. In most cases the world was unaware of their Jewish birth, until in 1933 they were dismissed wholesale, boycotted and driven into exile. Before that they had simply been celebrated " German " scientists, authors, musicians, actors, industrialists and business men. Many of them by their achievements had shed honour and glory on the German name. It was not only in the Olympic Games that German Jews battled for the German colours. They did the same in science, literature, technology, industry and commerce (especially when it was a question of capturing new markets for German goods), music and the art of the cinema.

As instances we may mention the film producers Ernst Lubitsch, Erich Pommer and Fritz Lang, whose pioneer work contributed greatly to the triumphant progress of German films throughout the world and who were naturally driven into exile after Hitler's victory. What they did for German films, the German Jews Otto Brahm, Leopold Jessner and Max Reinhardt did for the German theatre. (On the other hand Piscator is an " Aryan.") It may be mentioned as a piquant incident that Goebbels in addressing the Association for the Protection of German Film Producers described the films *Potemkin*, *The Rebel*, *The Nibelungs* and *Anna Karenina* as models of their kind, evidently ignorant that they were all the work of " non-Aryan " producers, Eisenstein, Kurt Bernhard and Lang.

Now an attempt is being made to eliminate everything " non-Aryan " from German culture. The young are to be trained, as Frick, the Reich Minister of the Interior, expressed it, " to turn away instinctively from everything racially alien." The great names of German-Jewish culture, living and dead, are no longer to be heard or read by the German people. When in the summer of 1934 Germany commemorated her explorers and colonisers, Emin Pasha (Eduard Schnitzer) and his work were passed over in silence. Felix Mendelssohn-Bartholdy, one of the most devoted servants of German culture, who made Leipzig a world-famous centre of German musical life, who resuscitated from oblivion one of the most glorious representatives of the Germanic spirit, Johann Sebastian Bach, and taught the English to love Beethoven and Schubert, may no longer be played in Germany, and his statue in front of the municipal theatre at Düsseldorf has been removed. His genuinely romantic music to *A Midsummer Night's Dream*, which hitherto has been generally regarded as an extraordinarily fine creation, has been pronounced unworthy of Shakespeare, and two German composers have been commissioned to replace it with " Aryan " music. And so on. Perhaps only practical considerations prevent the pulling down of buildings designed by Jewish architects. And only through an inconsistency is Christianity allowed to continue, though in a Nazified dress—in spite of its Jewish origin.

The Nazis, however, do not venture to carry their doctrines to their extreme logical conclusions. In medicine, for example. A Christian doctor writes ironically in a Riga paper : " A Nazi who gets syphilis must not allow himself to be cured with salvarsan, as this was discovered by the Jew Ehrlich. In fact, the very diagnosis of his disease is to be rejected, for the Wassermann reaction is also the work of a Jew. If the patient is suspected of having gonorrhœa he must not have the bacilli investigated, for it was Jewish physicians, Neisser and others, who discovered the gonococci. If he suffers from cardiac debility he must abstain from using the classical remedy digitalis, as that is derived from Ludwig Traube. If he has toothache he must refuse injections of cocaine, for this was a discovery of the Jew Karl Koller. Typhus cannot be treated, as to do so one would have to resort to the methods of the Jews Vidal and Weil. If your patient suffers from diabetes he must avoid insulin, which is an indirect result of the researches of the Jew Minkowsky. If he has headache he must abstain from using pyramidon and antipyrin, as Spiro and Filehne were Jews. If he suffers from convulsions he is incurable, as the remedy, chloral hydrate, was discovered by the Jew Oscar Liebreich. Similar conditions apply to psychiatry: psychoanalysis is the work of the Jew Freud. Furthermore he must abstain from profiting by the results of medical research carried out by Politzer, Bárány and Otto Warburg, the dermatologists Jadassohn, Bruno Bloch and Unna, the neurologists Mendl, Oppenheim, Kronecker, Benedikt, the lung specialist Fränkel, the surgeon Israel, the anatomist Henle, etc." Similar things might be said of many branches of science and cultural life.

CHAPTER XII

THE JEWS' FINANCIAL POWER

THE IDEA OF THE JEWS' enormous wealth and the great political power of Jewish finance is widely entertained even far outside antisemitic circles. At the same time as the German National-Socialists appealed to the middle classes to resist Jewish Marxism—with what right it was called Jewish will be shown in the next chapter—they tried to win over the workers by depicting capitalism as "Jewish." The fact that the most anti-Jewish States, Russia and Rumania, were able to place one international loan after another without altering their Jewish policy ought to have sufficed to make it clear to anyone that the talk of a world-dominating finance guided by Jewish interests must be nonsense. Nevertheless Fritsch, Hitler, Rosenberg, Feder, Goebbels and others disseminated the most fantastic assertions as to the power of Jewish world-finance and its diabolical tactics. A highly esteemed German-Jewish writer on economics, Richard Lewinsohn (Morus), has indeed shown in a learned and acute inquiry, *Jüdische Weltfinans?* (1925), how absurd are these conceptions, but the antisemitic campaign of hatred and lies shouted everything down.

The following may be cited as typical. On December 25th, 1909, Walter Rathenau wrote in the *Neue Freie Presse* an article, afterwards reprinted in his well-known book *Zur Kritik der Zeit*, in which he called attention to the power of the economic oligarchy in the world: "Three hundred men," he wrote, "who all know each other, control the economic destiny (*die wirtschaftlichen Geschicke*) of the Continent and appoint their successors from among their own circle." He saw in this a danger against which he would offer a warning. Of Jews not a word was said. Nevertheless the antisemitic agitators took hold of this. They assumed offhand that the word *men* in this connection must mean *Jews*, and soon the quotation in its falsified dress went the round of the antisemitic papers. Some of them simply changed the word *men* into *Jews*. Dr. Roesicke (*Bund der Landwirte*) wrote: "Three hundred Jewish bank directors"; in the *Kreuz-Zeitung* of September 7th, 1925, the three hundred men became "one thousand, who are all Jews"; others equated the three hundred with the "Elders of Zion." Of course Rathenau himself was one of the last-named, and naturally his words were to be regarded as an exposure and a boast! Rathenau, accustomed as he was to be the victim of infamous treatment, wrote on October 3rd, 1921, with reference to this: "It must be an unprecedented thing in the history of falsification that a person who utters a warning should be made responsible for the very thing against which that warning was given."

In the Nazi theory of Antisemitism the Jews constitute a close corporation, a kind of secret conspiracy, with the object of getting all the wealth of the world into their own hands, for which in their opinion God himself has given them leave. With this in view they have insinuated themselves into practically every country and snatched political power either by themselves taking possession of government offices or by controlling the country's economy and finances, thus making the Christian statesmen entirely dependent on them. As Jews are relatively rare in the higher official posts, it must be the latter method which is usually employed. They make a show of being patriots, but serve, though secretly, only the invisible Jewish World State. The men in control of this—a universal super-government, secret of course!—actually control the nations of the world, though the latter in their blindness have not yet realised this. Lewinsohn, on whose book, mentioned above, the following statements are mainly based, justly remarks on the oddity of the same persons who claim to oppose the materialist view of history as fundamentally false and depraving, imagining statesmen to be merely puppets in the hands of those who control finance and economy.

The man in the street often imagines that industrialists, especially the chiefs of industries working for export, are national and beneficial to the State, while he has doubts of the great bankers in the former respect. It is not at all clear to the plain man what the banks' business really consists of. In National-Socialist propaganda bank capital is described as unproductive, international, Jewish (*raffendes Kapital*), whereas industrial capital (and agricultural capital) is said to be productive, national and Aryan (*schaffendes Kapital*). The National-Socialist movement, we must remember, was dependent on the financial support of the great industrialists ! Millions of debt-encumbered farmers as well as townsmen were tempted by the Nazi promises of breaking the bonds of interest-slavery and incited against the " Jewish " holders of mortgages, represented to be a band of parasites who did no " work." As a matter of fact there is no opposition between industrial capital and loan capital, since the banks' capital must be placed in productive undertakings in order to yield interest and is thus just as beneficial to the national economy as industrial capital. The great industrialists are, of course, numerously represented on the boards of the great banks, and vice versa. Moreover it must be noted that in our day not only the banks but the great industries are extremely international in character. It is true that great industrial undertakings, syndicates and trusts are often controlled by banks, but the rôles are often reversed. The statement that industry is controlled by Jewish or " Judaised " capital is without foundation.

The tendency has been for capital to be concentrated in fewer and fewer persons or groups of an international type. It has become customary for manufacturers in a certain country and a certain branch first to agree upon prices, areas of distribution and so on, and then to make similar agreements with similar foreign combinations in the same branch of industry in order thereby to avoid mutual competition and to monopolise the market. Before the World War German industry was engaged in over a hundred international combinations of this sort. These, as it appears from the investigations of Professor Robert Liefmann, the chief authority on international cartels, were preponderantly " *Judenreine*," that is, free from Jewish interests. In one case only a great Jewish financier took a decisive part in concluding one of these international agreements: when the American Mercantile Marine Company, in other words Morgan's trust, was preparing to crush its German competitors, as it had already done with its English and French, Ballin with the concurrence of the Kaiser and the German government arranged an agreement between this trust and the two German lines, the Hamburg-America and the Norddeutscher Lloyd, which saved these from cut-throat competition. It may be worth pointing out that the munitions industry, which in all countries was practically " *Judenrein*," was internationally combined from 1901 to 1913 with the United Harvey Co. The manufacturers of explosives were also combined in a cartel, to which Nobel's dynamite trust belonged. It should also be pointed out that immediately before the war the German " Jew-free " munitions industry delivered armour plates for the British navy, at a lower price, by the way, than that charged to Germany. Transactions of this kind are not " Jewish " but are characteristic of international capitalism generally. In 1922 Hugo Stinnes, a pure " Aryan," by agreement with the chief of the French reparations commission, the Marquis de Lubersac, undertook to deliver material to the amount of 1,500 million gold marks, for which he was to receive a commission of six per cent, or 90 million gold marks. One could fill many pages with similar proofs of the international character of " Aryan " industry. They show amongst other things how absurd it was to set up Stinnes as a kind of national hero in opposition to the " international Jew " Rathenau, as was often done in the post-War German Press.

A special class of international trusts is that in which the same undertaking deals both with production and distribution. Two of these overshadow all the rest in importance: the American Standard Oil Company and the Anglo-Dutch Royal Dutch-Shell Combine. These are not the servants of the banking organisations but their masters. The oil industry, too, is now practically entirely " Aryan," since the Rothschilds and Sir Marcus Samuel have ceased to take part in it. Here, as we know, Rockefeller is supreme.

There is however one banking group, but only one, which is at the same time a power of the first rank in industry: the purely " Aryan " Morgan trust, which is thought to control the property of a fifth part of the American people and which employs hundreds of thousands of workpeople. It is the world's biggest lender and underwriter of loans. We know how after the war it saved the French currency by a great loan. In comparison with this trust its European equivalents seem fairly unimportant. Lewinsohn goes through them all, including the purely " Aryan " Kreuger match trust. The Jews' influence in these is extremely insignificant. It is non-Jews almost entirely who are at the head of all important international cartels and trusts.

The same applied to the Weimar Republic. According to the official statistics of the German department of economy (*Reichswirtschaftministerium*) there were in 1931 no less than 2,500 cartels of a mainly industrial nature and about 300 concerned with wholesale trade. Precisely those branches in which Jews are most interested, the textile industry for

instance, are least internationalised. The ten largest undertakings were practically " Jew-free." Before the World War
the Jews were rather thinly represented in German industry,
after the war they became still rarer.

When we come to banking, Jewish influence is greater. An
eminent writer on finance, Paul Einzig, has recently inquired
into the part here played by Jews, with special reference to
three antisemitic theses : that the Jews have complete control
of the banks; that the Jewish bankers are combined in a sort
of ring for the defence of Jewish interests, and that they use
their power to the detriment of the countries in which they
operate.

The Jews' influence in the banking world varies very
much, according to Einzig, in different countries, but nowhere is complete control in their hands. Their influence is
not in proportion to the Jewish population but decidedly
greater, which is natural, since the Jews have been
specialists in banking from of old. In countries whose
population has no aptitude for this side of economic
activity, their importance is relatively great, otherwise it
is quite small.

England is one of the countries where in this respect the
Jews are of least importance. For Englishmen and still more
Scotsmen are very able in this field. No Jews are among the
governors of the Bank of England, and hardly any are on the
boards of the " Big Five." Those Anglo-Jewish banking firms
which are of international importance can be counted on the
fingers of one hand : N. M. Rothschild & Sons, Samuel
Montagu & Co., Seligman Brothers, and S. Japhet & Co.
In the financial life of London the Jews are only predominant
in the gold and silver market. The money market is controlled
for the most part by non-Jews. There are many Jewish firms
of bill brokers, but they are far outnumbered by the non-
Jewish.

In France the leading business banks are not under Jewish
influence, although they are not so exclusively non-Jewish as

the English clearing-house banks. Three Jewish banking firms are very prominent: those of Rothschild, Lazard Frères and Dreyfus, but the Protestant banks are at least of equal importance.

In the banking world of Switzerland the Jews play a very small part, but the contrary is the case with the private banks of Holland. The influence of the German banks in Amsterdam after the war was mainly Jewish.

In the United States several Jewish financial experts have come to the front, Bernard Baruch for instance, who during the war was in charge of raw materials, and Paul Warburg, who was the real author of the Federal Reserve system. But neither they nor any other Jewish financiers have controlled the economic life of the United States. The great Jewish banking firm of Kuhn, Loeb & Co. occupies a place by itself among Jewish banks. Apart from this house they are not of much account, and generally speaking Jewish financial influence in America is far smaller than is commonly believed.

In Central and Eastern Europe on the other hand Jewish banking houses play a very important part. Their influence is greatest in Austria and Hungary. In those countries one may reasonably speak of a dominating Jewish influence over the banks. In Rumania and in the Balkan States Jewish (Sephardic) banking firms are prominent, except in Greece; for the Greeks are themselves " born bankers."

In Germany the Jews have had a great share both in commercial and in private banking. Many of the old banker families of Frankfort-on-Main are Jewish, as are the Warburgs of Hamburg, the Berliner Handels-Geschäft, the firms of Bleichröder and Mendelssohn in Berlin, and several others. Many Jews have sat on the boards of the four, since 1929 three, great German banks known as D-banks from the initial letters of their names. But as a rule the influence of the Jews on the German money market is recklessly overestimated. In 1927 Hans Priester showed that it was in no way comparable to that of the non-Jews. In the leading banks the Jewish directors were in a decided minority. Only during the short period when, at the close of inflation and on the stabilising of the German currency, Jacob Michael appeared as a lender on a large scale, had Jewish capital any great influence on the German money market. Since Hitler's victory the Jews have to a great extent been driven out of the commercial banks.

Ever since the commencement of assimilation and Jewish emancipation, that is, ever since the Jews began their organic growth as citizens of the States in which they lived, the internationalism which distinguished Jewish banking has been on the decline. In proportion as it still exists—in such cases as the German-American banking firm of Warburg—it evidently performs a function in the national economy, and the State concerned may profit thereby. Only those who like the German National-Socialists are hostile to almost any form of internationalism can see anything anti-national in it.

Far from holding together, the Jewish banks compete with one another in precisely the same way as the Christian banks. Large and well-known Jewish banking houses often join national and international banking syndicates, most of whose members are non-Jews. Before the crisis N. M. Rothschild's emissions were managed partly by the non-Jewish banks J. Henry Schröder & Co. and Baring Brothers. The arrangement was regarded as permanent. It was jocularly alluded to as " the trinity." That the Jewish banks are banded together against the Christian world is pure fiction.

The same may be said of the statement that they are injurious to the countries concerned. In Germany, where formerly the Jews had more influence in the banking world than in other countries, the banks have been extraordinarily active in stimulating the trade and industry of the country, thereby of course serving their own interests as well. Especially by giving German exporters long credits the commercial banks, largely controlled by Jews, displayed an aggressive German nationalism which became proverbial. The Jewish and semi-Jewish banking houses contributed greatly to the growth of German heavy industry in the decades preceding the war. Their German-Jewish banking interests coincided with those of Germany, as the Anglo-Jewish with those of England, and so on. When Germany grew rich, its bankers grew rich. Germany's defeat and poverty hit them too. It is not to be wondered at that in English banking circles the elimination of Jews from German banking is generally regarded as a German mistake, since their activities have been greatly to the advantage of Germany.

It has already been emphasised that the World War and the crisis had an extremely injurious effect economically upon Jewry, especially in Eastern Europe, but also in Germany. Those Jews who made money out of the War were far fewer than those who lost over it; a fact which ought to be stressed, since one often hears the contrary asserted. The War was not even lucrative to the Jewish bankers (nor to the " Aryan "). The World War cost such an enormous sum every day that even the money of a Morgan would not have sufficed to finance it for long. The governments took the matter in hand, levied huge taxes and, degrading the banks into the position of their tools, issued great loans, paying the interest in paper-money which was continually depreciating in value.

When, as the War proceeded, the German Government took charge of the distribution of goods, tradesmen finally became a kind of Government officials, with no chances of making large profits. In the branches most open to clandestine dealing (bakers, butchers, grocers), Jewish traders were only sparsely represented. It was not so much the shopkeepers as the producers who made fortunes during the war, especially those who did business with the War Office, which for reasons of economy took care to avoid middlemen.

The demand for a special tax on war profits was started by the way in the Press of the Left—as early as 1915—which has generally been described as the " Jew Press." Those who produced things necessary for the army naturally made most money. In a few of the industries which produced such goods, Jews were relatively numerous, namely in the leather and textile trades and in some metal industries. But " heavy " industry, where most of the money was made, was almost entirely " Aryan." This also applied to the chemical industry, which profited by the discoveries made during the war by the two Jewish scientists, Haber and Caro. Hugo Stinnes too, who was to play such a dominating part in the post-War period, succeeded thanks to his intimate connections with governments and headquarters in making large profits by making purchases for the army in neutral countries. As has been said, Stinnes was a pure " Aryan." The two great undertakings which were under Jewish management, the Hamburg-America Line (Ballin) and the Allgemeine Elektricitätgesellschaft (Walter Rathenau and Felix Deutsch), both suffered severely from the war.

It has been pointed out above how the War led to financial capital being outstripped by industrial capital. Both indeed were predominantly " Aryan," but the latter far more than the former. Thus the War meant a further decline for German-Jewish finance.

The War was followed by inflation, which of course involved violent derangements of people's fortunes. Naturally the Jews were singled out as the originators of inflation and the ones who were making most out of it. The hard-hearted Jew who speculates in the distress of others is, as we know, a type which the Antisemites are fond of drawing. That the Jews intentionally or unintentionally occasioned inflation in Germany is an allegation that no initiated person can any longer maintain, since the antecedent history of inflation has now become known: the men who were formally and actually responsible for the unfortunate fiscal, monetary and banking policy which brought it about—above all Haven-stein, governor of the Reichsbank, Hermes, Minister of Finance, and Helfferich, financial adviser to the Chancellor Cuno—were all " Aryans," and the man who by his un-scrupulous tricks, now found out, caused the disastrous fall of the mark in April 1923 was Hugo Stinnes, Germany's greatest " inflation profiteer." A number of Jewish jobbers naturally made fortunes during this time, but there was not a single Jew among the big inflation kings in Germany. Lewinsohn, who has investigated the matter in detail, points out that what happened was the very reverse of what the Antisemites love to imagine: it was not a case of Jews working with Christian dummies and auxiliaries, but of " Aryan " specu-lators employing Jews. (As a rule of course they used non-Jews.) Thus for instance Stinnes's assistant was a Jew, Camillo Castiglioni, who by the way carried on an inter-necine struggle with his fellow-Jew, the Austrian Siegmund Bosel—one example among many of how much truth there is in the alleged solidarity of the " secret Jewish finance inter-national." In general the luck of the inflation profiteers, both Jewish and " Aryan," was of short duration. Easy come, easy go. The class of society which suffered most from in-flation was, as we know, the middle class, both upper and lower. The owners of floating capital were the heaviest losers. But the great majority of Jews belonged precisely to the middle class, and the wealthy among them were seldom owners of real estate, but precisely " finance capitalists." It is clear therefore that on an average the Jewish population was harder hit by inflation than the " Aryan."

It is perhaps hardly necessary to point out that the German Antisemites represented the Dawes plan as part of the Jewish scheme for obtaining power and its acceptance as a sign of the mastery of " Jewish " world finance over the German people. It was now declared that Morgan, who of course was described as a Jew—he and his whole firm are purely " Aryan "—had won financial control over Germany ! Actually the firm's function was confined to acting as the issuing house of the loan which Germany placed in New York after the acceptance of the Dawes plan, whereby the Reich was able once more to enjoy foreign credit. No financial control of any kind was bound up with this transaction. Neither Mellon, the U.S. Secretary of the Treasury, nor any other leading personality on the Dawes Commission was a Jew. The same applies to the Young plan, which of course was also described as " an instrument of international Jewish financial capital," and even as " the Talmud of Economy." But a number of Mellon's advisers and experts were Jews, and these of course were made out to be a kind of dictators. Of the fourteen chief delegates to the Paris Conference of 1929, when the Young plan was drawn up, not a single one was a Jew. It is true that Carl Melchior of the banking firm of Warburg in Hamburg took part as a substitute. Then as on subsequent occasions he distinguished himself as the cleverest and most energetic of those who defended German interests. No Jew besides Carl Melchior was given a place on the board of the international bank at Basle, which was the real instrument for carrying out the Young plan. This plan therefore did not lead to any increase of Jewish influence, but rather the contrary.

Even in circles friendly to the Jews it is commonly supposed that they are a rich people. According to the Antisemites their wealth is enormous. It is stated for example that the Jews possess ninety per cent of the world's floating capital and that man for man a Jew is 450 times richer than a non-Jew, assertions the absurdity of which is patent to anyone who has some idea of the distribution of the world's wealth, but which nevertheless have played and still play an important part in antisemitic agitation. On the other hand, anyone who has seriously occupied himself with contemporary Jewish political problems has been overwhelmingly impressed by the boundless poverty and misery of the Jewish people regarded as a whole. Jewish plutocracy is far less rich and far less numerous than is generally imagined, and the Jewish middle class is very far from being so well off as is believed by those who only know it from Western Europe and America.

As we know, America now leads in finance. Ford and the Rockefellers, father and son, are undoubtedly the richest men in the world, next to whom comes the Duke of Westminster. Among American millionaires in 1922 we have to go to the ninth place before coming to a Jew, the lately deceased Otto Kahn. Out of New York's 199 millionaires, paying 100,000 dollars or upwards in income-tax, there were in 1925 no more than nineteen Jews, a figure far lower than one would expect from their proportion of the city's population. In the financial world of America the Jews play an important but by no means preponderant part. There is no Jewish Morgan. And there, as in Europe, it is not Jewish bankers who dominate economic life, but " non-Jewish industrialists, railroad kings, steel magnates and oil lords."

Among the Jewish families of Europe the house of Rothschild notoriously occupied a special position during the nineteenth century. Their financial power culminated about the middle of that century. Since then it has declined very considerably and is now entirely eclipsed by that of the " Aryan " Americans. According to James Burnley's often quoted statistics, of the world's forty-four richest men in 1905, seven were Jews, of whom five were Rothschilds. Of the latter two were in England, two in France and one in Austria. They occupied the 11th, 17th, 18th, 32nd and 41st places and owned altogether 1,150,000,000 marks. They thus had a good many superiors and equals among non-Jews. But as this did not suit Nazi propaganda, Fritsch and other Antisemites put the Rothschilds' fortune at forty milliards. It need hardly be pointed out that even in its most flourishing period the house of Rothschild did not possess a twentieth part of this sum. But the forty milliards were cleverly exploited in antisemitic propaganda, as for instance in a leaflet published by the Nazi author Dietrich Eckhart on April 5th, 1919, and directed against "interest-slavery," which Gottfried Feder reprinted in 1933 in his *Kampf gegen die Hochfinanz*. Eckhart effectively contrasts German industrial capital, which he estimates at not quite 12 milliards, and the poor 250 millions of the Krupp family, with these 40 milliards, which he sees multiplying indefinitely if the system be not broken ! It may be noted that even before the World War the power of the house of Rothschild had declined to such an extent that even Rudolf Martin, to whom the Nazis are fond of referring, found occasion in 1912 to make the following remarks: " Thirty years ago many a well-known political economist still considered the Roths-childs a plutocratic danger to the civilised world. Now the Rothschild fortunes are divided among an ever greater number of eminent families, both Jewish and aristocratic, and in ever smaller shares. . . . The world-dominion of the House of Rothschild is a thing of the past. The successors of the Rothschild family are being outstripped in wealth more and more by others." He might have added that financial magnates are everywhere in retreat before the great leaders of industry.

According to the authority just quoted, among 223 millionaires with more than ten million marks in Prussia in the year 1912 there were just 46 Jews, which however included members of the christianised families of Mendels-sohn, Bleichröder and Weinberg, some of whom were of partly non-Jewish descent. Only two of the forty-six had more than fifty million marks : Baron Max von Goldschmidt-Rothschild and Eduard Beit von Speyer. Thus the percent-age of plutocrats among German Jews was considerably greater than among non-Jews, though in no way pre-dominant; and this applies in an even greater degree to their racial kinsmen in England, France and other countries before the World War. Since the War the wealth of the

Jewish plutocracy as well as the prosperity of the middle class has decreased enormously—for reasons already discussed. But not even before 1914 did the Jews possess any capitalistic monopoly in the world.

Against the few hundred Jewish millionaires in Europe, South Africa and the United States and the relatively well-off middle class in Western and Central Europe we have to put the Eastern Jewish proletariat, reckoned in millions, which was hit not only by the difficulties of the depression, but also by special legislation, political, social and economic, which reduced it to such extreme misery as to be utterly beyond relief, even if Jewish solidarity were such as is imagined by the Antisemites and by many a Judæophile, and if Jewish wealth were many times greater than it actually is. We may ask ourselves whether there is any people on earth which consists to so great an extent of proletarians as the Jewish, the people who are so often supposed to consist of Rothschilds great and small. Either the talk of a great Jewish solidarity or that of the wealth of the Jewish people must be a myth, or else both ideas are erroneous. Unfortunately the last alternative is true. Even since Palestine has become practically the only country which is to some extent open to Jewish emigrants—and millions of Jews ask nothing better than to be allowed to emigrate !—the annual Jewish contributions to this work of rebirth and liberation amount to a sum which at present, in spite of intense publicity, does not exceed half a million pounds—a mere fraction of the budget of a small European State !

To sum up: there are no doubt many Jews who are rich, and many who take an important part in economic life, but nearly half the Jewish people are not merely poor, but desperately poor. One of those best acquainted with the social-economic problems of contemporary Jewry, Jacob Lestschinsky, arrives at the conclusion that of the Jews in Europe and America at least two millions are proletarians, leaving their wives and children out of account. It is the non-Jews who own the largest fortunes and are the real leaders both of financial and industrial life. No scientifically trained man can dispute Richard Lewinsohn's conclusion, " that there can be no question of any one-sided financial International of Jewish colour, and that the alleged Jewish sway over international economy (and finance) is nothing but a stupid antisemitic fable."

CHAPTER XIII

"THE JEWISH INTERNATIONAL," WORLD POLICY AND THE WORLD WAR

IN HIS BOOK, already referred to, *Die Protokolle der Weisen von Zion und die jüdische Weltpolitik,* which after Hitler's victory was published in a new edition revised by A. Philipp —20th thousand !—Alfred Rosenberg annotates this forgery in his own way, which makes this work of his undoubtedly one of the most preposterous books in the world's literature— side by side with that of Ford, written in the same spirit but, as we have said, withdrawn by the author himself as mendacious. But it has often been proved that preposterous books and senseless accusations make the very best propaganda when popular passions run high.

Rosenberg's fixed idea is that the Jews form a secret world-conspiracy and have been very near to realising their ancient Satanic plans, and ridden by this idea he tries page after page to prove its truth, using a mass of quotations from Jewish books and papers. As many Jews before the World War declared that they could see it coming and said so publicly—as no doubt did thousands of " Aryans "—it is clear to Rosenberg that they had made up their minds to bring it about. The book bears a significant motto, taken from *The Jewish World's* comments on Lord Robert Cecil's famous utterance that posterity would regard two results of the World War as specially fortunate and significant, namely the foundation of the League of Nations and the re-establishment of Jewish Palestine. (Of course the League of Nations is also controlled by the Jews or their nominees and equally

of course it is a link in the Jewish plan of world-conquest !)
Referring to the fact that the nations were far from having
these objects in mind when they took up arms in 1914, the
paper in question wrote: " It is remarkable to note the
difference, as Lord Robert Cecil puts it, of the purposes men
intended to serve when they helped in inflicting that
tragedy of tragedies upon the world, and what it is likely
history will conclude was the result of what they did."
Rosenberg of course sees in these words a proof that the
secret Jewish World State with diabolical cunning inveigled
first the nations into destroying one another and then the
peace negotiators into realising the objects for which the
Jews had brought the war about. The whole of Rosenberg's
book is written in this spirit. Obviously we have here a
typical case of persecution mania. But the remarkable thing
is that this preaching was, and is, greedily accepted by
millions of Germans and that on the National-Socialist
capture of the German State it became, so to speak, official.
Indeed Rosenberg's book, as already mentioned, has been
made a text-book in the Prussian schools ! It is in this spirit
that the youth of Germany is now to be educated.

Rosenberg enumerates many leading Jewish statesmen,
politicians and higher officials, especially in Western Europe,
Italy and the United States, where Jewish birth does not
stand in the way of advancement. It revolts him that the
State has benefited by these men's ability. In every distinction conferred upon a Jew he sees an anomaly, and for that
very reason a proof that Jews are the real masters of the
State in question. But as they are only a fraction of the
" Aryan " officials and leading politicians and are only
exceptionally to be found in the highest official posts, he
tries to make out that, as private secretaries to leading
statesmen or in other relatively subordinate positions, they
are the actual rulers and in secret collusion with one another
form a Jewish International which governs the world.
" Within the bounds of this survey," he writes by way of

introduction, " it should be emphasised that the parallel appearance of Baruch-Montague-Rathenau is altogether astounding. Just as the Jew Baruch emerges from obscurity and becomes dictator of the American World-State,[1] just as Montague, as Minister of Munitions, practically controlled the British army, so the Jew Rathenau appeared before the German Kaiser a few days after the outbreak of war with a cut-and-dried plan of war-economy." After that Montague and Baruch saw to it that Russia did not get enough munitions to prevent her bleeding to death, and " Jewish usury headquarters in Berlin," which were in the pay of the Germanophobe Northcliffe, took care that Germany did not defeat Russia too quickly. Thus Jewry succeeded in murdering its two enemies, imperial Germany and antisemitic Russia. Similar assertions are to be found in superfluity in Nazi writings of the same type as Rosenberg's book, for instance in Wilhelm Meister's *Judas Schuldbuch*.

Just as it was—and is—an axiom among German Nazis that the Jewish " World-International " desired the destruction of Germany, so were the Russian and French Antisemites convinced that its object was the very reverse. It was for this reason that Tsarist Antisemitism dealt so hardly with Russian and Polish Jews during the war, regarding them as pro-German. While the Dreyfus affair was in progress the French antisemitic papers used to call the French Jews (and Protestants) William II's myrmidons, who were trying to undermine the strength of the French army in order to facilitate the conquest of the country by the Germans. Examples are numerous. I choose a couple of recent date.

During 1932, while the German Antisemites were trying to stir up savage hatred against " World Jewry," which was alleged to desire the annihilation of Germany, an out-and-out British nationalist, the late J. L. Maxse, made in the *National Review* a violent attack on " international Jewish

[1] Bernard Baruch was chairman of the War Industries Board.

high finance" in general and in particular on Anglo-Jewish finance, "the London German Jews," whom he described significantly enough as "the German garrison in the city of London." For in his opinion they were extremely Germanophile ! The Anglo-Jewish financiers, according to Maxse, were almost all of German descent and only cared for their former country, lending it vast sums, which were frozen there and which they were now trying to rescue, counteracting the legitimate French claims against Germany for reparations. This "German garrison" used its influence in the Press, in society and in Government circles to evoke Germanophile feelings. At about the same time both the French nationalists and the American farmers' organs were making similar charges against American-Jewish finance.

The following example is no less typical. Year after year the German Antisemites with Hitler at their head tried to convince the German nation that Jewish world finance in alliance with the Freemasons was working in intimate association with liberal France with the object of ruining Germany. On July 23rd, 1933, Count Reventlow, one of the most active propagandists for "The Protocols of the Elders of Zion," explained in his paper the *Reichswart* how France and England were being induced and seduced by the Jewish International in association with the Freemasons into working for the ruin of Germany even after the treaty of Versailles. But at the same time one of the wealthiest and then most active Antisemites in France, the scent manufacturer and newspaper king François Coty, explained in the *Figaro* (July 13th and 24th) how Jewish world finance entirely espoused the interests of Germany and therefore constituted an immense danger to France. As the real instigator of American Germanophile policy (for according to the French nationalist view the treaty of Versailles, mainly through American influence, was far too lenient to Germany, since the Reich was allowed to continue united) Coty indicated the Jewish financiers in the United States and above all

" the financial dictator " Baruch. According to Coty the diplomats and presidents of the United States dance to the piping of these men and of the masonic lodges. The depression and the Hoover moratorium, so advantageous to Germany, were according to Coty the work of America's leading Jewish bankers, Kuhn, Loeb & Co., and their allies the masonic lodges !

Thus in the view of the German Antisemites the Jewish financial International is extremely hostile to Germany, and in that of the Antisemites of the victorious Powers it is extremely friendly to the same nation. It is not very difficult, however, to arbitrate between them. The answer has already been given in the last chapter: there is no Jewish " finance International." European and American high finance, which are not of Jewish invention, form a net spread over the world, in which there are a number of Jewish meshes among the rest. But making all allowance for good faith, it is an outrage on truth to single out just those men who hold these meshes in their hands and say: " Look how the Jew has his finger everywhere and pulls the strings that bind the nations " (Lewinsohn). In every country the Jewish financiers are just as much bound up with their country as the " Aryan," for the Jewish capitalist has the same interests as the non-Jewish. On the other hand the assertions of the Anglo-Saxon and French Antisemites contain just this grain of truth, that after the collapse of Germany a remarkable number of influential Jews were strongly in favour of a peace of understanding instead of a victors' peace—Georg Brandes, who for that matter opposed his friend Clemenceau, was only one among many—and that after the peace they raised their voices for a lenient treatment of Germany. It may be added that the Eastern Jewish masses, on account of their Yiddish speech and Germanised culture, entertained sympathies for Germany, to which the legal security of the Jews' position in imperial Germany powerfully contributed.

That in such circumstances the Nazi talk of a Jewish International working against Germany could win a hearing in that country can only be explained by the fact that antisemitic agitation had stifled reason and judgment. Antisemitic hatred was specially directed against the most prominent men of German Jewish finance, Walter Rathenau and Max Warburg, both enthusiastic German patriots. That the third of Germany's most eminent Jewish citizens, Albert Ballin, did not suffer the same fate was due to his taking his own life in despair after the defeat of Germany and the Kaiser's abdication.

After Rathenau had been murdered by the Antisemites in 1922, this hatred was concentrated upon Warburg, who by the way, was associated with the German National Party. He was described as a leader of the anti-German Jewish finance International, therefore a traitor to his country, and was bespattered with dirt as Rathenau had been before him. With what right may be judged from the account given in his *Memoirs* by the last Imperial Chancellor, Prince Max of Baden, of the negotiations which preceded the armistice. Warburg did his utmost to convince the representative of General Headquarters, Colonel von Haeften, of the necessity of not giving in, but was unsuccessful. At the conference with the Imperial Chancellor, Warburg finally said, after vainly urging his opinion against von Haeften: " It strikes me as odd that to-day I, a civilian, should be appealing to the soldiers to fight on. My only son, who is now undergoing his training, will be in the trenches within a month; all the same, I implore you not to give in now." Prince Max also tells us of Rathenau's despair when the German front gave way—he cried like a child—but at the same time he " lashed his inventive mind " for a possibility of avoiding the armistice. On October 7th Rathenau published an article in the *Vossische Zeitung*, in which he drew up directions for a levy in mass. " This," wrote Prince Max, " was a cry from the heart of a great patriot." This episode throws a strange light on the Nazi story of the undefeated German army, which the Jewish traitors and their tools the Marxists brought to naught by a stab in the back. But, as Christian von Dohm remarked nearly 150 years ago, it is an old custom to blame the Jews for defeat in war.

But, of course, World-Jewry is also responsible for the outbreak of the War according to Nazi doctrine, and Theodor Fritsch openly declared that the Jews are preventing a real investigation of war-guilt for fear of being unmasked. It seems the Nazis have forgotten that precisely those circles in which Antisemitism flourished and still flourishes were in favour of action in the years preceding 1914 and praised war for its hardening effect on the nations. And they suppress or refuse to see the fact that with few exceptions the Jews were engaged before the War in just such occupations as profited by a peaceful state of things; that, as shown above, Jewish finance and still more the Jewish masses did not gain but lost by the war, and that for nearly half of Jewry, the World War meant a complete catastrophe, one of the most terrible misfortunes that have ever befallen this, the most stricken people in the world's history.

The only gain which the War brought the Jews was the Balfour declaration (November 2nd, 1917), whereby the Jewish people were guaranteed a national home in Palestine. According to Rosenberg, the Balfour declaration was not drawn up by the British Government, but by the Zionist leaders, and then submitted to Balfour, who, of course, had only to sign it. If this had been so, the Jews would certainly not have got " a Jewish national home in Palestine," but Palestine would have become what Weizmann hoped to see it: just as Jewish as America is American or England, English. Thus the Balfour declaration itself implied far less than the Zionists hoped for. Besides, it must be noted that the most influential sections of American and European Jewry, including English, were against the re-establishment of Jewish Palestine. This applied to Edwin Montagu, the only Jewish member of the British Cabinet. In 1922 the whole eastern portion of Palestine was separated from the " national home " and made into a distinct State, Transjordan. Since then, as we know, the British Government has made one concession after another to the Palestine Arabs, so that at times the future of the Jewish national home has been seriously threatened. Now that Transjordan is separated from it, Palestine constitutes only a hundred-and-seventieth part of the Arabs' huge, thinly populated territory, much of which was presented to them by the victors in the World War. The Jews now ask to be allowed to own and cultivate this one-hundred-and-seventieth part, not alone, but together with the Arabs already settled there. To refuse them this would be robbing the poor man of his one lamb. But only the utmost efforts of the Jews and their British friends have been able of recent years to prevent the British Government sacrificing the land of Jewish hopes on the altar of British imperialism. The Jewish people, which is united on this point since the non-Zionists joined the Zionists in 1929, is politically so weak as only to be able with difficulty to defend its right to build up its own future in this little country, which is not much larger than Wales. If it had only a thousandth part of the power that is ascribed to it, then no doubt it would not have been forced to content itself with " a national home " *in* Palestine, but would have had its own Jewish State on both sides of the Jordan, even if this State would have been a very small one and quite insignificant compared with the Arab dominions. Ought one to laugh or to weep on hearing a people so feeble politically, which moreover has consisted generation after generation to a greater extent than any other nation of proletarians sunk in the deepest material misery, represented as the rulers of the world ? Ought one to laugh or be angry when it is made responsible for the World War, which more than any others it had reason to fear and which brought upon it unspeakable misery ?

The Jews, of course, feel mutually united by a common religion and a common destiny. (No doubt there are many Jewish individuals who have lost this feeling, but they can hardly be in a majority). But at the same time they are closely bound by their feelings and interests to the country whose language is their mother-tongue and whose civilisation has become a part of themselves. The Jews expelled from Germany feel as a rule just as homeless outside the frontiers of Germany as any " Aryan " exiles.

For millenniums the Jews have been without a united political leadership, a misfortune, in Theodor Herzl's opinion, more fatal than any persecutions. It has not yet been possible to realise the plans of a Jewish World Congress. Even if this were brought about, it would be powerless without the goodwill of the non-Jewish nations in giving ear to its appeals.

The Jewish people desires no world-dominion, in fact, there is certainly not a single Jew in the whole world who entertains such a thought. It is not merely their religion which enjoins on the Jews to promote the welfare of the city to which God has led them (Jeremiah, xxix, 7). It is an axiom of political economy that its welfare must be their welfare; in other words that an economic—to say nothing of an ideal—community of interest exists among all the inhabitants of a country. The erroneous idea of the Jews lacking this kind of solidarity may perhaps be explained as an atavism from a time when it was unusual for Jewish families to live in a country generation after generation, so that as a rule they did not take root there but were migrants and were so described. Afterwards this error has given birth to another: that the Jews form an International hostile to the non-Jewish nations, a dogma contrary to all reason, which could hardly win general acceptance except in disturbed times when the voice of hatred drowns all others.

Formerly the Jews were much more internationally inclined than now. Broadly speaking it is now only the Eastern

Jews and, since 1933, the German Jews, who merit the appellation of the wandering people. The touch of internationalism which this people, scattered all over the earth, has preserved and which, as pointed out above, is by no means synonymous with the *ibi patria ubi bene* of shallow cosmopolitanism, may claim to be regarded from a human point of view not simply as a deficiency but also as an asset. A man who has acquainted himself with foreign peoples and civilisations takes as a rule a freer view of the world. He is better protected from national prejudices and nationalistic agitation than the mentally insular. And it is certainly not fortuitous that Jews in particular have shown themselves possessed of a sense for ideas that embrace the whole of mankind, Their history has trained them to this. (Christianity was the creation of Jews; they have played a prominent part in the history of Socialism and the pacifist movement. Zamenhof, the inventor of Esperanto, was a Jew.) It is true that they have thus brought down on themselves the hatred of extreme nationalists in various countries. But the genuinely Jewish idea of the brotherhood of man, which is derived from their religion, is too lofty to be sacrificed for tactical reasons on the altar of opportunism.

CHAPTER XIV

THE JEWS AND RADICALISM

ON ACCOUNT of the relatively important part played by the Jews in the revolutions which accompanied the World War in Russia, Austria, Hungary and Germany, and still more on account of the far greater share that was falsely attributed to them, the question of Jewish radicalism was much discussed after the close of the War. At about the same time as the Antisemite George Batault in *Le Problème Juif* (1921) exhaustively treated " *le judaïsme* " as synonymous with " *l'esprit de rèvolte*," Jacob Wassermann in his autobiographical *My Life as German and Jew* admitted that the Jews were the Jacobins of the age, and explained Jewish radicalism as inherited Messianism transposed into the social sphere, a view which Batault also maintained, independently of Wassermann.

The social legislation of the Old Testament and its prophetical writings seem obviously to support the theory of a disposition to Radicalism on the part of the Jews. It has been said with justice that Moses, 1,250 years before Christ, was the first to proclaim the rights of man and that—the words are Cardinal Faulhaber's in his celebrated Advent sermon of 1933 on the social values of the Old Testament—the cradle of humaneness stood not in Hellas but in Palestine. The nation is to be a holy nation, every human being has a value as a human being, one person is socially responsible for another, mutual help is the duty of all. Therefore above all the weak are to be protected, the widow and the fatherless, the stranger, the poor, even the slave. It is significant that everywhere else in the ancient world the slave was regarded as an animal or a chattel, but in ancient Israel he was looked upon as a human being, generally as a member of the family, even if he was a heathen. A man who ill-treated a slave was punished, the penalty for killing one was death. If anyone knocked out one of his slave's teeth, the slave was set free. On leaving service he was to receive gifts: sheep, seed, wine. A slave who fled to the land of Israel was not to be given up to his master, and, like the stranger in distress, he was free to choose his place of residence. Compare with this the martyrdom of Roman slaves, of which Mommsen said that in comparison all the sufferings of negro slaves were a drop in the ocean.

Mercy, loving-kindness and justice to all the weak and poor are enjoined over and over again with extraordinary emphasis as a maxim in private life, but they also characterise the whole social legislation in an unparalleled way. It is forbidden to wait till the morrow before giving the day-labourer his wage or returning one's neighbour's cloak, if one has taken it as a pledge; it is forbidden to curse the deaf or put stones in the way of the blind.

The owner is not to reap his fields and vineyards to the last ear of corn or the last grape; gleaning is the part of the stranger and of the poor man, as is all that grows in the corners of the field. On the sabbath the stranger, the labourer and the beasts are also to enjoy rest. Every third year all landowners are to pay tithes, not to the authorities, as might be supposed from analogy, but to the Levites, who own no land, and to the widows and fatherless. Every seventh year, the sabbath year, when it is unlawful to sow one's field or prune one's vineyard, everything that grows of its own accord is to be given to the servants and to strangers in the land. But the most radical provisions against the exploitation of the poor and the amassing of fortunes are to be found in the laws that in every seventh year all debts are to be cancelled; that those who are enslaved for non-payment of debt shall then be set free, and that in every fiftieth year, the year of jubilee, every family shall regain possession, without redemption, of the land it has been compelled to sell. For all land is God's land—in modern parlance, national property—and it must not be degraded into a commodity. If we add that it was forbidden to take interest from fellow-countrymen,[1] it will scarcely appear an exaggeration to describe the ancient Jewish social order as inspired by a unique ethical-religious Radicalism. The Bible cannot be said to regard the rich as inferior, but it evidently prefers the poor. The social obligations of the rich are demonstratively emphasised: the poor are to receive their part, not as a favour but as a lawful right. In fact, according to later biblical interpretation poverty itself ought to be extirpated as conflicting with the idea of social justice. The view that all men are equal in the sight of God led logically to the principle of social equality.

Doubtless these statutes were unable to check an economic development independent of the law: the Jewish State like the rest of the Near East was drawn into a course that was in a certain degree capitalistic. An oppressive rich man's class arose. But the law was still alive, and so was its spirit. The preachings of the Prophets against kings and the powerful classes form a vehement protest in the name of justice and religion against the proletarianisation of the lower classes and the weakening of the sense of human solidarity, a social and ethical programme of extraordinary future importance both for Judaism and for Christianity. Old Testament " nationalism," narrow at the outset—what nationalism was not narrow at the outset?—rings out in the Prophets as a lofty and moving universalist message, reinforced by their feeling of social justice. All the peoples of the earth are to

[1] It was not forbidden to take interest from Phœnician merchants and other foreigners, as these employed their money in the pursuit of gain and themselves took interest; for which reason mutual relations between Jews and non-Jews were impossible.

worship God and to be penetrated with the spirit of charity and human solidarity. " The idea of the supremacy of monotheism," says a Swedish-Jewish author, Stig Bendixon, " was thus no abstract idea which merely proclaimed the thought of a single God for all, it was also bound up with the dream of a future international realm of justice, liberty and peace."

It is also a fact that from the most ancient times to our own day a remarkable number of Jews have been possessed by a powerful ethico-social emotion, real prophet and saviour natures, distinguished by intense idealism and boundless altruism. This also applies to many revolutionary Jews of our time, who figure in antisemitic literature as morally deficient subverters of society, and whom he who writes these lines has often attacked in speech and in print as fantastic visionaries or as Jews without sufficient sense of proportion. One of the noblest and most profound of them, the philosopher Gustav Landauer, who was murdered on the overthrow of the Soviet Republic in Bavaria—he was by the way an anti-Marxian Socialist—was governed, nay, possessed as perhaps no other of his contemporaries by the idea of the liberation of mankind from its thraldom and its re-birth in love, dignity and beauty. A person who during the Communist period at Munich saw Landauer speaking not only to the masses but also to small groups and individuals, " always ready to help, encourage, teach, console," said that nothing had ever moved him so much as the sheer goodness and humanity which emanated from this genuinely Jewish prophetic figure. This Socialism, far more ethical and social than political, represents one side of " Jewish " Radicalism, which in discussion is too often neglected in favour of that which is represented by Marx, for instance, or by the handful of Russian-Jewish terrorists who, seen through the antisemitic magnifying glass, have been multiplied a thousandfold, and who are no more typical of the Jewish people than are Kreuger and his associates of the Swedish. In the eyes of Fritz Kahn, himself a Radical, who in his able but extremely subjective book *Die Juden als Rasse und Kulturvolk* (1920) accepts entirely the hypothesis of Radicalism as a Jewish racial quality, even the de-Judaised or Judæophobe leaders of Jewish birth are possessed of a Jewish ethos in which he sees one of mankind's most precious treasures and an evidence that in the future, as in the past, the Jews have a great mission to perform in the service of man. Moses, Jesus and the impassioned altruist Marx are according to this writer the chief upholders of the idea of social justice, the idea of the kingdom of God on earth, though Marx's religiousness was of a secularised kind. In Marx's Jewish successors he—like the Antisemites—sees representatives of the true Jewish spirit. These revolutionaries were as a rule men from relatively well-to-do circles who, led, in his opinion, by sympathy and a sense of justice, that is by ideal conviction, went over to the proletariat; and neither the caricature of them drawn by the bourgeois Press nor the shameful death which many of them suffered, will degrade them in the eyes of posterity. They have illustrious predecessors: Jeremiah was stoned; Jesus died on the cross between two criminals; Spinoza was excommunicated.

That this social-ethical Radicalism is not extinct in our day is shown by its prominence among the Zionist agricultural youth of Palestine, which has organised itself to a great extent in collectivist combinations, *kvuzoth* as they are called, in which not only labour but also property is shared in common. (The resemblance with the " Communism " of the Essenes and of primitive Christianity is striking.) Many a Jewish youth and girl emigrated to Palestine not merely from motives of Jewish nationalism, in order to re-establish the Jewish people in the land of their fathers, but to realise the idea of a model social order on a basis of justice; a new society, " *die wahrhafte Gemeinschaft*," which bears witness, as Martin Buber has expressed it, that God lives and works within us.

A distinction must be drawn between this social-ethical Communism, which seeks to produce its effect more by the force of example than by propaganda and which has a certain right to be called Jewish, and political Communism, which in contrast to the former is founded on the theory of the class war, force, the dictatorship of the proletariat and drastic centralisation. The totalitarian State, in which the individual counts for nothing, is in direct conflict with Old Testament views—see for instance Deuteronomy xx, 5–8— and with the tradition of Jewish civilisation. The fact, however, that this form of Communism has also attracted a number of Jews, especially young Eastern Jews, is doubtless due in the first place to the Communist State's principle of disregarding race and religion. Hundreds of thousands of young Eastern Jews are humanly speaking condemned to permanent unemployment, since opportunities of work are reserved for non-Jews. They are also under the spiritual pressure of Antisemitism. Their situation is terrible. They think that a victory of Communism in Poland or Rumania means to them a place in a factory, a Government post, opportunities for study, in short, a life worthy of a human being, a future. America has closed its doors to immigrants. Palestine can only receive a few tens of thousands a year. Where are they to turn ?

I recently asked a Galician Jew, an anti-Communist, whether Communism was rife among the Jews of Poland. He replied: " No. But it is remarkable how many young Jews of intellectual and moral distinction are Communists." I rejoined: " It is out of the question that Communism should gain the upper hand in Poland. The Polish Jews' conversion to Communism is a kind of romantic flight from reality." To which he answered: " That is true. But the reality is just what is so distractingly hopeless." In such circumstances there is in truth no need to seek an explanation in the theory of a special Jewish racial disposition to Radicalism. And in this connection it deserves to be

Q A

emphasised that Communism is only embraced by any
important number of Jews in those countries in which
despair is prevalent.

The hypothesis of the Jews' racially conditioned tendency
to Radicalism is of course, like all theories of fixed psychical
racial qualities, incapable of scientific proof and should
therefore not be resorted to when, as here, the matter admits
of natural explanation without it. There is much evidence
against the hypothesis. According to ancient Jewish ideas it
is a mortal sin to sell oneself to the revolutionaries, to
" Korah's company." The orthodox Jew is the least revolutionary of men. And the conservative Disraeli, who in spite
of his fantastic racial chauvinism was probably a far better
judge of Jewish nature than Rosenberg or Hitler, asserted
his conviction, in his novel *Coningsby*, that the Jews are by
nature Conservatives and that injurious treatment alone is
able to turn them into Radicals. The Jews' political leanings
in all those countries in which Antisemitism has not embittered their lives, in America, Italy, Western Europe,
Scandinavia—especially in Sweden, where for generations
their treatment has been gentlemanlike—appear to bear
out his words. Probably in none of these countries are they
on an average more radical than the non-Jewish members
of the same social classes as they belong to. Of the thirty-
nine Jewish members of the British House of Commons in
1930, sixteen belonged to the Conservative, twenty-one to the
Liberal, and two to the Labour Party, in addition to which
there were two former Liberals, one of whom went over to
the Labour Party and the other to the Conservatives.
(Jewish Radicalism in the United States, which plays a
certain part in the American Labour movement, is princi-
pally of Eastern Jewish origin.) A Swedish Jew is not surprised that Disraeli became leader of the Conservatives in
England, that Goldschmidt allied himself with the aristocratic agrarians of Denmark, or that Italian Jews sympathise
with Mussolini, all which things are likely to arouse the

astonishment of an Eastern or a German Jew, who is accustomed to see in practically every Conservative an Antisemite. Thus Jewish Radicalism is no universally Jewish phenomenon. No doubt there are to be found everywhere individual radical Jews, as there are radical non-Jews, but a "Jewish," in the sense of a racially determined, Radicalism exists only in Eastern Europe and Germany, where the Conservative and Nationalist Parties are hostile to the Jews. We must therefore conclude that, if the Jews are " by nature " disposed to Radicalism, which is very doubtful, it requires certain special conditions to bring out this tendency.

As a rule the tradition of Jewish civilisation does not seem to have had much influence on the politically radical Jews of our time. On the other hand there is no doubt that the consciousness of belonging to a slighted human group has predisposed many a wronged and insulted Jewish child to adopt a radical attitude of opposition to the State and society and caused many Jews and Jewesses from well-to-do homes to have a feeling of solidarity, not indeed with their racial kinsfolk, for as a rule they have been indifferent to them, but to the persecuted and down-trodden proletariat, with the outcasts of society; a fact of extreme importance for an understanding not only of Eastern-Jewish but also of German-Jewish Radicalism.

.   .   .   .

Destructive Jewish Radicalism, lashed as much by Jewish-minded Jews as by Antisemites, is an evil to be resisted, all the more as experience shows that in this sphere again Jews often occupy leading positions. But it is, to put it mildly, a misuse of words to characterise these Radicals, detached from Judaism and Jewry, as representatives of the " Jewish " spirit. Voltaire, as we know, meant by Jewish spirit the very opposite: rigid, superstitious traditionalism. And it is a disastrous mistake to suppose they can be defeated by bloody

or " dry " pogroms. This destructive Radicalism is a product
of abnormal circumstances and can only be extirpated by
the removal of these. This cannot be done by " re-ghettoising " the Jewish masses, but by making them productive.
There is a physical Jewish distress: their boundless poverty,
especially in Eastern Europe. There is also a moral Jewish
distress: " an ancient civilised people cries out for justice
and is met by scorn, hatred and contempt, which embitter
the soul and drive the oppressed into the arms of the
revolutionary parties " (Richard Lichtheim). But it is
assuredly not merely morally reprehensible but also politically unwise to treat the distressed as criminals.

It was a matter of course that at the time of their emancipation the Jews, the former pariahs, should sympathise
with the political tendencies from the victory of which they
expected liberty, equality and fraternity. The Jewish youth
of the period became predominantly liberal. The Liberals'
doctrine of liberty and still more of humanity touched
similar chords in their souls. In proportion as they felt
themselves to be the recipients of a Jewish inheritance, they
loved to imagine that the consciousness of the wrongs done
to their forefathers made them specially receptive of the
new emotions of liberty and justice, a view which was not
infrequently shared by their " Aryan " fellow-Liberals and
in which there may indeed be some truth.

So long as Conservatism was anti-Jewishly inclined, the
Jews obviously could not sympathise with it. There were no
doubt exceptions to this rule. The rabbi Salman Schneerson,
leader of the Hasids of White Russia, declared during
Napoleon's war against Alexander I: " If Bonaparte is
victorious, the Jews will be richer and their (social) position
will be improved, but in return the heart of our heavenly
Father will depart from them; if on the other hand our
Tzar Alexander is victorious, the hearts of the Jews will draw
near to our heavenly Father, although the poverty of Israel
will increase and its situation will be made worse." Even

those who are impressed by this ancient Jewish idealism must yet agree that the predominantly liberal attitude of European Jewry at that date was natural and reasonable.

In imperial Germany the Jews doubtless constituted, broadly speaking, an educated and well-to-do but nevertheless *déclassé* group of citizens, as it were " base-born," like the unprivileged classes in feudal times. As we have said, unless they accepted baptism they were practically excluded from the higher official posts, from professorships in the universities and from the corps of officers. In Wilhelmine Germany the last-named exclusion was a particular mark of loss of caste. As in international law they did not constitute a minority nation but were one with the German people and regarded themselves as Germans—we shall speak later of the Zionists' attitude—they felt their actual exclusion as an insult. Thus the assumptions of the emancipation period continued in Germany to determine the existence of Jewish Radicalism. The Liberals and Socialists disapproved of this exclusion. They maintained the democratic principle that every man ought to be judged only according to his intellectual and moral qualities as expressed in deeds. But no attention was paid to their opposition. In such circumstances the political attitude of German Jewry appears natural: German Jewry before 1918 was no more anti-monarchical or revolutionary than the unprivileged French bourgeoisie previous to 1789, but as a rule it acknowledged liberal and democratic principles. It did so also in its quality of a middle class. For German and especially Prussian Conservatism at that time entertained very largely a semi-feudal view of society, according to which the officers' caste, the high bureaucracy and the landed nobility were to control administrative and social life. And yet German Conservatism owes a heavy debt of gratitude to a German Jew, Friedrich Julius Stahl, the founder of the German Conservative Party. (He was baptised by the way, like Disraeli and Karl Marx.) On the centenary of his birth, his memory was honoured by

Conservative Germany, headed by the Conservative section of the Prussian *Herrenhaus*. Not without reason did the *Konservative Monatschrift* write a decade later (in August 1912) that no man, not even Karl Marx himself, had meant so much to any German party as Stahl. It was from this party that the German National People's Party was afterwards formed. No one who is acquainted with Jewish political leanings in non-antisemitic countries can doubt that German Jewry would have adhered to this party in great numbers, if it had not been antisemitic. Now those German Jews, who by nature or on account of their social position were predisposed to be conservatives, were compelled to go over to the other side; which, of course, furnished the Antisemites of the Weimar Republic with a welcome opportunity of discrediting both the Liberal and the Socialist Parties as representing " Jewish " interests.

It became particularly common to describe anti-capitalist Marxism as Jewish, which of course did not prevent people from branding its antithesis, capitalism, in the same way. The slogan of " Jewish Marxism " acquired a special significance when Hitler and his adherents in order to win over the workers went in for a " national " Socialism, which was played off against international Socialism, the latter being represented as Jewish and thus un-German and contemptible. With what right ? The circumstance that Marx was born a Jew—he was baptised at the age of six—is hardly sufficient to make international Socialism "Jewish." If it were so, then German Conservatism would also be Jewish, since Stahl was a Jew. Besides which, Marx was indifferent to everything Jewish, nay, hostile towards Judaism and the Jews, in whom, naïvely accepting the Antisemitic views of the outer world, he saw the incarnation of capitalism, the spirit of huckstering and mammonism, the objects of his burning hatred. Of his intellectual precursors not one was a Jew: not Saint-Simon, not Proudhon, not Louis Blanc, not Fourier, not Hegel, from whom he borrowed his method of research. This method, which Hegel himself called " dialectic," was not " Talmudic," nor was it solely negative, as everyone must admit who has studied Marx's writings. From the baptised Jew Ricardo, whose name is familiar as one of the leaders of the Manchester school, Marx no doubt derived strong impressions; but he formulated his socialist doctrines in conscious opposition to the view Ricardo represented. Marx's theory of the value of labour is a kind of perversion of Ricardo's. Nor can the circumstance that a striking number of socialist leaders in Eastern Europe and Germany were Jews—Marx, Lassalle, Adler, Bauer, and so on—justify the appellation " Jewish Marxism," for while Socialism is an international phenomenon, Jewish Radicalism, including Socialism, is, as we have said, locally circumscribed.

" Jewish materialism " has also become a favourite slogan, admirably suited from its ambiguity to serve for antisemitic agitation. In no respect does it correspond to reality. Perhaps it is most commonly intended to imply that the Jews are specially prone to making money and amassing a fortune. How this idea has arisen has already been pointed out, in Chapter III. Its truth naturally does not admit of proof. As evidence against its truth may be cited the high estimation in which intellectual values are held by pre-Talmudic, Talmudic and post-Talmudic Judaism, the Jews' well-known interest in education, science and art—Jewish patrons of art are strikingly numerous—and, as a well-known Swedish bishop expressed it, their " turn for charity." It can scarcely be asserted with justice that the Jews are more addicted than other people to a materialistic life of enjoyment, nor that the materialist view of history, that is, the view that all social and political development is ultimately determined by economic factors, can be regarded as characteristic of a people whose greatest contributions have been made in the intellectual sphere. Nor was it Jews who created or advanced philosophical materialism, that is to say, the view that all is matter and the spirit merely one of its products. The ancient materialist philosophers, Democritus, Epicurus and Lucretius, were no Jews, nor were the leading materialists of recent centuries, Holbach, Helvetius, Moleschott, Buchner, Karl Vogt, and others. (What a chance for antisemitic propaganda if any of them had been !) On the other hand, Jewish thinkers in all ages have combated materialist opinions, from the Prophets down to Hermann Cohen and Henri Bergson.

As in the political, so in the cultural field we find a relatively large number of Jews among the extremists. It is these in particular who represent what is called destructive or disintegrating (*zersetzende*) Jewry and who are therefore regarded, especially in conservative quarters, as liable to undermine the power of the State and society to resist spiritual decay. In this connection, however, it must be noted that even in Germany these extremists have never constituted more than a small minority of Jewry, and that their importance both quantitatively and qualitatively has been recklessly exaggerated in the service of propaganda. With the Germany of the good old times, its piety, purity of morals, frugality, loyalty to authority and the laws, and its patriotism—a tendentious rose-coloured picture of the past —was contrasted the Weimar Republic, the " Jew Republic," with its atheism, licentiousness, social and political unrest, its Communism, its cultural Bolshevism. Men did not or would not see that there was here no question of a " Judaising " of Germany, but of a transforming process, a " metropolising " of our whole civilisation, resulting in an intellectualisation and rationalisation of culture. The Jew was summarily equated with the typical city-dweller, the Jew and the Voltairian were the same. The destroyer, that was the Jew with his intellectualism hostile to all that was naïve and primitive, his corroding reflection, his unrestrained love of criticism, his scepticism, his blindness to national and irrational values, his cosmopolitanism, pacifism and defeatism. Not only those Antisemites who were blinded by hate and in reality knew nothing of Jewish mentality, regarded it as a corroding poison in German civilisation, but even German critics of eminence took the same view; Hans Blüher, for instance, who, while acknowledging the Jews' high moral qualifications, advocated as early as 1922 their total exclusion from the German national community and their " re-ghettoising." Others, such as the fanatically antisemitic literary historian Adolf Bartels, asserted that scornful Jewish critics of Heine's type were hostile to Germany, and Wilhelm Stapel launched the term "Jewish Anti-Germanism," which soon became a catchword. But this designation, which was obviously intended to exhibit Antisemitism as a reply to German-Jewish hatred of Germany, is misleading, since these scoffers were at least equally critical of everything Jewish, and no hatred of Germany existed in any German-Jewish circles, not even among the extremists who were least sympathetic or most hostile to Prussian militarist ideals.

The word "disintegrating" is extremely ambiguous. Much that was so described by militarist nationalism was, and is, regarded by its opponents as the reverse. The view is widely and, as I believe, rightly held outside the frontiers of Germany that precisely in influential German-Jewish intellectual circles a remarkable number of highly cultivated, broad-minded and humane men and women are to be found. Much that is described as "Jewish" cultural Bolshevism is only a modern metropolitan phenomenon with nothing distinctively Jewish about it ("Jazz-culture," sensationalism), novelties which have proved productive (expressionism), or actual scientific achievements which have been brought into disrepute by gossip or irresponsible reiteration. It is significant that Einstein's theory of relativity according to a recent Nazi publication of semi-official character has led to everything being regarded as relative, including morality.

There is no possibility of illustrating statistically to what extent German Jews have excelled other German journalists and authors as negative critics or supporters of extreme views in politics or morals. But the type exists and calls for an explanation.

When after the French Revolution the Jews made their entrance into Western society, they obviously had not assimilated its culture. For this reason many of them failed to understand conservative ways of thinking. This does not apply to those Jews who still clung to their inherited Jewish culture. These had, in a spiritual sense, firm ground under their feet. Apart from their social and financial position, they were a sort of conservative aristocrats. No wonder the anti-liberal Bismarck held them in special esteem as an intellectually noble human type. But many Jews flung aside everything Jewish in order to be entirely absorbed in the new world opened to them by emancipation. They accepted its culture, not merely with their brains but with affection and passion. But without knowing it they remained in a certain degree outsiders, perhaps less on account of difference of race than as consequence of their lack of Western cultural tradition. No doubt it is true that they assimilated the culture itself with extraordinary rapidity. Heine has shown us the reason: they had acquired, he says, through a tradition of two thousand years " a great civilisation of the heart," which resulted, when emancipation arrived, in their having nothing to learn in the way of feeling and only requiring to assimilate knowledge. But Heine, himself a representative of " Jewish " Radicalism, overlooked the fact that a real understanding of a culture demands more than knowledge and " the civilisation of the heart." The power of real assimilation is as a rule only possessed by him who in intimate association with the members of a civilisation—which means not merely the leaders of culture but the whole nation at work—has experienced the existence of that nation in its irrational diversity. But this was as a rule denied to the newly emancipated Jews, especially as they were largely metropolitan. Those of them who had broken away from Judaism, the Jews " without history " so to speak, were therefore often led, as critics of society, to play a part similar to that assigned by eighteenth-century philosophers to various fictitious exotic strangers, who were made to appear as representatives of " pure reason," evidently more clear-sighted than the Europeans themselves, to whom tradition and education had imparted a mass of " prejudices " difficult to eradicate. A remarkable number of Jewish-born critics of society during the nineteenth century might be taken for spiritual descendants of Rika and Usbek, the celebrated Persians in Montesquieu's Persian Letters. Cut off from the Jewish tradition, which as a rule they would not hear of, but without being organically incorporated in the non-Jewish, they very naturally showed less comprehension of the romantically national tendencies of the age than of the movements towards rationalism and universalism, which often found in them devoted apostles. During the nineteenth century, the Jews became to a great extent rationalists, which they had not been previously; a state of things which, as has been rightly emphasised by an eminent German-Jewish writer, Kurt Blumenfeld, was not due to any Jewish racial peculiarity, but to the special situation created by Jewish emancipation. And while in most countries they were admitted directly to governmental work, in Germany the Jews were excluded from the administration until 1917, and it was only as authors and journalists that they had opportunities of propounding their ideas.

If these radical Jews had not lost contact with Judaism they certainly would never have merited the reproach of having lacked respect for the special character and historical importance of the German nation, of having picked to pieces what their intellectual qualifications did not enable them to grasp. Only the man without history lacks a sense of proportion and reverence for national peculiarities. In vain did the groups who acknowledged Judaism urge tactful reticence upon these de-Judaised Jews, especially in criticism of purely German affairs. "The sense of proportion," wrote the Zionist author Max Brod, "the sense that it is not our own peculiarities that we are criticising in such cases, but the peculiarities of others, whose respectful, thankful, nay, intimate friends we are, but who are not identical with us—this sense of proportion ought never to desert us. One has no right to carry on a merciless polemic except against oneself and one's own peculiarities." But the misfortune was that these radical Jews did not feel themselves to be Jews at all, but simply Germans, and therefore paid no regard to the fact that large sections of the German people took a different view of them and therefore of their cultural and political opinions. Thus this class of Jews not only furnished the Antisemites with an argument against them but also did injury to the radical ideas they desired to serve. But it deserves to be emphasised that even among German Jews indifferent to Judaism, these representatives of "disintegration" only constituted a small minority, and that German Jewry as a whole was far from being made up of disrespectful, negative critics or of extremists.

Alfred Rosenberg published in 1930 a collection of cuttings from books and newspapers, mainly derived from German-Jewish writers and with a commentary by himself; he called it *Der Sumpf. Querschnitte durch das "Geistes"-Leben der November-Demokratie* ("The Morass. Sections through the so-called intellectual life of the November democracy.") Much of what it contains can only appear compromising in the light of fanatical misconstruction;[1] much is disgusting. But it would not be difficult to publish a collection of German-Jewish cuttings a thousand times as bulky and tending in a

---

[1] A particularly grotesque example is to be found on p. 171 f., where Leo Baeck, well known as one of the most respected men in contemporary religious Jewry, is made out to be a Bolshevik on the strength of an observation about the "revolutionary idea" of Judaism.

directly opposite direction, which would afford evidence of a pure and warm affection for Germany, the German people and German culture, of a fine understanding of and a sincere sympathy for the German nature as reflected in art and literature, history and custom. Even Hans Blüher acknowledges that the German Jews " love the German race with unhappy passion."

If the Jews on account of their race, history or special position in the world are more prone than others to feelings of social justice and universalist humanity, then they certainly have a task to perform even in, or perhaps more than ever in an age of nationalism and imperialism. The same applies to rationalism, against the hegemony of which in assimilated Jewry Jews too have reacted with justice (Buber's Hasid mysticism !) In an age of anti-intellectualism it is well to remember that rationalisation is not synonymous with the stifling of human emotional life but on the contrary may be accompanied by a rich development of the nobler emotional complexes at the expense of the unennobled instincts and impulses. Even a number of qualities which are ultimately due to the Jews' being less firmly rooted in the traditions of the non-Jewish nations, have not infrequently had a civilising effect. If the Jews on the one hand have a certain propensity for accepting the newest of the new, on the other they have shown in a striking manner an appreciation of geniuses who have not met with immediate recognition and would otherwise certainly have been neglected altogether; and this applies both to the great buying public and to the leaders of culture. As Jacob Wassermann has expressed it, the Jews have been " caryatids under almost every great name," in art, literature and science. (It is remarkable, though not very creditable, that, as the same author has emphasised, in doing so they have often shown a distrust, mingled with envy, of men of their own race.) It has also been frequently acknowledged in German, non-Jewish quarters, by Nietzsche and many others, that German culture could have been much poorer without these contributions from intellectual Jewry.

All radicalism and all Conservatism has its value and its danger. It is through the dialogue between them that the march of progress is maintained. So it has always been. Ever since 1790, when Edmund Burke flung out his brilliant but one-sided polemic against eighteenth-century Radicalism and the revolution, *Reflexions on the French Revolution*, their antagonism has been a conscious one. The struggle between romantic Conservatism and rationalist middle-class Liberalism was only an ideologically coloured phase of this ancient conflict. In this the Jews in all antisemitic countries have been forced over to the Left, where their support has been of value. An objective estimate of this value is well-nigh impossible, since it is bound to be coloured by the critic's own attitude to the struggle between old and new, between organic growth and rationalism, between empiricism and ideas. Like all Radicalism, that of the Jews has been both constructive and destructive in its effects. It appears that, when torn from its Jewish roots, it is apt to incline towards the negative, but when nourished and held in check by Jewish consciousness, it tends towards the positive.

CHAPTER XV

THE JEWS AND BOLSHEVISM

THE SPIRITUAL FATHERS of Bolshevism are not Jews. Marx, who, as we have said, was antipathetic to all things Jewish, is probably the only exception. The tutors of the radical and revolutionary Russians in atheism, materialism, nihilism, terrorism, socialism and anarchism were Russians, such as Alexander Herzen, Bielinsky, Pisarev, Tchernyshevsky and Bakunin, or Englishmen, Frenchmen and Germans, to some extent the same as had influenced the West in the 1870's and 80's, but who had a far more disintegrating effect in Russia than elsewhere. A fine judge of Slav nature, ex-President Masaryk, justly points out that their unprepared study of the German thinkers, Feuerbach, Strauss and Büchner had a devastating effect on the Russians, much the same as is often the case with primitive peoples on first meeting with European civilisation. These Germans were all " Aryans," as were the French and English Positivists. But above all, Bolshevism is a Russian phenomenon. Read J. H. Seraphim's instructive works on Bolshevism in the supplement to the *Handwörterbuch der Staatswissenschaften !* (Seraphim is an " Aryan.") His whole exposition of the matter forms a convincing proof of the correctness of its opening words : " The origins of Bolshevism lie deep down in the Russian nature and in the politico-economic structure of the Empire of the Tsars. To conceive it as merely a variant of proletarian Socialism of the Marxist school would be to disregard its distinctively national character."

Nor is it true that any great number of Nicholas II's five

million Jewish subjects, of whom about half lived in what is now Poland and the other border States, were Bolsheviks. But undoubtedly the great majority of them were hostile to imperial absolutism. The whole Jewish policy of Tsarist Russia was in a high degree calculated to throw the Jewish intelligentsia and the Jewish workers into the arms of the extremist parties. Can we be surprised that those who had been treated as pariahs and enemies of the State allied themselves with the enemies of Tsarist despotism, with those who were willing to efface their pariah marks and grant them citizenship and equality ? That the younger Jewish generation, especially the so-called intelligentsia and semi-intelligentsia, was driven in no small numbers into the Radical camp was perfectly natural and has already been pointed out in Chapter V. But by far the greater part of Russian Jewry was not merely non-Bolshevik but non-Socialist, a fact which is accounted for by its social structure: it consisted to a very great extent of lower middle-class tradesmen and artisans, many of whom, however, were in a state of extreme poverty. The provisional Jewish National Assembly of the Ukraine (1918), where two million Russian Jews were domiciled, numbered 63·2 per cent bourgeois and 36·8 per cent Socialists of various shades. Thus the Jews of the Ukraine were decidedly less socialist proportionally than the Swedes of to-day or the Ukrainian people of 1918: in the Ukrainian constituent National Assembly, the majority was socialist. We may reasonably ask ourselves whether any intellectually progressive people who had been treated as terribly as were the Jews under the last of the Tsars would have recruited the extremist parties to a less extent.

The great majority of Russian Jewry belonged to the constitutional democratic party, the " Cadet Party," which was bourgeois and liberal. Many, though of course not most, of its leaders were Jews; foremost among them, Maxim Vinaver, who after the triumph of Bolshevism became Foreign Minister in the anti-Bolshevist Crimea government;

Michael Herzenstein, one of the greatest specialists in the Russian agrarian question; Josef Hessen, who edited the party organ in Petrograd, his brother, Professor Vladimir Hessen and many more. Most of the Jewish workers and many of the intellectual and "semi-intellectual" Jewish proletariat belonged either to the social-revolutionary or to the Menshevik Party, both of which took their stand on social-democratic principles, were hostile to the anti-democratic Bolsheviks and were soon to be cruelly persecuted by them. In 1917–18, the Russian-Jewish Socialists numbered 60,000. Among the leaders of the Russian Social-Democrats also we find a large number of Jews famous in the history of the Labour movement and in that of Russian freedom, for instance, the Mensheviks Dan (Gurvitch), Paul Axelrod, Martov (Zederbaum), Liber (Goldmann), Abramovitch (Rein). Enemies of Tsarist tyranny, they opposed in turn its spiritual heirs: the Bolshevik dictatorship. These bourgeois or socialist anti-Bolsheviks were men no less remarkable than their communist opponents, whose names, thanks to the victory of Communism, have become known all over the world: Trotsky (Bronstein), Kamenev (Rosenfeld), Zinoviev (Radomyslsky), Litvinov (Wallach, not Finkelstein), Radek (Sobelsohn), Joffe and others.

Before the World War, the number of Jewish Bolsheviks was insignificant. Trotsky himself did not turn Bolshevik till 1917. Even in 1922, that is, after several years of intensive Bolshevising, the Jewish element only amounted to 19,526 members, or 5·2 per cent of the party, in spite of the fact that the Jews, in contrast to the rest of the Russian population, were very largely composed of town-dwellers, who were able to read and were thus more accessible to propaganda. All three Jewish workers' organisations: the Serz, the Zionist Poale-Zion and the greatest of them, the general league of Jewish workers, founded in 1897 and usually known simply as the Bund, declared against Bolshevism.

Russian Jewry had joyfully hailed the revolution of March

RA

12th (February 27th), which overthrew imperial despotism, introduced a democratic system in Russia and placed the Jewish population on a footing of equality with the rest of the inhabitants. The Bolshevik revolution of November 7th (October 25th) aroused dismay and indignation. And in fact the Bund vigorously opposed the Bolshevist defeatism which led to the peace of Brest-Litovsk. The Commissariat for the administration of Jewish affairs, appointed by Lenin's Government, issued a manifesto on March 15th, 1918, attacking the Jewish workers for their anti-Bolshevist attitude. The Jewish bourgeoisie, the majority of whom followed trades and professions which must inevitably be ruined in a communist Russia, were still more enraged against Bolshevism. In the Ukraine in 1918, the Jewish workers with arms in their hands made common cause with the Jewish bourgeois against Bolshevism—which did not prevent Petlyura and other White generals during the civil war of 1919 from labelling Bolshevism as Jewish. The chief of the notorious Cheka, the secret Bolshevik police, Moses Uritsky, a man of Jewish birth, was put out of the way by a Menshevik Jewish worker, Leonid Kannegiesser, and a social-revolutionary Jewess, Dora Kaplan, made an unsuccessful attempt on Lenin's life.

After the definite victory of Bolshevism in Russia, even the Jews had to submit to the Soviet régime. Many Russians did the same: White generals, high Tsarist officials, scientists, senators. Some of these excused their submission as a patriotic duty, others as an act of material necessity. All the Jewish traders, book-keepers, typists and so on, who, on trade being nationalised, were transformed into government employees, are no more Bolsheviks than corresponding officials in Sweden are Socialists under a Socialist Government.

A boundless misery swept over the Jewish as over the non-Jewish bourgeoisie, but as the Jewish population consisted to a far greater extent than the Christian of middle-class folk—two-fifths of the Jews of Russia lived by private trade, one-third by handicrafts—the putting in force of Communism meant a greater catastrophe for the Jews than for any other section of the Russian people. For in Soviet Russia the private traders constitute a class that is barely tolerated and subject to every kind of persecution, and the private craftsmen are little better off. In the public workshops, which are supplied with raw materials through the State, not one-third of the Jewish craftsmen were employed at the close of 1929. It throws a lurid light on the situation that no less than 35 per cent of Soviet Russia's 2,600,000 Jews belong to the category of *déclassés*, while the corresponding figure for the non-Jewish population is between 5 and 6 per cent. The *déclassés*, who include the former bourgeoisie, have no votes, no right to receive bread-cards, no right to hold offices, to be engaged as workmen in factories, to send their children to industrial schools, and so on. Their distress is appalling. It is regarded as certain that the whole Jewish town population of South Russia would have died of starvation in 1922, if the Jewish-American Joint Distribution Committee had not brought them assistance in the nick of time.

The fight against private trade is, as Boriz Brutzkus has pointed out, largely a fight against Russian Jewry. In fact, in the two Western Soviet republics, the Ukraine and West Russia, the Jews are practically the only representatives of private trade. Every concession to this trade therefore meant a better chance of survival for very large sections of distressed Russian Jewry. Thus during the two and a half years covered by the " New Economic Policy " (N.E.P.), that is, to the autumn of 1923, many Jews were saved who would otherwise have perished. But the reaction was terrible. At the beginning of 1924 the Government decided on a drastic anti-capitalist course, whereupon the O.G.P.U., the successor of the Cheka, came down upon the newly arisen, mainly Jewish bourgeoisie, confiscated their property and deported them by the thousand. A new N.E.P.-period, called " Neonep," which began in the spring of 1925, only lasted till the autumn of 1926. As has been rightly emphasised by the Nazi writer Fehst (see below), it was none other than the Jewish Bolshevik leaders Trotsky, Zinoviev, Kamenev, and Radek who pressed the doctrinaire anti-capitalist point of view in opposition to Lenin and others, who were inclined to a more realistic and opportunist policy.

As everyone knows, the Jews are strongly represented in the Soviet Russian bureaucracy and in the Komintern, especially in the higher grades, though by no means to the extent that is asserted in many tendentious antisemitic publications. (According to the fantastic statistics in Ford's *The International Jew*, in the year 1922 no fewer than 17 of the 22 people's commissars were Jews, whereas actually at that time there were in all 18 people's commissars, of whom two were Jews, Trotsky and Dovgalevsky.) The Jews, who mostly live in the towns, compose—the figures date from 1927—11 per cent of the Russian town population. But while, of course, the Russian country population need hardly be considered in the matter of public service, the Jews did not hold 11 per cent of official posts, but only 7 per cent, and both in the Ukraine and in White Russia the non-Jewish town population supplied a larger percentage of officials and government servants than the Jewish. (In 1930 the Jews composed 22·7 per cent of the town population of the Ukraine, Jewish government servants 20·5 per cent. Of the town population of White Russia they composed 40·1 per cent, of its officials 30·6 per cent.) As, however, the Jews, in spite of their only composing 1·8 per cent of the Russian population, play so important a part in politics and constitute 3·5 per cent of the Communist Party—49,627 members in the year 1929—we may reasonably inquire what may be the causes of this apparently strange fact.

One of them, perhaps the most important, has already been alluded to: the Russo-Jewish population is predominantly a town population, and, even more important, one that can read and write. This was of immense significance when the Bolsheviks had to set up a bureaucracy in place of the Tsarist and generally to provide substitutes for all the murdered or banished intelligentsia. Up to the close of the first Five-Year Plan one and a half million new experts of different kinds were appointed ! During and after the Bolshevik revolution, when the last became the first, it was quite natural that the Jewish " intelligentsia " and " semi-intelligentsia," which under Tsarism had been kept down and thus made radical, should come to the surface, and when the anti-Bolshevist movements of 1919 assumed a pronounced antisemitic character, a number of Jews, till then non-Bolshevist, were forced by circumstances to go over to Lenin and his men or to take service under them. Among the Russian proletariat, who upheld Bolshevism, the Jewish formed an aristocracy of education. Its place was thereby determined. Lenin himself gratefully acknowledged the great part played in particular by those Jews who were brought into the interior of Russia during the war, when it was necessary to fill the places in the abandoned chanceries. It is quite possible that without their help the Bolsheviks would not have been able to master the machinery of administration and thus would have succumbed to the White armies. This, as the situation then was, would have resulted in a war of extermination against the whole of Russian Jewry (which was predominantly anti-Bolshevist). But otherwise it was no advantage from a Jewish point of view that so many of the Bolshevik leaders were Jews.

The Bolshevist Jews belong to that category of Jewish Radicals whom we described in the last chapter as " without history." Even before the revolution they professed internationalism. They feel themselves to be the champions of the proletariat; some of them indeed feel as Russians and not as Jews. When after the triumph of Bolshevism Trotsky was waited upon by a deputation from the Jewish congregation of Petrograd headed by the two rabbis and the Cadet

Vinaver and asked to resign his position as a leader in view of the terrible reprisals to which his kinsmen would otherwise be exposed, he replied: " Go you home to your Jews and tell them I am not a Jew and I care nothing for the Jews and their fate." This is typical. It therefore amounts to a grotesque distortion of truth when Trotsky, Zinoviev and their like are described in antisemitic literature as possessed of a feeling of Jewish solidarity, as aiming indeed at Jewish world dominion, or when their Terror is represented as " Jewish " revenge.

A chapter in the passion of Soviet Russia's Jewry which was much discussed, especially in the Jewish Press of the 1920's, deals with the activities of the " Yevsektia " (Yevreskaya Sekziya), that is the Jewish section of the Communist Party. As this section, in contrast to the sections of the other nations of Soviet Russia, had no autonomous territory to administer, it concentrated on extirpating the Jewish petty tradesmen and combating the Jewish religion. In doing so it was naturally pursuing positive aims. But its methods were brutal in the extreme, as though its leaders had feared to be accused of partisanship by their Russian colleagues, and were obviously coloured by the old hostility of the ultra-radical Jews towards the Jewish bourgeoisie and the Jewish religion. When in their anti-clerical doctrinairianism they transformed the synagogues wholesale into workmen's clubs, liquidated the Jewish congregations and the Jewish religious, cultural and philanthropic institutions, they actually aimed a deathblow at the whole existence of Russian Jewry. All Hebrew educational work is forbidden. War is declared on the Hebrew language, partly as being the language of a cult, partly—in the case of modern Hebrew—as a bourgeois luxury product. All Hebrew books and newspapers are prohibited, irrespective of their contents. Against Zionism, which was adopted by a very large proportion of Russian Jewry, a relentless war of extermination has been carried on. This movement, which was officially declared to be of middle-class reactionary character and a tool in the hands of British imperialists, has been simply suppressed. Its leaders have been to a great extent deported. Many have been driven to commit suicide. No wonder the dissolution of the Yevsektia in 1930 was felt as a liberation by Russian Jewry, who had every reason to acknowledge the truth of the saying that there is no enemy like those of one's own kin.

It is obvious that the Bolshevist leaders of Jewish birth are not to be regarded in any way as protectors of Jewish interests or as leaders of the Jewish people, whose existence or extinction is a matter of indifference to them and in whose fate they do not feel themselves bound up. But to the great masses of Russians they appear in the first place as Jews, and the ill-will towards the Bolshevik régime which is widespread even among those masses has had for one of its results a gradually growing Antisemitism. The fact that ever since Lenin came into power antisemitic agitation has been prohibited as counter-revolutionary is not sufficient to prevent Antisemitism from spreading, seeing that the Russian workers, especially in times of unemployment, wish to keep the factory jobs for themselves and the peasants dislike seeing Russian land in the hands of non-Russian farmers. But foreign countries too, where a great deal is heard of the Jewish Bolsheviks and their influence but very little of the Russo-Jewish masses and their misery, have been given a false picture of " Jewish " Bolshevism. The Nazi agitation has contributed to this and does so still.

This also applies to Nazi " scholarship." A book published in 1934 by Herman Fehst, lecturer at the German political college, and entitled *Bolschewismus und Judentum—Das Jüdische Element in der Führerschaft des Bolschewismus*, makes this very clear. It is true that the publishers, that is, the " Institute for the Study of the Jewish Question " and the " League of German Anti-Communist Associations," declare in their preface that Bolshevism must not be conceived as the result of a Jewish " intrigue " (" *eine jüdische Mache* "), which by the way is a remarkable Nazi admission, nor does the author deny that Lenin and Stalin, both non-Jews, must be regarded as real dictators; although he endeavours, on frail enough grounds, to make it seem credible or at least not incredible that Lenin's maternal grandfather was of Jewish birth, and describes Stalin's power as waning and about to be supplanted by that of the Jewish Kaganovitch. In his first chapter too, he rightly lays stress on the Jewish Bolsheviks having broken with Judaism, both religious and national. Nevertheless we are given to understand that they still hold together in their quality of Jews and try to favour what is specifically Jewish; in fact, they are supposed to revel in the thought of the Jews' great power and to do what they can to further it. Even the Yevsektia is depicted in this spirit. If two Bolshevist factions are in conflict, both with Jews at their head, the author sees in this an example of the Jews' " well-known policy of partition," whereby they are assured of victory whatever the outcome may be ! We are given the impression that, if they came together in private, they would talk things over in the manner of the " Elders of Zion," and it is expressly asserted, though without any attempt at proof, that they have the fullest support of World Jewry. The author assures us that everything nationally Russian is being extirpated, while everything Jewish is praised and promoted, as the result of the purposeful efforts of the Bolshevist Jews. As nonsense of this sort finds credit with a person of scientific training—the book is evidently written in good faith—we need not be surprised that similar views are widely disseminated among the masses in Russia. It may be mentioned by the way that the Jews are described as monsters of malignity and that the book closes with a prophecy of the fall of " Jewish " Bolshevism and its replacement by a Russian National-Socialism.

In justice it should be added that not all German National-Socialists are so lacking in discernment as Fehst. In the

August 1934 number of the Nazi review *Erwachendes Europa*, published later than his book, a writer emphasises that the Jews of Soviet Russia " are by no means the real rulers, but occupy almost everywhere the second or third rank. On account of their linguistic ability and suppleness alone they are the most skilful negotiators with foreign countries, and they are useful as advisers and assistants in economic affairs and finance. . . . They are the executive organs, but are far from being the leaders."

.   .   .   .

The Tsarist Government, which desired to annihilate Russian Jewry, welded it together; the Bolshevist, which makes no distinctions among the various peoples of Russia, has to all seeming brought it to the edge of the abyss. About half its numbers live on the verge of starvation, on doles, without a future. Jewish youth receives no Jewish education, though perhaps there may still be some Yiddish-speaking schools. It is becoming alien and indifferent to all things Jewish, apparently doomed before long to be wiped out as Jews. A great number of the young are unemployed and receive no industrial training. No doubt the Government has tried to rescue the most proletarian-minded of the ruined Jewish masses, partly by wholesale colonisation in the Crimea and in the Far East, of which more in a subsequent chapter.

But even if in this way it should succeed in saving a relatively large number of families, this will scarcely suffice to check the threatened extinction of Russian Jewry. This can only be averted by a peaceful liquidation of Communism. If the Red régime should be overthrown, it would probably be replaced by a White régime with resultant pogroms on a grand scale.

Simon Dubnov, the greatest historian of Russian Jewry, who is now living in exile, sums up the situation of the Russian Jews in the following words: " Two and a half million men and women are placed between an appalling present and an even more appalling future, faced by the choice between a Red and a White dictatorship, between dying out and dying a violent death. Never before has the Jewish people been confronted with a more terrible alternative."

CHAPTER XVI

THE TALMUD AS AN ANTISEMITIC
ARGUMENT

THE REMAINS of ancient Israelitish literature which
have been preserved and are known as the Old Testament
reflect a development covering many centuries. In many
passages of the oldest scriptures we meet with a singularly
hard and vindictive god, a barbaric warrior spirit, a morality
which, like that of other primitive tribes, recognises as its
" neighbour " only a member of its own kindred, or at least
gives him a preference over strangers. (Even in the laws of
Vestergötland, which moreover are a relatively late production and the result of a long and in many ways impres-
sive progress in jurisprudence, it costs a great deal more to
kill a West Goth than a stranger.) In this respect the history
of the Jewish people is like that of all others. But by degrees
there appears a process which is unique in the history of the
world. The god of the warring nation makes way for an
ideal image of holiness, justice and mercy; the warrior spirit
is softened and gives place to a profound, fervent longing
for peace and humanity; national exclusiveness weakens and
yields to a universalism embracing all mankind. Even Amos
—more than seven hundred years before Christ—preached
that God cares for all peoples. " Are ye not as children of
the Ethiopians unto me, O children of Israel, saith the
Lord. Have not I brought up Israel out of the land of
Egypt? and the Philistines from Caphtor, and the Syrians
from Kir?" (Amos ix, 7). The Prophets insist that sacrifices
are as nothing compared with the spirit, and that God's

message of salvation is addressed to all peoples (Isaiah xlix, 6). In the Pentateuch it is emphasised that God loves the stranger (Deuteronomy x, 18; Deuteronomy xxvii, 19 is significant); that the stranger in Israel is to be treated like a native, since the Israelites themselves were strangers in Egypt (and therefore ought to know how hard is the lot of the stranger), or again because all men are created in God's image and descended from the same human pair, thus being brothers. This last idea, as Michael Guttmann has elucidated, was destined to be of fundamental importance in the development of Judaism. Philo's words are typical: " It is incumbent on the Jews to pray and offer sacrifice for all mankind." The vision of a mighty Jewish realm, which floated before Israel under the impression of the powerful kingdom of David, gave way to another: a Messianic kingdom of serenity, in which the nations beat their swords into ploughshares and all mankind was filled with the knowledge of God. Even Israel's hereditary enemies are included in God's great love. Proto-Isaiah in a lofty vision makes God himself stretch out his hands over them in blessing: " Blessed be Egypt my people, and Assyria the work of my hands, and Israel mine inheritance " (Isaiah xix, 25).

The noblest of all Old Testament commandments: " Thou shalt love thy neighbour as thyself," is understood by the Jew as including his relations with the non-Jewish world. The words which St. Matthew's Gospel or, more probably, a later insertion therein, puts in the mouth of Jesus: " Ye have heard that it hath been said, Thou shalt love thy neighbour, and hate thine enemy," are without any kind of support in biblical or post-biblical Jewish literature. The attempts which have been made to interpret the words as a popular maxim current among the generality of Israelites in the time of Jesus—they are thus explained in Strack-Billerbeck's *Kommentar zum neuen Testament aus Talmud und Midrasch*—have always been contested from the Jewish side.

The fall of the Jewish kingdom, the destruction of the Temple, the dispersion of the people and the resulting danger that the Jews, who considered themselves called to uphold the Torah (the doctrine), might founder in the sea of nations, led to a supreme effort to save the life of the threatened Jewish nation behind the protective ramparts of the ceremonial law. This was the beginning of the rabbinical-Talmudic epoch with the isolation and exclusivism that were forced on it by circumstances. Its chief literary product is the Babylonian Talmud, which was compiled approximately between 450 B.C. and A.D. 500. It is a voluminous work: 6,000 folio pages in Lazarus Goldschmidt's well-known German translation; in the second edition, twelve closely printed volumes, of which nine have already appeared, each of 800 to 1,000 pages. The Talmud is not a book but a whole literature, including the most varied, often contradictory, opinions on a great variety of subjects; an echo of nearly a thousand years' discussions in the schools on things great and small, lofty and lowly, expressing " the most varied shades of piety and ethical thinking, casual dialogues of a general nature, private utterances of teachers totally devoid of any binding implication " (Ehrenpreis). The Talmud has been aptly compared with a huge—uncollated—collection of minutes of discussions. It was only in the sixteenth century that a writer, Josef Karo, succeeded in producing a ritual codex compendium, the *Shulchan Aruch*, which, with a commentary, was accepted as a standard by traditionalist Jewry.

Surrounded by a hostile world, defeated, oppressed, despised, the Jews clung to the thought that in spite of all they were still God's chosen people, an idea which, as we know, was already of fundamental importance in biblical times and at a primitive stage was conceived as an alliance in a literal sense between Israel and its tribal deity, but was afterwards developed, deepened and sublimated. This, by the way, is no peculiar distinction of the Jews. In fact, " the belief in selection was expressed far more definitely and exclusively by other nations (of antiquity) than by the Israelites " (M. Guttmann). As we know, many modern nations also regard themselves as chosen or "called," in other words as being charged with a special mission among the nations. The Jews considered that their selection was concerned with religion. They felt themselves to be the preachers of ethical monotheism throughout the world, the bearers of a religious message to humanity, and in fact their greatest contribution to history has taken this form. For both Christianity and Mohammedanism are of Jewish origin. The Jewish liturgy too, is full of expressions of gratitude for Israel's selection, but always in connection with the religious and moral obligations involved therein. This implies no sort of self-glorification or depreciation of other peoples. A pagan who studies and lives according to the Torah is pronounced by the Talmud to stand higher than the high priest himself who fails to do so.

On the other hand it cannot be denied that certain parts of the Talmud are marked by a Judæocentric view of history and of the world which appear altogether strange to us, whether Jews or Christians. Simon Dubnov, who has strikingly compared this with the equally explicable but abandoned geocentric cosmology, has rightly described it as a reaction against the hatred and contempt of the surrounding world for the heretical Jewish people, against whom was laid the terrible charge of deicide. Church and State vied with each other in humiliating this people, in representing it to be iniquitous and reprobate. In the Roman laws of the fifth and sixth centuries the Jews are described as inferior, vile and infamous (*inferiores, infames, turpes*), their worship as a blasphemous assembly (*sacrilegi coetus*), and marriage with a Jew as shameful cohabitation (*consortium turpitudinis*). The Fathers of the Church in their preaching and writings denounced the Jewish religion as a work of Satan and the Jews as destined for eternal torment in hell. Happily the Jews did not reply in the same tone. But in the face of this constant talk of their unworthiness they overemphasised their position as God's elect, persevering in their proud isolation. Only in this way was it possible for them to bear the burden of humiliation without being spiritually destroyed.

It is natural that there is no lack in the Talmud of bitter words against Israel's tormentors and oppressors, that not all of the 2,500 men of the most varied temperaments and views who had a hand in its composition are broad-minded, magnanimous, forgiving and noble. No nation that has been attacked has ever been able to rise to a supermundane gentleness, not even the highly civilised nations of the World War. We cannot therefore reasonably ask this of the Jews of late antiquity and the Dark Ages. But bitterness against the oppressors is not the prevailing mark of the Talmud. On the contrary: it is there insisted that not only the Jews, but the pious of all nations shall enter into salvation, a saying referable to the first or second century A.D. which has been adopted in the codices of the Jewish religion, based on the Talmud, and has thus become a normal part of Jewish doctrine. And among the pious are counted all those who keep what are called the commandments of Noah; that is, the precepts which God was believed, before the Sinai revelation, to have revealed to the sons of Noah; that is, to all men: observation of the principle of rectitude, prohibition of the worship of idols, of the denial of God, murder, theft, unchastity and the eating of blood. The pious and wise non-Jew is also honoured as one filled with God's spirit. " I call God to witness," so runs a rabbinical saying even earlier than the Talmud, " that both the heathen and the Israelite, the man and the woman, the man-servant and the maid-servant can only become partakers of the holy spirit through moral actions." The biblical reservations regarding the Moabites, Edomites, Ammonites and Egyptians are explained away by stating that after Sennacherib the nations became inter-mingled. As early as the third century Rabbi Jochanan taught that the heathens outside

Palestine were not to be regarded as such: they were only carrying on the customs inherited from their ancestors. Thus the term idolators, to which were attached the inhuman enactments of a bygone age, was so restricted as to be practically abolished. What this meant was formulated by a thirteenth-century Talmud commentator, Rabbi Menachem Meiri, in the following sentence: " Any member of a people which leads a moral and religious life " (keeps the commandments of Noah) " and worships God in some way, ought, even if its faith differs from ours, to be regarded in every respect as an Israelite." Any injury to the rights of the foreigner is an injury to God's. All things are to be done which contribute to the glorification of God's name; all that tends to the profanation of his name is to be avoided. Honesty in all dealings with Jews and non-Jews alike is prescribed as an imperative duty. Any fraud implies a profanation of God's name.

The distinction made by the authors of the Talmud between Israel and " the nations," that is, non-Jews, has its counterpart in the attitude of Christendom towards the Jewish and later towards the Mohammedan world, and never stifled the universalist idea. According to the Talmud, God caused all mankind to be descended from a single human pair, so that no one might be able to say to another: " My father is nobler than thine," and God forbade the angels to rejoice over the destruction of the Egyptian host in the Red Sea: " The work of my hands is drowning in the sea and you would sing a song ! " The saying of Hillel to the pagan who wished to learn the whole Torah off-hand, is widely known: " Do not unto thy neighbour that which is hateful to thyself. That is the whole doctrine; all else is explanation." Everyone who has any idea at all of the way Jews are brought up knows that such teaching as this and above all the venerable Old Testament commandment: " Love thy neighbour as thyself" indicate all over the world the attitude of Judaism to non-Jewish humanity.

We have already touched upon the campaign of persecution against the Talmud which has played a great part
in the history of Antisemitism ever since Eisenmenger's
notorious *Entdecktes Judentum*. On some occasions it has
attracted general attention, especially during the early
1880's, when Professor Rohling of Vienna, inspired to some
extent by the " revelations " of a Jewish renegade of criminal
type, Aron Briman (" Dr. Justus ") was actively engaged in
Antisemitic and anti-Talmudic literary production, which
resulted in a celebrated law case and a crushing defeat for
the falsifiers and slanderers. Several of the most eminent
scholars of that time were called before the court as experts.
Their sworn statements, accompanied by about five hundred
literally translated quotations from the Talmud, are to this
day an excellent authority for anyone wishing to inquire
into the authenticity of the accusations made against the
Talmud. Their evidence is all the more weighty as the experts were Christian theologians or Christian orientalists
of world-wide reputation, such as Nöldecke, Wünsche,
Strack and Franz Delitzsch. The first-named of these
described Rohling's translations as " a piece of baseness,"
and Strack characterised them as " a singular combination
of ignorance, blind hatred and malevolence." When Rohling
declared that he took his oath to the correctness of his
translations, Strack replied, in his pamphlet against the
ritual murder lie, *Das Blut im Glauben und Aberglauben der
Menschkeit* (fourth edition, 1892): " I publicly accuse
Rohling of perjury and gross falsification." Delitzsch described Briman's work as " a network of infernal lies " and
flung these indignant words at him and Rohling: " But the
God of truth still lives, and exalted at his right hand, Christ
still lives, who will know how to defend his honour against the
slanderers of his name. . . . A Rohling and a Justus (who
think they are serving him with their lies) shall die through
their lies."

But here, as so often in the history of national hatred, it
Sᴀ

proved that those blinded by hatred pay no attention to arguments and facts. The falsified quotations from the Talmud continued to be used for purposes of agitation, as though they had never been exposed. It is significant that the assertion (described as untrue even by Eisenmenger) that on the Day of Atonement, the Jews consider themselves released from all oaths sworn during the preceding year, still crops up occasionally as a " proved " fact. A Jewish author, Alexander Guttmann, has collected and illustrated under the title of " Talmud Quotations Exposed " (*Enthüllte Talmudcitate*) a hundred and ten of the quotations from the Talmud or from literature based thereon most commonly used for propaganda purposes, according to which the Jews are supposed to regard all non-Jews as their enemies, nay, as beasts, against whom everything is permissible: robbery, murder, perjury, rape—crimes which of course have not been approved by any Talmudic teacher, but on the contrary condemned, no matter against whom they may be committed. For the general public knows extremely little about the Talmud; and this applies to the Jews of our day (except the orthodox Eastern Jews). These know no more about this voluminous literature than the average Christian knows about the writings of the Church Fathers. Most of them have never even seen a Talmud. It has also to be considered that the Talmud is extremely difficult of interpretation, as, for one thing, its Hebrew or Aramaic text is unpointed (without vowels), and for another, its whole world is so different from ours. This provides an easy task not only for falsifiers but also for perverters of the text. They tear quotations from their context, cite only the beginning or the end, according to their requirements, take the statements of only one side from the " protocols of discussion " and exhibit them as a Talmudic " commandment," wilfully overlook the psychological background of the quotations, make it appear that the sayings directed against idolaters refer to those who profess the Christian religion, and so on.

They pounce down on offensive passages—there are not many of them, by the way—or on such as they falsely consider offensive, and make it appear as if these were dominating or guiding principles for the Jews of our day. It is as though one were to judge Christianity from the fanatical heretic-burners of the Middle Ages, or the Protestants of our time from the most orthodox zealots of the sixteenth or from the witch trials of the seventeenth century. What cannot one " prove " by such methods ! Rohling, who hated Protestantism as well as Judaism, " proved " in the same fashion that the Reformers were morally defective, and declared in his book *Der Antichrist und das Ende der Welt:* " Wherever Protestantism sets its foot, the grass withers. A spiritual void, the deterioration of holy morals, a terrible desperation of heart are its fruits. A Protestant who lives according to Luther's precepts is a monster."

Professor Ismar Elbogen has recounted a typical episode of 1920, when Adolf Dinter had published his notorious novel (of which 250,000 copies were afterwards sold) *Die Sünde wider das Blut,* wherein the Jews were exhibited as Satanic race-polluters, living in accordance with the Talmudic saying: " The seed of a non-Jew is to be regarded as that of an animal." This sentence by no means implies what Dinter believed, but had reference to the legal position of Jewish women violated by non-Jews and to that of their children, a problem which not infrequently became actual in view of the outlawed position of Jews in the Middle Ages, and the formula itself was a reflection of Ezekiel xxiii, 20. Professor Strack addressed a letter to Elbogen asking for information about the quotation in question, which by the way, is not to be found in the Talmud itself but in one of its commentaries, adding that he was aware of the existence in the Talmud of temperamental utterances, which were not to be weighed too nicely. Thus Strack, one of the world's most eminent Christian Talmudists, was unacquainted with this quotation, as was also Elbogen, one of the leading Jewish scholars of the time, who for forty years had made a study of the Talmud and had passed his examination as a rabbi, twenty years before. But Dinter evidently lived in the belief that the sentence in question, which he grossly misconstrued, was characteristic of the Talmud and a sort of guiding star to the Jews.

The falsified and perverted quotations from the Talmud are naturally intended to exhibit the Jews in the most detestable light, especially as given to self-glorification and cruelty, qualities which as a rule the disseminators of national hatred are fond of attributing to their opponents. It is significant that the Bolshevik Terror is often represented as "Jewish." We have already referred several times to the alleged overrating of self. As a rule it is probable that the Jews, at least the assimilated ones, are inclined to go to the opposite extreme, a result of their often regarding themselves with the eyes of a surrounding world which is ignorant of and antipathetic to Jewish nature and Jewish history. It is extremely rare to come upon any expression of Jewish chauvinism in modern Jewish literature. But of all accusations against the Jews that of cruelty is perhaps the most unjust. Not only is it the fact that crimes of cruelty are particularly rare among the Jews, as is shown by criminal statistics. It is significant that the authors of the Talmud, who of course, were not able formally to repeal a biblical commandment, out of respect for human life stipulated on such evidence in capital cases as made the death penalty practically a dead letter. Kindness and clemency towards all creatures is a virtue constantly inculcated in the Talmud and in post-Talmudic literature; kindness and clemency towards Jews and non-Jews, and especially towards all who are weak and suffering, towards strangers, widows, fatherless, and not least towards animals. This last deserves to be emphasised, since the Jewish method of slaughter, prescribed in the Talmud, is often described as cruel, even as the outcome of "Asiatic sadism," in spite of the declarations of a number of modern physiologists and veterinary authorities that it is just as merciful as the slaughter-mask, and that until the latter apparatus was invented and brought into use it was undoubtedly the most humane in the world. But it was not only in the case of beasts that were to be slaughtered that the Talmud prescribed the greatest forbearance it was possible to exercise. In the spirit of the Old Testament tradition it is directed, for example, that no one is to sit down to table before his beasts have been fed, and all hunting for pleasure is forbidden, as is even the keeping of animals in cages. Tenderness towards animals is one of the distinctive marks of the pious—Proverbs xii, 10—and Israel has been characterised with good reason as the world's oldest society for the protection of animals.

There are no secret Jewish scriptures or doctrines. Professor Strack, who is, as we have said, one of the greatest Christian Talmudic scholars of the present day, states in his *Einleitung in Talmud und Midrasch* (1921): "Judaism does not possess any written work or oral tradition whatsoever that is inaccessible to Christians. The Jews are at no pains to conceal anything from the Christians, nor could they do so. For the correctness of this statement I pledge my honour as a man and a scholar." Nor is the Talmud a book with seven seals. He who cannot study it in the original tongue can do so in translation, and the curious has at his disposal an abundant literature by Christian and Jewish Talmud specialists. But the anti-Talmudic lampoons issued from the workshops of antisemitic amateurs are valueless to him who seeks information about the true state of the case. The racy words which Johann Reuchlin, one of the greatest of German sixteenth-century humanists, flung at the Antisemites of his day on their attacking the Talmud, have lost none of their force: "The Talmud is not there for any scurvy fellow to run over it with unwashen feet and say he knows it all."

CHAPTER XVII

THE JEWS AND THE "PRODUCTIVE" INDUSTRIES

As we know, the Jews are thought to have a special turn for trade. Broadly speaking this is probably correct, but only as a generalisation. In the first place it should be noted that the Jews present an extraordinary diversity of types, a thing which is constantly overlooked. As is the case with other peoples, a great number of them are altogether lacking in commercial talent. The more or less "unpractical" students and dreamers, the Jewish "idealists" ill-equipped for the struggle for existence, are and have always been legion. The Talmudic scholar, who devotes his whole life to study without a thought of gain, has been of frequent occurrence even to our own day, and his spiritual descendants are numerous even among modern Jews. There are also many Jews whom nature designed for labourers and craftsmen, but who have been forced by circumstances to devote themselves to shopkeeping. Furthermore, it must be noted that other ancient peoples who have reached a high degree of economic civilisation, such as the Armenians, the Syrians, the Indians, the Greeks and the Chinese, have a pronounced gift for trade, or, to put it more accurately, have a mentality which adapts them for trade among other things. For, as Ruppin insists, man has no innate gift for any particular occupation. Our talents in the beginning are not directed towards any definite goal; only life can give man an object for his activity. This also applies in the highest degree to the Jews. The causes of their becoming a commercial people are above all of a historical nature. They did not become a predominantly commercial people until practically all other occupations were closed to them.

The view that owing to their spiritual disposition and to its noblest product, the Jewish religion, the Jews are peculiarly predisposed to capitalist methods and theories, has found its most talented supporter in the German political economist Werner Sombart. According to his striking work *Die Juden und das Wirtschaftsleben* (1911), long before the birth of economic liberalism, while the Western nations still adhered, officially at least, to the doctrine proclaimed by the Church that the profit on goods must not be greater than was warranted by the cost of production ("*justum praetium*"), and that the pursuit of riches was sinful, the Jews both in theory and practice had adopted the principles which later found general acceptance, as to free competition, advertising, the legitimacy of speculative profits, as well as the commercialising of industry and its liberation from all religious considerations. Max Weber had previously maintained that the Puritans were the fathers of modern capitalism, since they were the first to regard the pursuit of the greatest possible pecuniary profit as conduct agreeable to God and success in this field as a token of divine grace. According to Sombart it is the Jews who are the real creators of modern capitalism. He describes them as possessed of a way of thinking detached from instinctive life, as a race indifferent to metaphysics, determined in its actions by gross considerations of utility, predisposed by its whole racial mentality first to conceive and then actively to contribute to the formation of the capitalist system. He considers the expulsion of the Jews from Spain and Portugal at the close of the Middle Ages and the settling of the emigrants in Northern Europe to be the real cause of the former countries' decline, of the prosperity of the commercial States of Northern Europe and of the appearance of modern capitalism. " Israel passes over Europe like the sun," writes Sombart; "wherever it appears new life shoots up, but when it is withdrawn all that once flourished withers away."

Sombart's book gave rise to an extensive scholarly literature on the importance of the Jews in the development of commerce and particularly of capitalism, and on the Jews' ethical-religious attitude to problems connected therewith. In the latter respect we may now regard Sombart's book as totally mistaken. The criticism, mild indeed in its form, which the German-Jewish religious philosopher Julius Guttmann devoted to Sombart's work was particularly annihilating, but the political economist and economic historians were scarcely less severe. The Nestor of German political economy, Lujo Brentano, proved in his book *Die Anfänge des modernen Kapitalismus* (1916) that the capitalist spirit, as Sombart conceives it, was fully developed (without Jewish co-operation) as early as the time of the fourth Crusade and that even then, knights and burgesses alike were scarcely to be surpassed for greed of gain and relentless exploitation. The Jews have at times played a significant part in economic life, especially in the working of the credit system and the expansion of international trade; but there can now be no doubt that Sombart exaggerated their importance enormously. That Jews, Moors, Huguenots and Puritans played so conspicuous and to some extent so similar a part in the field of commerce cannot be fortuitous: no other arena was open to the Jews, and the same is true, though not in the same degree, of other dissenters.

· · · · · · ·

Before the Babylon captivity the Jews were a nation of herdsmen, craftsmen and agriculturists. The last-named were held in highest esteem. God himself instructs the husbandman (Isaiah xxviii, 26). Everyone who has read the Bible knows what importance is there attached to cornfields, fig-trees, olive-groves and vineyards, as also to flocks and herds and pastures. The tribe of Zebulon was famous for its sailors, that of Issachar for its porters; both categories were often employed in the Phœnician service. Handicrafts are of later date than cattle-breeding and agriculture. Here foreigners were the teachers, in the same way as German craftsmen taught the Swedes in the earlier Middle Ages; but soon native men became metal-workers, potters, weavers, masons, carpenters, and so on. On the other hand trade was still insignificant. Ancient Israel, to borrow Max Weber's happy phrase, was in all essentials " a confederacy of free peasants," a democratic republic even under the monarchy, supported by a free commonalty, divided into tribes. Like Switzerland, ancient Palestine was a small, free peasant country, squeezed in between great Powers, and in the centuries before Christ the sons of Jewish peasants, like the Swiss of a later age, often took service in foreign armies, where they were valued for their loyalty. Sombart's view, that the Jews were never agriculturists, not even in pre-exilian Palestine, nor in Babylonia, is completely refuted by a great number of inquirers and moreover is contradicted by the direct testimony of the Bible.

Only in exile, in Babylonia and in the Hellenistic world, did the Jews become traders to any great extent. It came about gradually. The Jews of Babylonia were always agriculturists for the greater part, as were those of Palestine. Even in the second century A.D. there were numbers of Jews in Egypt who lived as landowners, tenant farmers and agriculturists.

Babylon, a country which had reached a high state of economic development, saw the beginning of the evolution of the Jews into a commercial people; or, as Brentano expressed it: " the importance of the people of Israel in economic history begins " with the Babylonian captivity. But Alexandria was to be the only great Jewish centre of trade in antiquity. That city also contained great numbers of Jewish craftsmen; in the synagogue there were special benches for weavers, smiths of different kinds, workers in gold and silver, and others.

The transformation from agriculture to commerce and moneylending was regarded with disfavour by Jewish moralists even after Jews had been established for centuries as traders in all important Hellenistic cities. All shopkeeping was despised by the old rabbis, in fact it was placed on a level with robbery; and usury was looked upon as sin whether the borrower were Jew or not. But commercialisation could not be checked. There was no room for the surplus Jewish population in Palestine. Young Jews, who in earlier centuries would have served abroad as mercenaries, now emigrated as traders. In more recent times the Swiss afford a parallel, and an even closer one is furnished by the Scots, who are often called England's Jews on account of their important share in the economic life of Great Britain. When Alexander the Great and the Hellenistic rulers who succeeded him had brought about a commercial union between Europe and the Near East, the situation of Palestine became advantageous commercially, and their exile led the Jews to the centres of European trade. At that time there were no United States or Canada, countries with virgin soil waiting for the immigrant. The Hellenistic kingdoms were highly developed economically. Moreover the Jews, after the overthrow of their State, had no political organisation capable of facilitating a wholesale Jewish colonisation outside Palestine. They were obliged to flock to the cities—like the Russian, Italian and Eastern Jewish emigrants in pre-war America. Thus the change in a choice of occupation to which the history of the Jews in antiquity bears witness are in no way exceptional in their implications, especially as during the whole period a very large section of them appears to have been still engaged in agriculture. It did not occur to anyone in antiquity or in the early Middle Ages that the Jews had a special turn for trade.

In the Germanic States of the Dark Ages, conditions were similar. According to Ignaz Schipper the Jews were far more important as transmitters of the relatively high agricultural civilisation of the Romans than in the domain of commerce. Until far on in the Middle Ages we find Jewish agriculturists in Europe; in Spain, France, Italy and other countries. It is significant that the very first Jewish colonies in Poland were, as Schipper has shown, more agricultural than mercantile in character. In the Byzantine empire, the Jews were prominent as craftsmen, especially as silk-weavers; and the same is true of the Jewish blacksmiths and coppersmiths of Sicily, the Jewish weavers, dyers, goldsmiths, armourers and so on in the Spanish peninsula and in Southern France.

The Talmud sings the praises of labour. " Labour stands high, it honours its master." The rabbis ought to devote a third part of their day to manual labour. Craftsmanship is praised: " He who does not have his son taught a craft is like a father who brings up his son to be a robber." A number of the greatest Talmudic teachers were craftsmen or simple labourers: stonemasons, woodcutters—such was Hillel—builders' labourers, shoemakers, smiths, joiners, et cetera. Spinoza the lens-polisher is a typically Jewish case.

We have already told how the social and economic situation of the Jews was radically transformed during the Crusades; how they became, or rather were forced to become a nation for the most part of petty tradesmen, middlemen and moneylenders, a fluctuating element among the settled population of Europe. As a rule they did not venture to settle in the country districts. In most countries they were forbidden to acquire land—in Sweden the prohibition was not abolished until 1860—and the threat of expulsion, which continually hung over their heads, made it necessary for them to place their estate in floating capital. During the earlier commercialised centuries of the modern age, new opportunities were opened to the Jews, but almost exclusively in the mercantile sphere. Only after the gradual achievement of Jewish emancipation were non-mercantile careers thrown open to them in most countries. They then consisted in the whole of Central and Western Europe mainly of town-dwellers and belonged as a rule to the middle class. This to a great extent determined and still determines their choice of an occupation.

In the non-antisemitic countries, the Jews' choice of a profession tends more and more to follow the same lines as that of the non-Jewish town-dwelling middle class. The Jews now assert themselves even in callings which formerly were by custom closed to Jews in many countries after their emancipation. I take one example among many. The Jewish population of France during the World War amounted to 95,000. But Jewish generals on the active list of the French army amounted to fourteen, colonels to forty-six, and officers of lower rank were also numerous. The high command of the French army testified officially to their character in these terms: a talent for organisation, a distinguished bearing, resolution, intrepidity, brilliant ability as commanders, contempt of death, coolness in the greatest danger, a shining example to their men, reckless daring in the most perilous undertakings.

In Eastern Europe, where economic development has followed a course of its own, the Jews' occupational distribution shows great divergences from that of Central and Western Europe; but practically everywhere it is one-sided, or, if we like to call it so, " abnormal "; though it should be remarked that this is the result of a process in which the Jews more than other peoples have been the object rather than the subject. If we consider the Jews of the whole world as a unity, the abnormality of the situation will doubtless be less apparent, since among them all occupational groups are relatively abundantly occupied, although the proportions between them differ from the ordinary.

Trade still plays a very important part, but it is by no means so paramount as before emancipation. In Soviet Russia, 60·2 per cent of the Jewish population follows non-mercantile occupations; in Subcarpathian-Russia, which was ceded by Hungary to Czechoslovakia in 1920, 60·9 per cent; in Rumania, 49·8 per cent; in Poland, 49·3 per cent; in Hungary, 45·8 per cent; in Slovakia, 43·9 per cent; in Latvia, 38·4 per cent; in Bohemia-Moravia, 34·1 per cent, and in Germany, 31·6 per cent. Thus of all these seven millions of Jews, more than half make their living in non-mercantile occupations. This is also the case with the Jews of France and Belgium, where the majority of the Jewish congregations is made up of immigrant Eastern Jews, who are largely labourers. In Amsterdam, where a great part of the Jews have been engaged for centuries in diamond-cutting, the corresponding figure is 65 per cent. Of the Jews in the United States, about half are thought to be employed in industry and 60 per cent in all to be engaged in non-mercantile occupations. The great number of craftsmen among the Eastern Jews is striking. Those living in Poland-Russia in 1898 were estimated at over half a million, with their dependants, 1,793,937; that is, as has been mentioned in another connection, 35·43 per cent of the total Jewish population. Among the Jewish population of Galicia in 1910, handicrafts and industry were two and a half times more numerously represented than among the non-Jewish. Of the craftsmen of Rumania in 1908, no less than 19·6 per cent were Jews, 25,184 out of 127,841. The smiths of Lithuania are as a rule Jews. In 1921, 31·6 per cent of Poland's wage-earning Jews were engaged in handicrafts and industry. In America, the number of Jewish craftsmen before the War was estimated at approximately 300,000.

The Eastern Jews are largely industrial workers. In Poland, where the Jews constitute 10·4 per cent of the population, they account for 14·6 per cent of the country's workers; in Rumania the corresponding figures are 4·5 per cent and 10·5 per cent; in Subcarpathian-Russia, 15·4 per cent and 20 per cent. In Bohemia, on the other hand, the corresponding figures are 1·2 per cent and 0·2 per cent, and in Germany, 1 per cent and 0·3 per cent.

It is therefore incorrect to say that the majority of Jews

follow mercantile occupations. (It must be added that the term " unproductive " as applied to these occupations is extremely misleading.) But at any rate, Jewish occupational distribution is in many respects unfortunate and in need of reformation. Doubtless it need not be regarded as in itself a bad thing that the occupational distribution of the Jews does not coincide in all points with that of the non-Jewish world; that a proportionally far greater number of them than of their Christian fellow-countrymen are business men, lawyers, doctors, artists and journalists, in certain countries academic professors also, although this too may obviously involve certain risks. The disquieting factors are, first that Jewish occupations in Eastern Europe are overcrowded and that partly as a result of this, a huge Jewish proletariat has been created which is in the greatest need of productivisation; secondly, that the Jews have become predominantly a town-dwelling people, more than that, a people inhabiting great cities; thirdly and above all, that as a consequence of this they have lost touch with the land, which is a misfortune alike from a hygienic and from a psychological point of view. For the nervous, intellectual town-dweller is not fitted to be the nucleus of a nation. The instinctive element resulting from the tie with nature cannot be rationalised away without detriment to a people.

The productivisation of the Jewish masses, which is the essential antecedent to a general Jewish regeneration, physical and spiritual, has in the main followed two lines: it has been sought—above all through industrial schools and the granting of credit—to transform young men not yet trained to a craft, or those who have no craft, such as Eastern Jews who make their living as hawkers, into competent craftsmen, or else to settle them as agriculturists. In the former case, it was a question of continuing a never interrupted Eastern Jewish tradition, in the latter of reviving one abandoned centuries ago. Before the World War, apart from the great annual emigration, it was above all the transference of young men to qualified handicraft and, though on a smaller scale, to industry, which contributed to keep Eastern Jewry above water.

That the Eastern Jews in general prefer handicraft to factory work is due in the first place to their feeling more at home in the workshop with its patriarchal conditions than in the factory, where the worker is merely a number; secondly to their liking for a non-mechanical task requiring competence and affording opportunities for personal initiative; thirdly, to the fact that the Christian workers, even in factories owned by Jews, dislike seeing Jewish workers occupy places formerly given to their Christian fellows; and fourthly, to the factories being at work on the Jewish day of rest.

Before the World War, Jewish organisations for the productivisation of the Eastern Jews had accomplished a great work. No fewer than 125,000 Jewish master-craftsmen were members of Jewish credit institutions immediately previous to the War. But the War was devastating in its effects on Eastern Jewish handicraft, and in spite of great efforts it has not been possible to restore it to its former level. The progressive industrialisation of Eastern Europe, the cutting-off of Russia from Poland, which before the War used to export thither the products of Jewish handicrafts in great quantities, the exclusion of the Jews even from handicraft, when unemployment made offers of work a privilege primarily reserved for the Christian population, all this has co-operated in the decline of Eastern Jewish handicraft. The transference of the Jewish craftsmen to factory work, which may be said to be in full swing in Russia and to some extent also in Rumania, is evidently destined to take place in Poland too, in the event of Russia again becoming an export market. This is not the place to discuss the trend in this direction at greater length. The important thing from our point of view is the Jewish effort towards productivisation.

This is shown even more plainly in the attempts to create a Jewish race of agriculturists, a struggle which at first appeared quixotic against rooted and, as many people thought, ineradicable habits. The history of European colonisation abounds in examples of difficulties proving insuperable, when, in periods of unemployment for instance, it was sought to transform a town-dwelling population into one of agriculturists, even in the case of town-dwellers, whose ancestors a few generations back had been peasants, and to whom agriculture was therefore not so entirely strange as it usually is to the Jews of our day. It may suffice to refer to the British Government's attempts after the War to place exsoldiers as colonists in Canada and Australia; an experiment the success of which was very moderate, although half as much again was estimated for every family as is the case with Jewish families established in Palestine. Experience shows that a man who is not born on the soil, ingrained with the peasant tradition, as a rule finds it hard to feel at home in agriculture. The countryman's whole rhythm of life is different from that of the town-dweller. The special difficulties accompanying colonisation have also to be considered: it is relatively easy to take over a farm or small holding that has already been worked, but exceedingly arduous to break ground as a pioneer. The colonist has to put in more work than the settled farmer, in spite of being handicapped by his whole previous life. He does not know the soil he is to work; he cannot profit by parents' experience; his children and his wife cannot give him the same help in his labours. It is not surprising that the attempts to render the Jewish masses productive by transferring them to agriculture have been far from uniformly successful. The remarkable thing is that they have prospered to some extent, and indeed, as far as Palestine is concerned, have been brilliantly successful.

Apart from a few insignificant earlier attempts, the efforts to create a Jewish agricultural population belong to the nineteenth and twentieth centuries. At the beginning of the nineteenth century, there were practically no Jewish agriculturists. Now their number with that of their families is estimated at 430,000, a result brought about in the main by certain government measures—in Russia by Alexander I, Nicholas I and the Bolsheviks—and by Jewish organisations formed to this end, of which two in particular deserve mention: the society founded by Russian Jews for emigration to Palestine and known as " Bilu " (1882), and the Jewish Colonisation Association (" Ica ") founded by Baron Hirsch in 1891.

The oldest Jewish agricultural centres are situated in South Russia, in the Governments of Cherson and Yeka- terinoslav, where in 1897 about 32,000 Jews were living as agriculturists in 38 colonies. In Bessarabia, Lithuania and the Ukraine there were also similar colonies. In 1914 the Eastern Jewish agricultural population amounted in all to 185,000 souls. The War and post-War pogroms brought great devastation on this to some extent very promising colonisation. Some colonies were entirely exterminated, two for instance in Yekaterinoslav each of 1,000 inhabitants. Only the largest colonies in Cherson had the power and the arms to defend themselves against the pogrom bands. Most of the colonies, however, are in existence, but have not re- gained their former prosperity. In 1924, a new colonising movement was started in Russia, compelled by the whole- sale pauperisation which had overtaken the Jewish trades- men and craftsmen on the enforcement of the communist system. The American Jews in particular—America had not yet been hit by the economic crisis—intervened to save what could be saved. The American Joint Distribution Commit- tee, founded specially for the rescue of Eastern Jewish vic- tims of the War, formed a special organisation for this purpose, the Agro-Joint, and other Jewish philanthropic associations also took a part. Between 1924 and 1927, 12,500 Jewish families were transferred to agriculture, about half of them in the Southern Ukraine and one-third in the Northern Crimea. The Bolshevik Government, which natu- rally approves of this movement and has even tried to further it, has nevertheless since 1929 caused much confusion and injury through various acts of interference in favour of collectivised agriculture. It intends to continue the annual transference of a great number of Jewish families to agriculture, in Biro-Bidyan, amongst other places, in the Far East near the Chinese frontier; an undertaking which, however, Agro-Joint and Ica refuse to support. The Russian peasants nevertheless dislike seeing Russian land in the occupation of Jewish colonists, especially as a great many non-Jewish Russians are in need of it.

Other Eastern Jewish agricultural centres are to be found in Poland, Lithuania, Rumania (Bessarabia) and Subcarpathian-Russia. In the last-named country, the Jewish agriculturists amount to over 25,000, nearly 27 per cent of the whole Jewish population and nearly 6 per cent of the total population. This is the highest percentage of Jewish agriculturists in the whole world. In all probability, says Arthur Ruppin, they are the most unpretending and primitive of all Jewish tillers of the soil. Their holdings are so small that they are obliged to fall back on subsidiary employments like those of the small-holders in the Norrland saw-mill districts: felling timber and carting.

Among the best results of Eastern Jewish colonisation, we may also reckon the fifteen flourishing colonies in Argentina, which were founded with the support of Ica by Russian Jewish emigrants in 1890. They now count about 20,000 souls, besides about 13,000 Jews who live in the colonies but have other occupations. Here cattle-raising is more important than agriculture. The healthy outdoor life of these Jewish colonies forms a glaring contrast to the confined ghetto life which the colonists remember in their youth or of which the younger have heard their parents speak. In Brazil, there are two Jewish agricultural colonies with 1,000 inhabitants in all. Most of the approximately 10,000 Jewish families living by agriculture in the United States—scattered among the rest of the population—and some 5,000 families in Canada, are of Eastern Jewish origin. In all they amount to about 55,000 souls.

As to the future, it is difficult to express an opinion. Certain authorities consider that even in Russia there will not be much cultivable land available for those who desire it. One thing is certain, that if the development of Eastern Jewish agriculture is checked, it will not be because those who practise it are unequal to the task. On the contrary, it has been shown that Jews are well fitted for agriculture, that is, intensive agriculture. Their lack of farming tradition is compensated by the ease with which, in contrast to their Russian neighbours or to the Indians and half-breeds of South America, they know how to profit by the advance of agrarian science. On the other hand, it is true that the colonies of which we have spoken were brought into being by the economic distress of the Eastern Jews and not by love of agriculture as such. We might, therefore, imagine a wholesale flight from Jewish agriculture in the event of a general improvement in the situation. But such a proceeding is equally to be apprehended wherever a town population has been forced to adopt agriculture from necessity, and thus could not be regarded as specially distinctive of the Jews. On the other hand, the colonisation of Palestine is typically Jewish and at the same time a shining manifestation of the Jewish will to regeneration under the banner of productive labour.

Space does not permit me to give an account here of the origin and progress of the Jewish renaissance and of Zionism, nor to describe how Jewish, and especially Eastern Jewish, youth was thrilled with the idea of training itself to become pioneers (*chaluzim*) who with their own hands were to transform Palestine, till then neglected and largely waste, into a prosperous realm, a home for a reborn Jewish nation and a reborn Jewish civilisation. The object was to form a coherent Jewish population in Palestine with agriculture as its economic foundation and Hebrew as its national language. The underlying idea was—and is—the reunion of the Jewish people with the soil, the formation of a race filled with moral earnestness and Jewish emotion, tanned by the sun, braced by the wind, with strong arms and hands hardened by labour. But what a few decades ago was only a dream has now become reality.

The actual immigration began in 1882, at first a little band mainly dependent on philanthropy, afterwards on a steadily increasing scale, inspired with the idea of national regeneration. A Jewish industry was created in Palestine, Jewish arts and crafts, a system of Jewish education, a number of industrial schools, a Jewish university (1929), but above all Jewish agriculture. It was not as in South Russia or Argentina a case of Jewish emigrants who chose agriculture in order to make a livelihood worthy of human beings. The young men and girls who emigrated to Palestine generally had a prospect of making a far better living and leading an infinitely more comfortable life if they stayed where they were or emigrated to America, especially as many of them were highly educated. But they had taken service under a lofty idea and acted in accordance therewith. In 1908, the same year in which the Jewish city of Tel-Aviv, which now has over 100,000 inhabitants, was founded among the sand-dunes near Jaffa, the first collectivist union of agricultural workers entered upon its heroic task in Palestine. The Jewish pioneers had at last found the right form for their work of reconstruction. They saw that the present generation would have to sacrifice itself for the next, if the Jewish country was to be built up with Jewish hands, " conquered through labour " as their watchword ran; but they were prepared to make the sacrifice. They flocked to Palestine in their thousands and began its conquest, not with sword and spear like their ancestors in the time of Joshua, but with pick and spade. Under their hands, desert and marsh were converted into fields of waving corn, richly laden vineyards and verdant orange-groves. Some of them were killed by Bedouins, malaria claimed many victims, the weaker succumbed to hardships and privations. But there were always fresh recruits, enthusiastic young men and girls, to take the places of the fallen. It is an epic well worth dwelling upon.

I will confine myself to a single, significant episode.

On May 5th, 1891, the newly appointed engineer Ussishkin with his wife and five other young Jews started on a reconnoitring ride through the Valley of Kishon to explore the great plain which extends from Haifa to Akko. They wished to study the possibilities of a Jewish colonisation in this valley and to negotiate with the owners as to its eventual acquisition.

Desolate and abandoned for centuries the great valley lay before them. Round about stretched morasses and sandy wastes. Dry desert scrub here and there was the only sign of life. Far in the distance Carmel met the eye, dead and bare, without grass, trees or bushes, without the smallest sign of human occupation. The town of Haifa itself was insignificant and poor and full of dirt and misery. Only one colony in its neighbourhood attracted the attention of the little party by its beauty. It was German.

After traversing the valley all day long the Jewish party returned to the hotel late in the evening and the night was spent in long discussions of the possibility of developing the tract. It was concluded that a brilliant future was in store for this valley. It was in the centre of the country and the most suitable place for constructing a great modern port on the Mediterranean; and there was the great hinterland of Jezreel, which was then entirely deserted and unfertile, waiting to be awakened from its sleep of two thousand years.

Early next morning Ussishkin took a walk through the German village and greeted a peasant who was working among his vines. The latter however replied with an unfriendly mien: " I expect you're one of those who were riding through the Akko valley yesterday. I understand you're thinking of buying it." " What's your opinion about this valley ? " asked Ussishkin. The German peasant answered with a scornful laugh: " It's not in your line ! It won't do for Jews ! It's not your way to make sacrifices; I mean, really sacrifice yourselves to get a thing going. You wait till others have made the sacrifice, and then you come and buy it all up."

" This answer," writes Ussishkin, " was like a stinging box on the ears. I turned pale with shame and pain but replied calmly: ' If you live long enough you will see how profoundly mistaken you are. There may be a grain of truth in your words, if you're thinking of the Jews who for thousands of years have been living in dispersion and in the most inhuman circumstances, but it's a base slander if you mean it of those who are trying to reconstruct our ancient land from its ruins.' "

Ussishkin returned in agitation to his friends at the hotel and told them of his interview with the German. " Never shall I forget those words," he exclaimed. The little circle of trustworthy and devoted friends then swore a solemn oath to each other that they would dedicate their whole strength to the great object of shaming the doubter's words.

And they kept their oath. Carmel and the surrounding district is now covered with flourishing Jewish colonies, and at its foot stands a scientific institution of the first rank, the Hebrew technical college, which trains engineers for the ever-increasing needs of the country.

On the outbreak of the World War, the Jewish colonists numbered about 12,000 and the nucleus had been formed of a Jewish farmer class which as regards self-sacrifice, industry and agricultural achievement was second to none in the world and constituted a moral and intellectual élite of the Jewish people. The Jews of Palestine have learnt the difficult art of self-administration and have proved socially and economically constructive. The economic advance of Palestine in the period immediately preceding the World War was due above all to them.

Since the War, as everyone knows, Jewish Palestine has made extraordinary strides. It is a real oasis in the desert of unemployment and shaky State finances. This land, formerly in great part desert, shorn of its forests and with its rivers unutilised, will humanly speaking, though not rich in itself, once more flow with milk and honey. But the world, which is astonished at this achievement, is far too apt to forget that it is a work, not of profit-seeking capitalists, but of creative Jewish idealists, of the rank and file of the Jewish people, who in spite of their poverty collect money for the acquisition of land, and above all of agriculturally trained Jewish youth.

The Jewish agricultural colonies in Palestine now number over 150 with a population of about 40,000. The British Government, as we know, puts the brake on immigration, chiefly out of regard for the Arabs. Even allowing for this, it is obvious that the progress of Jewish agriculture in Palestine cannot be rapid, but is a matter of decades, especially as it involves a systematic exploitation of the country's irrigation resources. In many cases a long process of experimentation is required, to find suitable types of colony and methods of cultivation. The Jewish colonists in Emek and the Jordan valley, who, moreover, benefited by the experience of older colonies, required a decade to produce a wheat which increased their crop by one-half, and a race of cows which gave three to four times as much milk as those of the fellahin. But even now an almost unbroken belt of Jewish colonies stretches northward from Tel-Aviv along the coast. It is, however, no longer Emek Jezreel, the Galilean plateau converted into a fertile land by Jewish pioneers, which attracts most attention, nor the orange zone of Sharon created by the fourth Polish-Jewish immigration (1925), but Vadi Chavarith, the coastal district of central Palestine acquired by the Jewish national fund, south of the old colony of Chedera. In Hebrew, this part of Palestine is known as Emek Chefer, a name which is already superseding the old one. It is hoped that in the future Emek Chefer will be able to rival Emek Jezreel and Emek Hasharon. But it is still in the initial stage, as it was only in June 1933 that the Jewish colonists broke ground there. Large tracts are still bog or dry prairie full of weeds. Within a few years these will certainly be transformed into fertile cornfields and orange-groves, a living witness to the Zionist strength and enthusiasm which animates these young Jews. By the sea, where is now a waste of sand-dunes, a town is to be built. It is hoped that the lowland of the Haifa bay will also be converted into a prosperous Jewish colony in the near future, as well as the great tract around Lake Merom in Northern Palestine, now partly consisting of malaria-stricken fens, which has lately (December 1934) been thrown open to Jewish colonisation, on condition that the Jews drain, or irrigate as the case may be, the districts allotted to the Arabs, as well as their own.

At the time of writing more than 100,000 pioneers (*chaluzim*), trained or undergoing training, are waiting for an opportunity of emigrating to Palestine—an extraordinarily capable and enthusiastic body of young workers, nine-tenths of them Eastern Jews, who are in every respect the opposite of what the Jews are represented to be in the misconceptions of Antisemites.

An extremely discriminating non-Jewish authority, a widely known Swiss engineer by name Rudolf Phister, who built the famous Spullersee works and has since been Pinchas Ruthenberg's assistant in the erection of the Jordan power station, one of the most important events in the history of Palestinian industry, has also spoken not long ago of Jewish workers in the most appreciative way.

" In the erection of the first Jordan power station," said Phister, " only Jewish labour was employed. The workmen were divided into groups, each under a foreman. It was a pleasant surprise to the engineer in charge of the work to find these men eager to learn, full of enthusiasm, astonishingly quick to grasp a job which had previously been entirely strange to them and which they performed with the greatest diligence. Most of our workmen had attended secondary schools in their younger days, and had thus received a good preparatory training; and their boundless devotion to the work made them quick to adapt themselves to the heavy manual labour. The most important operations, such as the mechanical excavation of soil, the transport of the same, all quarrying and digging, were done by contract, and in spite of the unfavourable climate (the Jordan valley is tropical) our men were soon able to equal the maximum performances of European labourers. . . .

The workmen deserve special commendation for the sobriety and the profound moral earnestness which distinguish their conduct. A particularly interesting point is that according to my experience a Jewish workman is only able to execute a piece of work when he has been accurately informed of its object. Thus his brain has to grasp what his hands are doing. Wherever I have worked, in Switzerland, in Spain, in Austria, I have taken pains to come in close contact with the workmen and to gain their confidence. In this respect my experience of the Jewish workmen in Palestine has been extremely pleasant. To my great joy I have arrived at the conviction that the Jewish worker sees in his labour not merely a means of subsistence, but that he has constantly before his eyes the services he may thereby render to his country and thus contribute to its progress. For this reason he makes it his duty to understand the whole plan of the work and its progression. As I have already remarked, he wants to grasp with his brain what he is accomplishing with his hands. This need of intellectual explanation made me understand why the workmen, as soon as a job is finished, have so many questions to put to the engineer.

It is unnecessary to point out the importance of these cordial relations between workmen and engineers and this thirst for knowledge while the work is in progress. In this way there was established an intimate co-operation between the manual and the intellectual worker.

But I have also found interesting qualities in the Jewish worker outside the actual field of his work. In his fervent devotion to the Zionist cause he has taken upon himself an immense task: that of the pioneer. And he still has time at the close of the day, a day filled with hard labour, to educate his mind and develop his personality.

How much the workers of other countries might learn from the intimate family life and the moral seriousness of the Jewish worker's outlook !

When the work was at its height we had 700 Jewish work-men. Under them were 200 Arabs as helpers. The purely human relations between the Company and the workers were marked by great respect for our chief, Herr Pinchas Ruthen-berg, a respect and affection which also included the Arab workers.

The construction of the first Jordan power station, which was accomplished by Jewish labour but also gave the Arabs opportunities of employment, proved, while the work was in progress, the possibility of a co-operation free from friction between the two Semitic races of the country. It is obvious that the impulse given to industry by the provision of cheap electric power will in every way benefit all the inhabitants of the country."

Thus does an impartial man speak of Jewish workers, whom, in contrast to the case of a Hitler or a Rosenberg, he knows by experience. No one who does so will be surprised at his words; on the contrary, they are just what one would expect. His statements might be supplemented by many others in the same sense. For it is not true that the Jews naturally shun manual labour and are born to be shop-keepers. That is true of no nation. Like other people, they are the product of a historical development, in which, especially during the last two millenniums, they have been not the hammer but the anvil. In the decades immediately preceding the World War, Eastern Jewry, as already pointed out, was in a promising state, in spite of all violations of justice. The views of the young were changing. Peddling became unpopular. There was a desire, encouraged by societies working to this end, to learn a definite trade. Moneylenders, innkeepers, " men of straw " and idlers became fewer and fewer, the artisan class grew rapidly, and a class of Jewish industrial workers arose. By the turn of the century, Jewish craftsmen and industrial workers out-numbered the tradesmen, and of Jewish unskilled labourers there were about 100,000. But since the War the world has grown narrow. In those countries where the productivisation of the Jewish masses is specially called for, the cultivable land, in fact the very possibility of exercising a trade, is reserved to the non-Jewish population. For this reason the efforts to improve the unfortunate social-economic structure of the Jewish population meet with such great difficulties. That certain classes of the people hold fast to unfortunate inherited habits is very natural, a morbid symptom comparable to the opposition met with by the temperance reformers of the nineteenth century in their struggle against the national malady which was prevalent in their time among the Scandinavian and Anglo-Saxon peoples, the vice of drunkenness. The decisive point is not the patient's illness, but his power of reacting against it. Anyone who has made a close study of the modern Jewish question can scarcely doubt that the Jewish people is destined to be re-born through productive labour, if only it be not deprived of the external conditions necessary for such re-birth.

CHAPTER XVIII

THE FUTURE

THE IMPROVEMENT in the general situation, material and spiritual, of the Jewish people was above all a result of the economic and, to a certain extent the spiritual, transformation of European society which may be said to have begun in the latter half of the seventeenth century. The same factors which led to the advance of the third estate also favoured that of the Jews. The nineteenth century saw the culmination of the power of the middle class and also of the Jews' prosperity. It is not due to chance that the proletarianisation of the middle class in our time runs parallel to the decline of Jewry and the increase of Anti-semitism. The climax of Jewish prosperity occurred during the period of economic Liberalism; but in the present epoch, marked by strong nationalism, collectivism and State interference, the Jews have found themselves between the hammer and the anvil. Wherever the Jews are numerous and the world crisis makes itself specially felt—in Anti-semitic Poland as in the United States, where indignation at the Nazi persecutions is profound and genuine—the Jews are being forced out of their former positions in economic life and in culture. An American-Jewish writer, Selig Perlman, has made the observation that when a nation feels the pinch economically, it seizes upon those things which are supposed to divide fellow-citizens, race, religion, nationality, in order thereby to reduce the number of competitors. This is undoubtedly a correct observation. When the bunga-bunga tree yields abundantly the Australian blacks allow strangers to share its fruit; when the yield is moderate, they may not do so, and in time of famine they eat the stranger. Civilised man is the twin-brother of primitive man. At the same time the need often asserts itself of finding a moral excuse for dealing harshly with the excluded by exhibiting them in an odious light, in agreement with the laws of centrality- and difference-emotions, of which we spoke in the first chapter.

There is thus reason to suppose that Antisemitism will be lightened with the arrival of better times. But there is nothing to lead us to believe in its disappearance in a reasonably near future. Rather does it seem that Antisemitism must be regarded as inseparable from the existence of the Jews in dispersion. A Jewish writer, Josef Kastein, even believed he could observe a regular rhythmic alternation in the course of Antisemitism: at first the nations desire the assimilation of the Jews or at least do not oppose it, but when this has reached a certain point they begin to defend themselves against the alien influence in the State, and a period of Antisemitism commences. Even those who do not believe in historical " laws " of this sort must admit that the observation itself has a certain, though limited, validity.

In countries with a small Jewish population, there is of course no substantial basis for Antisemitism. But even there attempts are made, on the model of the German Nazis, to represent the Press and economic life as controlled by the Jews; grotesque assertions which are usually " proved " by freely invented statistics, while he who raises objection to the antisemitic lies is branded as bought by the Jews. It is important that more attention should be paid to this agitation than hitherto. It was mainly through antisemitic propaganda of hatred and lies that the German Nazis prepared the ground for Hitler, and their opponents benefited neither themselves, a free form of government nor the great traditions of humanity by ignoring the antisemitic side of the Nazi agitation.

While in Nazi Germany it is thought that the racially alien element ought to be removed from the German body politic, elsewhere the Jews' contributions to civilisation are appreciated in quite another way: not as an intrusion upon, but as an enrichment of the national culture. This applies in particular to the Netherlands, where the percentage of Jews is far higher than in Germany—in Germany 0·9 per cent, in the Netherlands, 1·7 per cent of the population—a country which stands high with the German Nazis, as the Nordic type is so strongly represented there. And in fact it is stated in the Nazi review *Erwachendes Europa*, July, 1934, that although the Jews of the Netherlands occupy high positions in nearly every branch, Antisemitism is scarcely noticeable, while on the other hand, they are regarded as a national asset the loss of which would be regretted.[1] When Hitlerite propaganda made its appearance in Holland, the States-General by an overwhelming majority passed a law penalising the dissemination of religious and racial hatred. As the Jews of the Netherlands resemble those of Germany in their level of culture and racial composition —the Sephardic element in both countries is insignificant— it is natural to suppose that specific circumstances, determined by German cultural tradition and post-War mentality, have occasioned in the Germans a supersensitiveness towards Jewish influence, the like of which is not found in any other country. How the English, the leading nation of Nordic type, have treated their Jews, is known to everyone. Benjamin Disraeli, who was not only a Jew but, in contrast to most of his racial kinsmen in England, of distinctly un-English appearance, became head of the Conservative Party, regenerated thanks to him, leader of the British nation in an extraordinarily fateful period of its history, and was honoured during his lifetime, and even more after his

[1] Even Dutch Naziism is for the most part non-antisemitic.

death as one of the Empire's most brilliant personalities
and greatest statesmen. Just before Germany announced
her withdrawal from the League of Nations the German
delegation at Geneva was obliged to listen to the speech of
the British representative, Ormsby-Gore, in which he
attacked German Antisemitism. The speaker declared that
as a conservative member of Parliament he had taken
part for many years in the annual ceremony of laying a
wreath at the foot of the statue which immortalises
Disraeli, a statesman who remained during his whole life
at once " a patriotic Englishman " and " the proudest of
Jews."

Rathenau on the other hand, whose whole appearance
was far more German than Jewish, was exposed as German
Minister for Foreign Affairs to a campaign of inordinate
hatred and antisemitic mud-throwing, till at last he was
struck down by the fatal bullets of his enemies. After Hitler's
victory homage was paid to the memory of the murderers.
The difference in the fate of Disraeli and of Rathenau is
characteristic not only of the treatment of Jews in the two
countries, but also of two different reactions to the " alien "
element. In one case the services of the " alien "—Scottish,
Welsh or Jewish—are sought after, in the other his extermination is the object. Which is the nobler course ? Which
is the wiser ? Of that the statesmen and the nations must
judge for themselves !

How the Jews themselves may contribute to the defeat of
Antisemitism is a question frequently discussed. The view
was generally held, not only during the period of emancipation but much later, that the Jews ought to give up everything Jewish except possibly what is purely religious. It
has been described above how in Germany this led to the
Jews as a rule feeling entirely German with a more or less
unessential Jewish admixture.

But particularly during the last two decades, when stress
has been laid more and more on the Jews' real or supposed

psycho-physical peculiarities, Nazi Antisemitism came to be
directed above all against those Jews who would not acknowledge their Jewishness but regarded themselves as Germans
pure and simple. It was considered that they sailed, doubtless
in good faith, under a false flag and that they therefore
exercised a peculiarly confusing and dangerous influence on
German life, German ideals, German " myths," whereas,
in the words of a non-Nazi writer, Prince Anton de Rohan,
" the Jew who acknowledges himself as such . . . nullifies
thereby most of the animosity aroused by his mimicry
(protective disguise), and appears as a valued, in many cases
a popular fellow-citizen, even to a conservative-national
(*volkbürgerlichen*) German." Furthermore the part played in
our day by a number of radical Jews who have renounced
their Judaism has induced many people who previously
held other views to look with favour on the modern tendency
which seeks to restore Judaism to its position of a main
value in the lives of young Jews, with all its problematical
and tragic implications, its intensified outlook and intro-
spection, its moral earnestness and inner wealth. In Sweden,
where the attitude of the Jews to the problem of assimilation
is similar to that of their kinsfolk in Germany, the matter
has not been discussed to any great extent. Fredrik Böök,
however, the most noted living critic in Sweden, has expressed himself on several occasions in the same spirit as
the Prince de Rohan. As a contrast to Georg Brandes, who
always insisted that things Jewish were without significance
to him, Böök has pointed out how Meir Goldschmidt,
Denmark's greatest Jewish poet, became a " good Dane "
for the very reason that he was a good Jew, devoted, grateful
and loyal in his relations both to what was Jewish and what
was Danish. Böök writes in the same way of Oscar Levertin,
the Swedish-Jewish literary historian, critic and poet, who
was no more inclined than Goldschmidt to deny his Jewish
nature: " Levertin's connection with our traditions was a
positive one and it has never been possible to stamp him as

a usurper. He was thus a better and more loyal Jew than
Brandes, a better and more loyal Swedish patriot than
Brandes was a Danish, and I cannot even see that he was
a worse European than Georg Brandes."

It does not follow however that if the German Jews had
adopted a tactful restraint when acting on behalf of the
German people, they would have been able to alter the
course of events. The view widely prevalent in Jewish and
non-Jewish circles that by acting in this way or that the
Jews might have been able to avert Antisemitism is based
on an illusion. For it is not the Jews who are hated, but an
imaginary image of them, which is confounded with the
reality, and the Jews' actual "faults" play a very unimportant part in the matter. It may indeed be true that
the Jewish people, like all others, is in duty bound to work
at its moral improvement; even more than others in fact,
since distress and oppression, of which it has had more than
its share, easily lead to demoralisation. The main thing is to
work for the productivisation of the suffering Jewish masses
and for the spiritual regeneration of the whole people, in
order that it may be equal to bearing its lot in the right
way, with humility and pride, ennobling constraint into
freedom. No work is more important for the Jews than this.
But a nation of sixteen millions can never avoid including
in its midst unsympathetic and inferior elements. When the
non-Jewish world feels the need of hating, of finding a scapegoat, it judges unfairly by these. In fact it is not at all certain
that Antisemitism would be weakened to any extent if the
Jews were to consist exclusively of angels in human form.
As we know, many Antisemites exclude all their Jewish
acquaintance from the general sentence of reprobation, and
German Antisemitism singled out two special victims,
Walter Rathenau and Max Warburg, who were both men
of high moral character and fervent German patriots. The
Christians of the Roman Empire, who were certainly not
morally worse than other people, were exposed to a hatred

Ua

similar to that reserved for the Jews of post-War Germany.
" If the Tiber rose to the walls of the city," writes Tertullian,
one of the Fathers of the Church, " if the inundation of the
Nile failed to give the fields enough water, if the heavens did
not send rain, if an earthquake occurred, if famine threatened, if pestilence raged, the cry resounded: ' Throw the
Christians to the lions ! ' "

Nor does it seem possible to get rid of Antisemitism by
the spread of enlightening literature. Passions are not to be
stilled by statistical figures. With facts and reasoning it is
possible no doubt to confute antisemitic assertions—this has
been widely done by the German Jews—but not to reach the
bed-rock of the subconscious, where hatred has its germs.
The terrible thing about hatred is that he who is seized with
it as a rule does not wish to be rid of it. He continues to
hate without regard to facts or arguments.

So, as far as we can see, this hatred will flourish for
generations and the struggle will surge backwards and
forwards. In this conflict the Western democracies have their
place assigned, unless they shut their eyes to the fact that
Antisemitism is a means of producing a reactionary national
psychosis; the Christian churches too, unless they will deny
their Master; all in fact who still regard humanity and
justice as the guiding stars of mankind.

It is a Nazi dogma that Jews and " Aryans " are divided
by the nature of their beliefs, their scepsis, and consequently
by their " myths " (dogmas). The dream of a realm of
peace, which of course presupposes nothing less than a
gradual modification of human mentality, is regarded as
one of these Jewish myths. But this has been a hope and a
guiding star for many millions of men of different races and
nations and one of the leading ideas of Christianity, indissolubly united with the great human traditions of mankind, in which too the greatest thinkers and poets of the

German people once lived and breathed. The idea triumphantly surmounts the boundaries which race and nation have
raised among men, nor will it submit, we may be sure, to
be confined in the future in the strait waistcoat of racial
dogmatism. We are not concerned here with the conflicts
of to-day, for the goal lies in the mists of the future and it is
doubtful if it can be attained, but rather with a tendency,
a mentality, an ideal aspiration, an evolution continuing
through thousands of years, though often checked, towards
a human solidarity elevated above nations, races and religions, a dream which was once shared by an Alfred Nobel.
National minorities and among them the Jewish people,
who are everywhere in a minority, are above all dependent
on this evolution. But it concerns us all. Is mankind, as
Grillparzer feared, to complete its course " from humanity
through nationality to bestiality " ? Or will the Caliban of
national hatred finally be vanquished by the bright powers
of life ? The fight for and against Antisemitism is but one
phase of this ancient conflict.

" In God's eyes," runs a saying of the Talmud often
quoted in Jewish educational literature, " the man stands
high who makes peace between men : between husband and
wife, between fathers and children, between masters and
servants, between neighbour and neighbour. But he stands
highest who establishes peace among the nations."

Ua*

NOTES AND ADDENDA

THE FOLLOWING LIST of authorities includes, first, the works of authors quoted in the text, and secondly, the most important books or articles on which the account has been based, especially such as are of an encyclopædic nature and furnished with a bibliography.

The best and most scholarly account of the history of the Jews is that written by SIMON DUBNOV and translated into German from the Russian MS.: *Weltgeschichte des jüdischen Volkes von seinen Uranfängen bis zur Gegenwart*, Berlin 1925–29, 10 vols. Among modern encyclopædias may be noted the *Jüdisches Lexikon*, I–V, Berlin, 1927–30, which is complete, and the *Encyclopædia Judaica*, Berlin, 1927–34, of which 10 vols. (as far as the letter L) have hitherto been published. The long articles on Antisemitism and on the different countries, all provided with full bibliographical references, in these two encyclopædias, together with Dubnov's above-mentioned work, are the chief authorities for the historical sections of the present book.

Page

9. WILHELM MARR. The first edition of Marr's pamphlet appeared in 1873, but it was the edition of 1879 which first attracted general attention. After a few years Marr turned away from Antisemitism " with a disgust which made him sick."

11. *The Marxist view*. See *Kommunismus und Judenfrage* in *Der Jud ist schuld? Diskussionsbuch über die Judenfrage*, pp. 272 ff., Basle, Berlin, Leipzig, Vienna, 1932.

13. WALTER HURT. *Truth about the Jews*, p. 172, Chicago, 1932.

14. DITLEF NIELSEN. Pontius Pilate, who according to the oldest New Testament sources bears the responsibility for the death of Jesus and is known to contemporary historians as the man who enforced a regular reign of terror in Palestine, until suspended by Vitellius, the Roman governor of Syria, and who certainly crucified a great number of Jews

suspected of rebellious tendencies, is represented in the later Gospels and still more in post-canonical literature as actually a friend of the great Jewish popular leader and reformer. In this Nielsen sees a perversion of history. According to him the words of the Apostles' Creed: "was crucified *under* Pontius Pilate," originally ran "was crucified *by* Pontius Pilate."

29. HEINRICH COUDENHOVE-KALERGI, *Das Wesen des Antisemitismus*, p. 28, Vienna, Leipzig, Paris, 1929. English translation, *Anti-Semitism throughout the Ages*, London, 1935.

29. *The Crusades.* Article *Kreuzzüge* in *Jüd. Lexikon*; and *Encyclopædia Judaica*.

32. *The share of Jewish credit in great undertakings.* JOSEPH JACOBS, *Jewish Contributions to Civilisation*, p. 207 f., Philadelphia, 1919.

33. COUDENHOVE-KALERGI, op. cit., pp. 134 f.

42. *An author of the close of the eighteenth century.* E. T. VON KORTUM, *Ueber Judenthum und Juden*, p. 90, Nuremberg, 1790.

46. *A Nazi writer.* WILLIAM GRAU in the *Völkischer Beobachter*, January 21st–22nd, 1934.

88. *The Transformation of Russian Jewry.* BORIS BRUTZKUS, *Die wirtschaftliche und soziale Lage der Juden in Russland vor und nach der Revolution* (in *Archiv für Sozialwissenschaft und Sozialpolitik*, Bd. 61, pp. 266 ff., Tübingen, 1929).

91. *The World War.* Article *Weltkrieg* in *Jüd. Lexikon*.

108ff.The chief authority is *Das Schwarzbuch, Tatsachen und Dokumente. Die Lage der Juden in Deutschland, 1933* (quoted as *Schwarzbuch*), published in Paris in 1934 by the Comité des Délégations Juives and based on extensive documentary material. Its statistical material is derived as a rule from HEINRICH SILBERGLEIT, *Die Bevölkerungs—und Berufsverhältnisse der Juden im deutschen Reich auf Grund von amtlichen Materialen bearbeitet, I, Freistaat Preussen*, Berlin, 1930.

109. *The German Jews in the World War.* Article *Judenzählung* in *Jüd. Lexikon*; article *Kriegsstatistik* in *Philo-Lexikon, Handbuch des jüdischen Wissens*, Berlin, 1935; article *Die Juden im Kriege* in *Jüdische Rundschau*, February 13th, 1934.

111. ARTHUR RUPPIN, *The Jews in the Modern World*, p. 302, London, 1934.

114. GOTTFRIED FEDER, *Die Juden. Nationalsozialistische Bibliothek,* Heft 45, p. 74, Munich, Berlin, 1933.
The history of the Swastika. W. NORMAN BROWN, *The Swastika. A Study of the Nazi Claims of its Aryan Origin,* New York, 1934.

114. GOTTFRIED FEDER, *Hitler's Official Programme,* London, 1934.

120. ALBERT OLSEN, *Antisemitisme og Racedogme i tysk Politik, Acta Jutlantica V:* 2, p. 30, 33, Copenhagen, 1933.

123. *" Non-Aryan "* films. In a few exceptional cases Goebbels has abstained from prohibiting successful foreign films which were not " Jew-free "; for instance, *La Maternelle,* whose Jewish producer was called in Germany, Benoit instead of Benoit-Lévy, and one of whose authors, Marie Epstein, was suppressed; also *La Bataille* and *Henry VIII,* both of which were made by Hungarian Jews.

124. *" By direct action . . ."* *Schwarzbuch,* p. 433.

127. The quotation from RATHENAU will be found in his *Nachgelassene Schriften,* I, p. 116, Berlin, 1928.

130. *" To the Jews science is only a business."* Thus the official *Preussische Zeitung. Schwarzbuch,* p. 256. Examples might be multiplied almost illimitably.
Since the above was written the " Nuremberg Laws " of September 15th, 1935, have come into force, marking the definitive expulsion of German Jewry from German political and social life. The Jews have been degraded into a kind of pariah. All intercourse with the " Aryan " part of the population is forbidden them. It would, however, be a mistake to suppose that these laws have placed a limit to the defamation and despoliation of the Jews. Rather are they to be regarded as a camouflage intended for foreign countries, under the shelter of which the ruling Nazi party can proceed with its work of ousting the Jews from the few fields of activity which have not yet been closed to them by law. A true and moving picture of the position of German Jews is given by High Commissioner James McDonald in his letter of resignation addressed to the League of Nations on December 27th, 1935, and reproduced at the end of this Appendix.

135. *The Tribes of Israel.* Certain inquirers count the tribes of Israel—perhaps rightly—among the descendants of Terah.

139. MAX MÜLLER, ROBERT HARTMANN and others. The literature on this subject is very abundant. One of the best and most lucid works is FRIEDRICH HERTZ, *Race and Civilisation,* London, 1928. The examples in the text are taken from this work, unless otherwise stated.

139. EDWARD MEYER, *Geschichte des Altertums,* I, p. 76, Berlin, 1907.

140. JULIUS GOLDSTEIN, *Rasse und Politik,* p. 149, Schlüchtern, 1921.

142. *The north-eastern third of France is more " Nordic " than South Germany.* CONSTANTIN BRUNNER, *Der Judenhass und die Juden,* p. 60, Berlin, 1918.

142. RENAN. In his famous work *Histoire générale et système comparé des langues sémitiques,* published in 1855, Renan assumed that the ancient peoples who spoke Semitic languages formed an anthropological group, and described them as a race without civilising power. This work, from which the author afterwards dissociated himself, was diligently exploited by Chamberlain and other racial Antisemites. In 1883 Renan declared : " L'histoire du peuple juif est une des plus belles qu'il y ait, et je ne regrette pas d'y avoir consacré ma vie " *Le Judaïsme comme race et religion* (in *Discours et conférences,* p. 361, Paris, 1919).

142. *Gobineauism in France.* HERTZ, op. cit., p. 7.

143. *Wagner's Antisemitism.* Article *Wagner* in *Jüd. Lexikon.*
The suggestive power of Wagner's music. ALBERT OLSEN, op. cit., p. 7.

144. HANS GÜNTHER, *Rassenkunde des deutschen Volkes,* 9, verbesserte Aufl., p. 21, Berlin.

146. FRITZ KAHN, *Die Juden als Rasse und Kulturvolk,* pp. 43 f., 107 f., Berlin, 1920.

147. BRUNNER, op. cit., pp. xx f.

148. *The alleged fairness of the Amorites.* RUPPIN, op. cit., pp. 8 ff.

148. DOKTOR RUDOLF, *Nationalsozialismus und Rasse,* Nationalsozialistische Bibliothek, Heft 31, 3. Aufl., Munich, 1934.

The first edition appeared before Hitler's assumption of power. In it the author declares, p. 49, that the rulers of Germany intend to shut the mouth of Nordic man and exterminate him, and that all measures taken against the Nazi party and its leaders from a racial point of view are to be understood in this sense.

149. *The history of the Nordic movement.* HANS GÜNTHER, *Der nordische Gedanke*, 2. umarbeitete Aufl., pp. 7 ff., Berlin, 1927. EUGEN FISCHER in a lecture: *Sozialanthropologie und ihre Bedeutung für den Staat*, Berlin, 1910.

149- Criticism mainly after FRIEDRICH HERTZ, *Hans Günther als*
160 *Rassenforscher*, 2. verbesserte Aufl., Berlin, 1930, and ALBERT OLSEN, op. cit., pp. 55 f.

160. CHAMBERLAIN, *Die Grundlagen*, § 93.

161. FRITZ LENZ in Baur-Fischer-Lenz, *Grundriss der menschlichen Erblichkeitslehre und Rassenhygiene*, 3. Aufl., pp. 521, 573, Berlin, 1927, Engl. trans., *Human Heredity*, pp. 623 ff., London and New York, 1931.

161. *Jewish competitors in the Olympic Games.* The Jewish world champions in boxing are Berney Ross (two championships), Max Baer, Maxie Rosenbloom, Jackie Brown.

162. FRITZ LENZ, op. cit., p. 365. Engl. trans., p. 676.

175. *Maurice Joly.* Article *Protokolle der Weisen von Zion* in *Jüd. Lexicon.*

175. *The comparison published by the Jewish community of Basle : Confrontation der " Geheimnisse der Weisen von Zion " (" Die zionistischen Protokolle ") mit ihrer Quelle " Dialogue aux Enfers entre Machiavel et Montesquieu." Der Nachweis der Fälschung.* Basle, 1933.

182. *The Berne trial.* Reported at length in the *Jüdische Rundschau*, November 2nd, 1934.

185. *Anti-German war propaganda.* CONSTANTIN BRUNNER, op. cit. The quotation from Miraquet's and Pergameni's school-book will be found in *Enquête sur les livres scolaires d'après guerre*, pp. 63 ff., 2. ed. Paris, 1925.

193. *Hitler's hatred of the Jews.* It is worth pointing out that Hitler often seems to regard his opponents as morally inferior. His

more recent utterances also bear witness to this. In *Der Angriff*, 1930, No. 55, he writes: " Even a Bismarck did not succeed in establishing friendly co-operation with France; one does not sleep under the same roof as a brigand." In *Der Angriff*, 1931, No. 186, he writes: " In dealing with France Germany can never pursue a policy of friendship. . . . . We will accept no praise from this scoundrelly neighbour France. . . . The Frenchman is in reality the Mephisto of mankind."

195- Unless otherwise stated, the statistical material is derived
206. from the *Schwarzbuch*.

196. FELIX THEILHABER, *Der Untergang der deutschen Judenheit*, Berlin, 1921.

197. *Sombart's investigations.* ALBERT OLSEN, op. cit., pp. 30 ff.

197. *The proletarianisation of the German-Jewish middle class.* KURT ZIELENZIGER, *Juden in der deutschen Wirtschaft*, pp. 275 ff. Berlin, 1930.

198–9. *Jews in the German administration. Anti-Anti, Tatsachen der Judenfrage*, published by the Centralverein deutscher Staatsbürger Jüd. Glaubens, 7. Aufl., p. 41, Berlin, 1932.

200. ARNOLD ZWEIG, *Bilanz der deutschen Judenheit*, p. 142, Amsterdam, 1934.

200. *German-Jewish physicians.* According to statistics recently published in the *Deutsches Aerzteblatt* and quoted in the *Jüdische Rundschau*, January 4th, 1935, on the outbreak of the National-Socialist revolution 13 per cent of the doctors in Germany were Jews, 6,488 out of 50,000, and 3,000 Jewish doctors were established in Berlin. According to the same sources 1,667 non-Aryan physicians were deprived of their panel practice and about 575 emigrated during 1933.

202. *Jewish influence in the German Press.* RICHARD LEWINSOHN (" Morus "), *Jüdische Weltfinanz ?*, pp. 91 ff.; *Handbuch der deutschen Tagespresse*, published by the Deutschen Institut für Zeitungskunde, Berlin, 1932.

205. *Criminal statistics.* That crimes of fraud are more frequent in several countries among the Jewish than among the non-Jewish population is natural, since the proportion of business men among the former is much higher than among the

latter. " The difference is only apparent between the criminality of the Jews in Western and Central Europe and that of their environment" (article *Kriminalität, Philo-Lexikon*). In Amsterdam, which has a large Jewish working population, crimes of fraud are 50 per cent more common among the non-Jewish than among the Jewish population. Article *Kriminalität der Juden* in *Jüd. Lexikon*.

206. The reader interested in the cultural contributions of the German Jews is referred to Zweig's work quoted above.

206. *Jewish Nobel Prizemen.* Article *Nobelpreisträger* in *Philo-Lexikon*. Altogether, up to the year 1933, 14 Jews and 6 half-Jews have received Nobel prizes, making 12 per cent of all Nobel prizemen.

207. *Jews in German films. Schwarzbuch*, pp. 426 ff.

210- In addition to Lewinsohn's work quoted in the text, the
225. article *Finanz und Bankwesen* in the *Encyclopædia Judaica* and the article *Finanzwesen, Anteil der Juden*, in *Jüd. Lexikon*, may be referred to.

211. *Substitution of the word " Jews " for " men."* See, e.g., OTTO HAUSER, *Geschichte des Judentums*, p. 496, Weimar 1921, and WILHELM MEISTER, *Judas Schuldbuch*, p. 197, Munich 1919. Rathenau's letter printed in *Walter Rathenaus Briefe*, II, pp. 332 f., Dresden 1926.

213. ROBERT LIEFMANN, *Cartels, Concerns and Trusts*, p. 30 f. London 1932.

215. PAUL EINZIG, *The Jews in International Banking* (in *The Banker*, Oct., 1933).

216. HANS PRIESTER in the review *Der Morgen*, 1927, heft 3.

222. *" Non-Jewish industrialists . . ."* Quoted from the above-mentioned article in *Jüd. Lexikon*.
   As Lewinsohn has shown, it was due to a mistake that Burnley included the Catholic Archbishop Kohn, a man of Jewish descent, among the forty-four richest men.

223. RUDOLF MARTIN, in the *Jahrbuch des Vermögens und Einkommens der Millionäre in Preussen*, II, p. 25, Berlin, 1925.

224. JACOB LESTSCHINSKY in the article *(Beruf-)Statistik der Juden, Jüd. Lexikon*, V, col. 697.

231. PRINCE MAX OF BADEN, *Memoirs*, II, pp. 13, 57. London, 1928.

236. " *Moses, 1250 years before Christ* . . ." FRITZ KAHN, op. cit., p. 179. The figure 1250 is naturally open to discussion. Cp. pp. 135 ff, above.

236. CARDINAL FAULHABER, *Judaism, Christianity and Germany*. Advent Sermon preached in the church of St. Michael in Munich, 1933; p. 68, London, 1934.

237-8. *Old Testament legislation and the Prophets*. KAHN, op. cit., pp. 179 ff.; FAULHABER, op. cit.; MICHAEL GUTTMANN, *Das Judentum und seine Umwelt*. Eine Darstellung der religiösen und rechtlichen Beziehungen zwischen Juden und Nichtjuden mit besonderer Berücksichtung der talmudisch-rabbinischen Quellen, I, Berlin, 1927. Articles *Arbeit, Armut, Kommunismus, Sklaven, Soziale Gesetzgebung der Juden, Sozialismus*, in *Jüd. Lexikon*.

239. *Landauer*. KAHN, op. cit., p. 199.

242. *Jewish members of Parliament*. Article *Parlamentarier, Jüdische*, in *Jüd. Lexikon*.

244. *Schneerson*. DUBNOV, op. cit., VIII, p. 376.

246. *Marx*. E. J. LESSER, *Karl Marx als Jude* (in the review *Der Jude*, 1924, pp. 173 ff.

248. *Tendentious rose-coloured picture*. ERIK NÖLTING, *Das " zersetzende " Judentum*, p. 23, Berlin, 1924.

249. HANS BLÜHER, *Secessio Judaica*. Philosophische Grundlegung der historischen Situation des Judentums und der antisemitischen Bewegung. 3. Aufl., Potsdam, 1933.

249. *Einstein*. The statement about his theory of relativity is to be found in *Feder*, op. cit., *Die Juden*, p. 66.

250. HEINE in a letter to Joseph Lehmann, Oct. 5th, 1854.

251. *Jews " without history."* ISAAK HEINEMANN in an article written for the *Jüdische Zeitung* and reproduced in the Norwegian-Jewish review *Hatikwo*, Nov., 1933: *Israel mellem folkene*. KURT BLUMENFELD in the *Jüdische Rundschau*, Sept. 9th, 1915.

253. HANS BLÜHER, op. cit., p. 23.

253. JACOB WASSERMANN, *My Life as German and Jew*, p. 154, London, 1934.

255- Authorities besides those quoted in the text: BRUTZKUS,
266. op. cit.; DIMITRI BULASCHOW (BENJAMIN SEGEL), *Judentum
und Bolschewismus*, 4. Aufl., Berlin, 1924; DUBNOV, op. cit.,
X, pp. 514 ff.; EDMOND FLEG, *Anthologie juive du moyen âge à
nos jours*, pp. 184 ff., Paris, 1923; articles *Bolschewismus*,
Kommunismus, *Revolution*, *Russland*, in *Jüd. Lexikon*.

262. *Yevsektia*. Article *Jewsekzia* in *Encyclopædia Judaica*.

265. *Erwachendes Europa*. CONSTANTIN VON STAMATI, *Sovjetrussische
Nationalitätenprobleme* (in *Erwachendes Europa*, Monatsschrift
für nationalsozialistische Weltanschauung, Aussenpolitik und
Auslandkunde, pp. 240 ff., 1934).

267- The chief authority is MICHAEL GUTTMAN, op. cit. All the
277. Talmud quotations in the text will be found there. See also
ALEXANDER GUTTMAN, *Enthüllte Talmudcitate*, Berlin, 1930;
HERTZ, op. cit., *Günther als Rassenforscher;* articles *Auser-
wähltes Volk*, *Fremder*, *Gesetze*, *Liebe deinen Nächsten wie dich
selbst*, *Sittlichkeit*, *Talmud*, in *Jüd. Lexikon*.

270. DUBNOV, op. cit., III, pp. 306 ff.

275. ISMAR ELBOGEN in op. cit. *Der Jud ist schuld?* p. 358.
Cp. A. GUTTMANN, op. cit., pp. 107 f.

276. *The Talmud's attitude to capital punishment.* M. GUTTMANN,
op. cit., pp. 39 f., 222, note 3.

276. *The Jewish method of slaughter.* Articles *Schächten*, *Schächtverbot*,
Tierschutz, in *Jüd. Lexikon*.

278- RUPPIN, op. cit., pp. 130 ff.; J. M. ISLER, *Rückkehr der Juden
290. zur Landswirtschaft*, Frankfort o. M. 1929; articles *Berufsumschichtung*, *Handel*, *Handwerk bei den Juden* (statistical information), *Kapitalismus und die Juden*, *Kolonien*, *Landwirtschaft*,
(Berufs-)Statistik der Juden (statistical information), *Wirt-
schafts- und Sozialgeschichte der Juden*, all in *Jüd. Lexikon*.

278. RUPPIN, op. cit., p. 31.

280. JULIUS GUTTMANN, *Archiv für Sozialwissenschaft und Sozialpolitik*, 1913, pp. 149 ff.

281. *Loyalty of Jewish mercenaries.* HERTZ, op. cit., *Race and
Civilization*, p. 275.

282. "*All shopkeeping was despised by the old rabbis.*" The passages
from the Talmud are collected in MATTHIAS MIESES, *Der

Jüdische Wucher und der Judenhass (in *Der Jude*, 1922, pp. 416 ff.).

284. *Tribute of the French command to Jewish officers.* B. SEGEL, op. cit., p. 176.

291. IGNAZ SCHIPPER, *Anfänge des Kapitalismus bei den abendländischen Juden im frühen Mittelalter*, Vienna, 1907.

293. *Ussishkin's expedition.* M. USSISHKIN, *Der Wille des Volkes* (in *Haifa, Vergangenheit, Gegenwart, Zukunft*, published by the Keven Kajemeth Lejisrael, pp. 30 f., Jerusalem, 1929).

294. *Jewish agricultural colonization in Palestine.* My work on *Zionism*, published in 1933, and the monthly reports in *Jüd. Krönika*.

296. RUDOLF PHISTER, *Züricher Jüd. Presszentrale*, Nov. 25th, 1932.

300. SELIG PERLMAN, *Our Economic Arena* (in *The Menorah Journal*, May, 1934).

301. *The bunga-bunga tree.* HERTZ, op. cit., *Race and Civilisation*, p. 70.

301. JOSEF KASTEIN, *History and Destiny of the Jews*, pp. 412 ff., London, 1933.

302. *Erwachendes Europa*, 1934, pp. 202 ff. FRIEDRICH OTTOMAR JUMMEL, *Die Niederlande und das neue Deutschland*.

303. *Rathenau's murderers.* At their uncovered grave the speaker declared that Rathenau desired " the annihilation of the German race." *Völkischer Beobachter*, Oct. 31st, 1933. *Assimilation as a remedy for Antisemitism.* This view is the basis of BERNARD LAZARE's well-known book, *L'antisémitisme, son histoire et ses causes*, Paris, 1894. The author's opinion that Antisemitism was really directed against insufficiently assimilated, " unenlightened " Jews, was disproved by the Dreyfus affair, and this, together with a more profound study of the Jewish question, induced the author radically to alter the views put forward in his book. It seems strange therefore that the new edition of Lazare's work (Paris, 1934) is unaltered, although the author himself before his death contemplated revising it in conformity with his new view of the question.

ANTON DE ROHAN. *Europäische Revue*, 1932, p. 459.

307. *An oft-quoted saying of the Talmud.* Mechilta to Exodus xx, 22.

MR. J. G. McDONALD'S LETTER

(see page 310)

London, Dec. 27.

Sir,—On October 26, 1933, the President of the Council of the League of Nations did me the honour to appoint me High Commissioner for Refugees (Jewish and Other) Coming from Germany, to " negotiate and direct " the " international collaboration " necessary to solve the " economic, financial, and social problem " of the refugees. I hereby beg to submit through you to the Council of the League my resignation from this office, to become effective as from December 31, 1935.

2. In the period of over two years since the establishment of the office, conditions in Germany which create refugees have developed so catastrophically that a reconsideration by the League of Nations of the entire situation is essential. The legislation and administrative and party action against " non-Aryans " were steadily intensified, and culminated in the autumn of 1935 when a series of new laws and decrees initiated a fresh wave of repression and persecution of a character which was not envisaged in 1933.

The intensified persecution in Germany threatens the pauperisation or exile of hundreds of thousands of Germans—men, women, and children—not only Jews but also the " non-Aryan " Christians treated as Jews, and Protestants and Catholics who in obedience to their faith and conscience dare to resist the absolute will of the National Socialist State.

3. Apart from all questions of principle and of religious persecution, one portentous fact confronts the community of States. More than half a million persons, against whom no charge can be made except that they are not what the National Socialists choose to regard as " Nordic," are being crushed. They cannot escape oppression by any act of their own free-will, for what has been called " the membership of non-Aryan race " cannot be changed or kept in abeyance.

Tens of thousands are to-day anxiously seeking ways to flee abroad; but, except for those prepared to sacrifice the whole or greater part of their savings, the official restrictions on export of capital effectively bar the road to escape, and the doors of most countries are closed against impoverished fugitives. Nevertheless, if the present pressure is not relieved, it is inconceivable that those who can flee will remain within Germany.

The task of saving these victims calls for renewed efforts of the philanthropic bodies. The private organisations, Jewish and Christian, may be expected to do their part if the Governments, acting through the League, make possible a solution. But in the new circumstances it will not be enough to continue the activities on behalf of those who flee from the Reich. Efforts must be made to remove or mitigate the causes which create German refugees. This could not have been any part of the work of the High Commissioner's office; nor, presumably, can it be a function of the body to which the League may decide to entrust future administrative activities on behalf of the refugees. It is a political function, which properly belongs to the League itself.

4. At the last meeting, on October 16, 1935, of the Permanent Committee of the Governing Body of the High Commission, at which my intention to resign was fully discussed, action was taken to liquidate the office of the High Commissioner at the end of January, 1936, or sooner if before that date the Council of the League had made other provision for the co-ordination of the activities on behalf of the refugees coming from Germany. It was the expectation of the Permanent Committee that the Committee of Experts provided for by the Assembly of 1935, to study the reorganisation of the activities on behalf of the " German " and of the " Nansen " refugees, would complete its investigations in time to present a plan for consideration, and, it was hoped, for action, by the Council at its meeting in January, 1936.

It has been the sense of the Governing Body that the work of assistance in the countries of refuge could be better carried forward by an organisation directly under the authority of the League. It is now clear that the effectiveness of the High Commissioner's efforts was weakened from the beginning by the compromise which was agreed upon at the time his office was set up—that is, the decision to separate it definitely from the League. This compromise was accepted in order to avoid the veto of Germany, which was then an active member of the League.

5. Progress has been made during the last three years in settling the refugees from Germany. Of the more than 80,000 who have already left the Reich approximately three-fourths have now found new homes—more than half of these in Palestine—or have been repatriated to their countries of origin. This accomplishment has been primarily the work of the refugees themselves and of the philanthropic organisations—Jewish and Christian—whose devoted labours have been ceaselessly carried on in many parts of the world. Probably not more than 15,000 refugees now remain unplaced. (An account of the work done for the refugees since April, 1933, is being published.)

6. The care and the settlement of these remaining thousands of

refugees could and would be borne by the already heavily burdened private organisations, were they not fearful that the number of refugees may be increased many times by new flights from Germany.

The facts which arouse these apprehensions are indisputable. They are evidenced clearly in the German laws, decrees, judicial decisions, and Party pronouncements and practices during the last two years. The culmination of these attacks on the Jews, the Christian " non-Aryans," and the political and religious dissenters was the new legislation announced at the Party Congress at Nuremberg last September. The core of that enactment was the law limiting citizenship to those who are " of German or cognate blood," and who also conform to the National Socialist conception of loyalty to the State. As the direct result in Germany not only the Jews, who now number about 435,000, but also tens of thousands of Christian " non-Aryans " who are classified as Jews, lost their citizenship, were disfranchised, and made ineligible to hold public office. Indirectly, through this new law, a constitutional basis was laid for unrestricted discriminations against all those whom the Party may wish to penalise.

The denationalisation by the German Government of thousands of German citizens has added to the hardships both of those remaining in Germany and of the refugees, and is an increasing burden on States which have admitted the refugees while in possession of German nationality.

7. Relentlessly the Jews and " non-Aryans " are excluded from all public offices, from the exercise of the liberal professions, and from any part in the cultural and intellectual life of Germany. Ostracised from social relations with " Aryans," they are subjected to every kind of humiliation. Neither sex nor age exempts them from discrimination. Even the Jewish and " non-Aryan " children do not escape cruel forms of segregation and persecution. In Party publications, directly sponsored by the Government, " Aryan " children are stirred to hate the Jews and the Christian " non-Aryans," to spy upon them and to attack them, and to incite their own parents to extirpate the Jews altogether.

8. It is being made increasingly difficult for Jews and " non-Aryans " in Germany to sustain life. Condemned to segregation within the four corners of the legal and social Ghetto which has now closed upon them, they are increasingly prevented from earning their living. Indeed more than half of the Jews remaining in Germany have already been deprived of their livelihood. In many parts of the country there is a systematic attempt at starvation of the Jewish population. In no field of economic activity is there any security whatsoever. For some time it has been impossible for Jewish business men and shopkeepers to carry on their trades in small towns. The campaign against any dealings with Jews is now systematically

prosecuted in the larger towns. Despite the restrictions upon migration from the provinces into the few largest cities where Jewish economic activity is not yet completely excluded, the Jews are fleeing to those cities because there only can they hope to escape, at least for a time, from the more brutal forms of persecution.

This influx has exhausted already the resources of the Jewish philanthropic and educational institutions in Germany. The victims of the terrorism are being driven to the point where, in utter anguish and despair, they may burst the frontiers in fresh waves of refugees.

9. Again, as so often during their long heroic and tragic history, the Jewish people are used as the scapegoat for political and partisan purposes. The National Socialists level against them charges of the most outrageous and untenable kind. They ignore all of the facts of the continuous loyalty of the Jews in Germany: for example, during the Empire when Jews helped to unify Germany and to make it strong; during the War when a percentage of Jewish youth as high as that of any other religious community in the Reich gave their lives for the Fatherland, and Jewish scientists and men of affairs helped so notably to enable Germany to prolong the struggle; and under the Republic when Jewish leaders aided in saving Germany from some of the worst effects of defeat. Instead, it has been found useful to attribute to the Jews the responsibility for the misery and dejection which the German people suffered during the last years of the War and the decade that followed. Though less than a one-hundredth part of the total population, the Jews are held responsible for all the adversity which the German people had to undergo. As in the Middle Ages, when they were massacred and expelled from German States as the cause of the Black Death, so to-day they are eliminated from the economic and cultural life of Germany and degraded on the ground that they were the cause of the German humiliation. So far does this hatred extend that even the Jewish war veterans who fought and were wounded in the front line trenches have been forced from their positions in the public services, and the names of the Jewish war dead may no longer be engraved on war memorials.

10. The attitude of the German Government is based not only on the theory of " Nordic race " supremacy and the desire to eliminate " foreign racial " elements from the life of the country; it rests also on the conception of the absolute subordination of the individual to the State. An influential section of the Party is actively promoting a revival of neo-Paganism which sets itself against both the Old Testament and parts of the New Testament. The conceptions of " blood, race, and soil," propagated with fanatical enthusiasm, menace not alone the Jews, but all those who remain defiantly loyal to the old ideals of religious and individual freedom.

Party leaders violently attack religious freedom in the State, and threaten the Church with political domination. Outstanding thinkers of the two great Christian communities in Germany and abroad raise their voices in protest against this attack which threatens to increase the number of refugees.

11. The developments since 1933, and in particular those following the Nuremberg legislation, call for fresh collective action in regard to the problem created by persecution in Germany. The moral authority of the League of Nations and of States Members of the League must be directed towards a determined appeal to the German Government in the name of humanity and of the principles of the public law of Europe. They must ask for a modification of policies which constitute a source of unrest and perplexity in the world, a challenge to the conscience of mankind, and a menace to the legitimate interests of the States affected by the immigration of German refugees.

12. Apart from the Upper Silesia Convention of May, 1922, Germany does not appear to be expressly bound by a treaty obligation providing for equal citizenship of racial, religious, or linguistic minorities. But the principle of respect for the rights of minorities has been during the last three centuries hardening into an obligation of the public law of Europe. That principle was recognised in some of the most important international instruments of the nineteenth century. I may refer to the provisions of the Congress of Vienna, the treaty of guarantee following upon the Union of Belgium and Holland, the collective recognition of the independence of Greece, the creation of the autonomous principalities of Moldavia and Wallachia. It was affirmed at the Congress of Berlin in 1878 in relation to newly recognised States. It was deliberately reaffirmed in the Peace Settlement of 1919, and in a series of special minorities treaties as a vital condition both of international justice and of the preservation of the peace of the world. In the case of newly created States its express recognition constituted a condition of admission to the League of Nations.

Neither was the attitude of Germany in this matter open to any doubt. During the Peace Conference the German Delegation, in urging the adoption of the principle of protection of minorities for the German population in the territories detached from Germany, declared spontaneously that " Germany on her part is resolved to treat minorities of alien origin in her territories according to the same principles." The Allied and Associated Powers expressly took note of that declaration. From the moment of her admission to the League Germany took the lead in securing the effectiveness of the principles of international protection of minorities.

13. The Assembly of the League in 1922 adopted a resolution which expressed the hope that " States not bound by specific legal obligations in the matter of minorities will nevertheless observe in the treatment of their own minorities at least as high a standard of justice and toleration as is required by the treaties in question." The

Assembly in 1933, when considering the question of the persecution of Jews in Germany in connection with the discussion on minorities, reaffirmed that resolution; and in order to dispel doubts whether it applied to the Jews in Germany voted, with the single dissent of Germany, in favour of a further resolution that the principle " must be applied without exception to all classes of nationals of a State which differ from the majority of the population in race, language, or religion."

The German Jews, although not claiming or desiring to be a minority, are within the scope of this principle because, as was stated at the Assembly, as soon as there is legal discrimination, a minority exists within the meaning of modern law.

14. It is not within my province to state to what extent the practice in this matter of the community of nations in the last one hundred years and of the League of Nations has become a rule of customary international law; neither am I called upon to judge how far the declarations and the conduct of Germany prior to 1933 are in themselves sufficient to establish legal presumptions. But both, I believe, are sufficient to establish an appeal to those broad considerations of humanity and of international peace which are the basis of the public law of Europe in the matter of racial and religious minorities.

The growing sufferings of the persecuted minority in Germany and the menace of the growing exodus call for friendly but firm intercession with the German Government, by all pacific means, on the part of the League of Nations, of its Member-States and other members of the community of nations.

Pity and reason alike must inspire the hope that intercession will meet with response. Without such response the problems caused by the persecution of the Jews and the " non-Aryans " will not be solved by philanthropic action, but will continue to constitute a danger to international peace and a source of injury to the legitimate interests of other States.

15. The efforts of the private organisations and of any League organisation for refugees can only mitigate a problem of growing gravity and complexity. In the present economic conditions of the world the European States, and even those oversea, have only a limited power of absorption of refugees. The problem must be tackled at its source if disaster is to be avoided.

This is the function of the League, which is essentially an association of States for the consideration of matters of common concern. The Covenant empowers the Council and the Assembly to deal with any matter within the sphere of activity of the League or affecting the peace of the world. The effort of the League to ensure respect for human personality, when not grounded on express provisions of the Covenant or international treaties, has a sure foundation in the fact that the protection of the individual from racial and religious intolerance is a vital condition of international peace and security.

16. I am appending to this letter a comprehensive analysis of the German legislation, administrative decrees, and jurisprudence, as well as of their effects on the problem of refugees.

17. I feel bound to conclude this letter on a personal note. Prior to my appointment as High Commissioner for Refugees Coming from Germany, and in particular during the fourteen years following the War, I gave in my former office frequent and tangible proof of my concern that justice be done to the German people. But convinced as I am that desperate suffering in the countries adjacent to Germany and an even more terrible human calamity within the German frontiers, are inevitable unless present tendencies in the Reich are checked or reversed, I cannot remain silent. I am convinced that it is the duty of the High Commissioner for German Refugees, in tendering his resignation, to express an opinion on the essential elements of the task with which the Council of the League entrusted him. When domestic policies threaten the demoralisation and exile of hundreds of thousands of human beings, considerations of diplomatic correctness must yield to those of common humanity. I should be recreant if I did not call attention to the actual situation, and plead that world opinion, acting through the League and its Member-States and other countries, move to avert the existing and impending tragedies.

> I have the honour to be, Sir,
> your obedient servant,
>
> JAMES G. McDONALD, High Commissioner for Refugees (Jewish and Other) Coming from Germany.